TWO GEORGES

TWO GEORGES

The Making of the Modern Monarchy

David Sinclair

Hodder & Stoughton

LONDON SYDNEY AUCKLAND TORONTO

British Library Cataloguing in Publication Data

Sinclair, David, *1945*–
    Two Georges: the making of the modern
    monarchy.
    1. Great Britain. Monarchy, 1660–1987
    I. Title
    354.4103'12'09

    ISBN 0-340-33240-9

First printed 1988

Published by Hodder and Stoughton,
a division of Hodder and Stoughton Ltd,
Mill Road, Dunton Green, Sevenoaks, Kent TN13 2YE
Editorial Office: 47 Bedford Square, London WC1B 3DP

Photoset by Rowland Phototypesetting Ltd,
Bury St Edmunds, Suffolk

Printed in Great Britain by St Edmundsbury Press Ltd,
Bury St Edmunds, Suffolk

This book is dedicated to
the memory of
my mother, 1920–1988

Pallida Mors aequo pulsat
pede pauperum tabernas
Regumque turris – Horace

CONTENTS

ILLUSTRATIONS

TWO GEORGES

INTRODUCTION

Monarchy and Mediocracy

'I am sure I cannot understand it,' King George V said in response to the overwhelming expressions of public loyalty and affection on the twenty-fifth anniversary of his accession. 'After all, I am only a very ordinary sort of fellow.' Yet in saying that he went some way towards understanding. A certain 'ordinariness' has been an important element in what the British people have demanded of their monarchs in the twentieth century. For the modern sovereign must be, as much as anything else, the embodiment of what are considered to be the ordinary, traditional values of the middle classes: 'the abiding virtues of hearth, home and service,' as the late Sir Arthur Bryant expressed them.[1]

This ideal of ordinariness is a curious feature of the British constitutional monarchy, one that is widely considered to be a source of strength in the institution because it allows the proverbial man-in-the-street to identify with the otherwise remote figure who is, by no right other than birth, the head of state. It is a perverse concept, requiring for its justification remarkable mental agility. Logically, it would surely be much easier for ordinary citizens to identify with a head of state raised to pre-eminence from among their number by their own choice – in the manner of an American president, for example – rather than with a figure whose antecedents and environment are such as the man-in-the-street cannot, in truth, relate to even in his imagination. To put it another way, the electoral method of appointing a head of state takes an ordinary person and endows him or her with greatness, while the monarchical system on the British 'democratic' model is obliged to reduce a person born to greatness to the level of the ordinary.

But, of course, that is not the whole story. Presidents are distinguishable by what they do or, in countries where the office is a non-executive one, usually by what they have done in the past. The British monarch, on the other hand, is distinguished only by what he or she *is*, since the modern theory of constitutional monarchy does not permit the sovereign to *do* anything. Perversity is thus compounded by paradox. At one and the same time, the monarch is, by definition, an extraordinary person – occupying solely as a result of being born a position hallowed by more than a thousand years of history – and, by democratic demand, a sort of paragon of ordinariness.

The origins of this peculiar and, to the strictly rational mind, untenable situation are complex. They are to be found partly in two conflicting strands of British history, one pressing for change and the other resisting it; partly in a kind of political confidence trick used to establish a cohesive state without precisely defining the rights and responsibilities of either its rulers or its citizens; and partly in a failure to understand, or even to ask the question, why a monarch is useful, necessary or desirable in a modern parliamentary democracy.

That the monarchy has survived at all is a testament to what the historian E. H. Carr characterised as the force of gradualism in shaping the political and social development of Britain. The institution might well have disappeared for ever more than three centuries ago, following the victory of the Parliamentarians in the Civil War, but the nation as a whole was not ready to abandon its traditions and embrace instead the radical regeneration envisaged by Oliver Cromwell. When the Lord Protector died in 1658, the English republic – and for most people even the idea of a republic – went with him. Thirty years later, the so-called Glorious Revolution that deposed the Catholic James II in favour of the Protestant William of Orange was a triumph of gradualism, and as such considerably more significant than the Civil War. As Paul Langford, of Lincoln College, Oxford, has pointed out, 'A perceptible sense of compromise, of the need to step back from the brink, carries over the centuries from the debates of the assembly which met in London in 1689' (subsequently turning itself into Parliament and establishing the reign of William and Mary). In Langford's words, 'the priority was plainly to find a common core of agreement' and, as a result, 'the substantive acceptance of parliamentary monarchy was achieved'.[2] Evolution, then, not revolution.

The implications of this fundamental choice cannot be overestimated. The monarchy was saved, but, to quote Langford again, 'First William and Mary, then Mary's sister Anne, and finally, after the death of the latter's son the Duke of Gloucester in 1700, the Electors of Hanover (descended from James I through the female line) all owed their title to the determination of the propertied classes.' What was important about this was that the composition of the propertied classes was changing, with the rise of what might be called the mediocracy – an educated middle class that saw itself, by virtue of its enterprise, industriousness, prudence and moderation, as a natural ruling elite. Throughout the eighteenth century and particularly in the early part of the nineteenth, this new, ambitious class expanded rapidly, gathering influence as it grew, until by the middle of the nineteenth century the mediocracy had become the dominant force in British political and social life.

It was not until the twentieth century, however, that the process begun by the 1688 revolution entered its climactic phase. The years between 1910, when George V succeeded to the throne, and 1952, when his son George VI died, saw the mediocracy achieve complete mastery and firmly establish the polity of the nation on a broad foundation of middle-class perceptions. The reigns of the two Georges encompassed both the removal of the remaining constitutional teeth of the old ruling class, the aristocracy, and the successful containment of the political power conceded to the working classes in order to legitimise the mediocratic concept of democracy. All this was to have a profound effect on the position of the monarchy, so that George V and George VI found themselves moving in previously unimaginable directions.

Since the Glorious Revolution, the history of the English crown has been one of gradual surrender of authority, reluctant no doubt, but brought about by the steadily applied pressure of the governing class and sometimes in return for cash. It is generally acknowledged that the last monarch with any real power in Britain was George III, who died in 1820. Queen Victoria, inspired by her far-sighted consort, Prince Albert, fought a determined rearguard action throughout her long reign on behalf of royal influence in political decision-making. By the 1880s, though, the confidence and ambition of the middle classes was such that further retreat on the part of the monarchy became inevitable. Although the few remaining prerogatives of the sovereign remained theoretically intact, the monarchy in effect was incorporated into the Civil Service, so that while it was still able to offer advice to government, ultimately it had no choice but to bow to the will of its political masters. In this way, the institution also came to symbolise the underlying philosophy and values of the ruling mediocracy.

It was not quite as simple as that, however. The second half of the nineteenth century had also seen the rise of revolutionary movements dedicated to sweeping social and political reform, through violence if necessary, that would destroy the establishment constructed by the

[3]

middle classes and distribute power among the masses. Anxious to maintain its position as the main engine of change – and convinced that it alone was worthy to govern – the mediocracy was obliged to apply some form of brake on the process it had itself begun. The result was the political confidence trick I mentioned earlier.

Under the influence of the Tory leader Benjamin Disraeli, some of the medieval mystique of monarchy was revived and the sovereign, in the person of Queen Victoria, was established as a sort of national icon, transcending the mundane and messy business of politics, towards which public loyalty and faith could be directed. As a result of this, some of the emotional bonds of tribalism were recreated. The people were encouraged to believe that the object of national allegiance was the monarch, not the state as represented by the government. This had a number of benefits for the ruling class.

First, the concept of statehood was embodied in the sovereign, which made it easier to 'sell' to the ill-educated and politically unsophisticated under-classes: people were more likely to respond to an appeal on behalf of a person rather than a political abstraction. Second, stability and moderation were ensured by divorcing support for the government from loyalty to the throne – making it possible for the citizen to oppose the policies of a particular administration without necessarily demanding the overthrow of the system. Third, the revival of the mystique of monarchy on old feudal principles reinforced the concept of elitism, the idea that there was a natural order of things which it would be dangerous to disturb. Fourth, and perhaps most important, loyalty to the sovereign implied adherence to the values and attitudes of the middle classes, with which the monarchy under Queen Victoria and Prince Albert had become so closely identified.

Thus began the process that would result in the confusion of images which has characterised public attitudes towards the monarchy – not to mention the attitudes of the royal family towards the public – in the twentieth century. The absence of a written constitution meant that there was nothing specific to which a new monarch could refer for guidance, nothing upon which he could build to develop sensibly the institution he represented. Each had to find his own balance between the roles of figurehead and public servant, spiritual leader and political puppet, instrument of change and defender of the status quo. Above all, each new sovereign had to find his own way of justifying his existence, reduced, as he was, to political irrelevance and dependent upon the continuing approval of government and people. Equally, the lack of a proper constitution defining the position of the monarchy in relation to the government and the citizen meant that the British people had no means of knowing what they could expect of their sovereigns or of judging their performance. The result has been the growth of a series of myths, legends, half-truths, misconceptions and misunderstandings that has left the British monarchy not knowing quite what its role is or what its future direction should be, while the British people spend part of their time worshipping their royal family and the rest of it trying to knock various members of it off their pedestals. The conflict between the ordinary and the extraordinary images of the monarchy has reached such a pitch that the very nature of the unprecedented popularity the institution has appeared to enjoy during this century may, in the end, imperil its survival. That its usefulness has already been severely restricted by the contradictions surrounding it seems beyond doubt.

It might seem odd that an institution apparently so dear to English hearts should have been allowed to reach such a state, stranger still that one so obviously popular should be subject to uncertainty as to its future. The fact is that during the past hundred years or so, the monarchy has been so taken for granted that its development has largely been either left to chance or manipulated according to the demands of short-term expediency. It is still widely assumed that a sovereign is essential to the British system of democracy, but few people have ever seriously considered why or how. Consequently, the evolution of the monarchy in modern times has been haphazard and, in a way, almost accidental.

For twenty years, the reign of Queen Victoria was given meaning and direction by Prince Albert, who had very clear and definite ideas about the role of the monarchy in the bourgeois state that was then being created. After Albert's death in 1861, however, the broken-hearted Queen relapsed into the idiosyncratic ways of her first three years on the throne, before her marriage, concentrating more on the niceties of her personal position than on the wider, public aspects of the institution in her charge. When finally, under the prompting of Disraeli, she did emerge into public view, it was mainly as a sort of living statue, an object of reverence and awe.

Upon Victoria's death in 1901, the crown passed to the ageing Edward VII, too set in his ways, too self-centred and too accustomed to a life of idleness and pleasure to be more than a caretaker king. His overwhelming presence, reminiscent in some superficial ways of Henry VIII, inspired public confidence and loyalty, while at the same time his large and generous personality, with its only too human failings, evoked in the mass of his subjects a new species of affection that was almost familial. He had little else to offer, however, and his effect on the development of the monarchy may be regarded as negligible.

Edward's successor, George V, was a much smaller figure, lacking both the personality and the style of his father, but it was he whom history chose to set the tone of the 'new' popular monarchy required by the now dominant mediocracy. The choice was accidental: George V was King Edward's second son and came to the throne only because his elder brother, the Duke of Clarence, died young. That historical accident, though, was crucially to affect the course of the monarchy.

At his accession in 1910, George V found the old certainties of Victorian and Edwardian England hard-pressed but by no means swept away, and he saw it as his function to support the retention of all that was good while encouraging the abandonment of the less attractive features of Victorian philosophy and practice. His eldest son, later King Edward VIII, characterised him as a man determined to make the nineteenth century last for ever.[3] That judgment, arising out of bitterness, frustration and misunderstanding for which King George himself was in some measure responsible, is simplistic. It is true that George V was almost obsessively conscious of tradition, convention and correct behaviour, and that he mourned the passing of the tranquillity, order and confidence that had marked most of Queen Victoria's reign. Those, however, were precisely the attitudes that the new bourgeois governing class could exploit in endowing their rule with legitimacy in the face of radical pressures from below. The Victorian era was presented as a quintessentially English idyll (it still is) and the mediocracy claimed for itself the guardianship of its 'values'. George V was both the symbol and the servant of such values.

Of course, some concessions had to be made in view of the growing challenge of socialism, but because of the King's position as the representative of all that was deemed best in Britain, combined with his status as the focus of public loyalty and the curious 'kinship' the mass of people now felt towards their royal family, the mediocracy could use the monarchy as a stabilising factor. Since it was the king who symbolised the state, while the government (and increasingly, in fact, the prime minister) actually ruled it, the populace could be persuaded that the interests of the state were best served by allegiance to the monarch, irrespective of what the government did. Given that George V was deemed to represent an ideal – of justice, fairness, peace and, above all, moderation – to which all were meant to aspire, the pace and scale of change that threatened the power of the governing class could be restrained: gradualism in action again. Thus the mediocracy was allowed time to protect its position within the framework of change. Beneath the cloak of 'democratisation' demanded by a working class growing ever more vocal and activist, the power structure remained the same.

This delicate balance was upset by King Edward VIII. The circumstances surrounding his abdication destroyed the notion of permanence and continuity and dented the concept of selfless service to state and people that was required of the monarch in return for public loyalty. The crisis did something else, too. By encouraging factionalism to the extent that there was talk of forming a 'King's Party' to fight an election on the issue of Edward's proposed marriage to a divorced American woman, it threatened to bring the monarchy into the centre of the political arena. That, of course, was regarded as a very serious danger by the mediocratic Establishment. The prospect of a king appealing directly to the people, over the heads of his government, raised the spectre of royal powers long buried under the weight of parliamentary domination. It was therefore essential that Edward VIII be disposed of and the old illusions restored.

Fortunately for the governing class, those illusions had become so firmly rooted that most people understood the monarch must have no real power. That was why the once-popular Edward was forgotten so quickly after his abdication and the loyalty and affection he had commanded were transferred immediately to his sucessor, George VI. The prime minister of the day, Stanley Baldwin, captured the mood exactly when asked what was to happen about the coronation ceremony that had been planned for Edward VIII. 'Same day,' he said. 'New king.' There was no danger of any widespread loyalty to Edward as the 'king across the water', as had been the case with the previous abdicant, James II. Under what has been described as the legal fiction of the constitutional monarchy, it does not matter much *who* occupies the throne so long as he or she has an hereditary right to it and is prepared to play by the rules.

George VI, like his father, was more than willing to accept the constraints and demands of constitutional monarchy. However, unlike George V, he had not come to the throne in calm, orderly succession and, as he put it himself, he was utterly unprepared for kingship. Many influential people doubted whether he had the ability or the temperament to become a symbol of national unity at a time when the divisions between capital and labour in Britain were acute, the peoples of the old Empire were in rebellious mood and most of Europe was in the grip of dictatorship, either communist or fascist. What they saw was a slight, shy man, untrained in kingcraft and matters of state, hardly able to speak in public because of a severe nervous stammer.

[7]

'With the existing King we knew where we were,' the press baron Lord Beaverbrook grumbled after the abdication of Edward VIII. 'We knew his defects and his limitations. But with a new King we have to start all over again. And maybe we will find ourselves up against a new lot of defects of a different kind.'

But the deficiencies in the personality of George VI were of the sort that would cause more harm to himself than to government or people, while his virtues fitted him perfectly for the role to which he was called so summarily. Even more than his father had been, he was resolved to be 'the people's king' and he knew rather more about 'the people' than George V had known. As Duke of York he had founded camps which brought together boys from public schools and from the urban slums with the aim of fostering better understanding between social classes, and he had visited industrial areas, factories and mines with such dedication that his brother had nicknamed him 'The Foreman'. He disliked formality – 'No more high hat business,' he said, when setting off on a tour of the United States and Canada – and he sometimes disconcerted officials by changing the programme of his visits so as to spend more time rubbing shoulders with the crowds gathered to see him. In royal terms, this was innovative, even slightly revolutionary, but in the social conditions of fifty years ago it could not have been more welcome.

In addition, George VI was a natural conciliator and a fervent supporter of widespread co-operation in pursuit of common goals. On his desk he had a motto taken from the Book of Isaiah: 'They helped every one his neighbour and every one said to his brother, Be of good courage.' The cause of unity, of 'sticking together' in the face of adversity, was a constant theme of his public utterances and private thoughts. The doubts about him quickly faded. The mediocracy realised that it had found its ideal rallying-point. The modern perception of the monarchy was in the making.

George V and George VI are remembered, if at all, as 'good' kings, yet no one can point to any particular achievement of either of their reigns. They did not shape their times, but were shaped by them and, as a result, the passivity of the monarchy became an accepted fact. George V and, even more so, George VI slavishly made themselves available to the ever increasing demands of a constitutional fiction, and in so doing denied the most positive features of the system they were so dedicated to upholding. This book will explore how the monarchy, in the words of Sir Arthur Bryant again, 'more than any other single factor . . . has accounted for the astonishing steadiness and resilience of the nation during the present stormy century'.[4] Yet it will also be a record of opportunities missed, of beneficial change delayed or diverted, of unhealthy reverence for the past and a refusal genuinely to come to terms with the new world and seek a meaningful role in it.

The noted constitutional lawyer Sir Ivor Jennings pointed out that the 'romance' surrounding the monarchy, medieval in character but surviving to this day, is not without its disadvantages. For one thing, the idea of royalty has perpetuated a class system founded on birth, honour and privilege which mass education and the rise of a meritocracy has fundamentally failed to change and which remains one of Britain's greatest handicaps in the modern world – not least in the sphere of economics, since the system bases qualitative judgments on grounds other than the contributions people actually make to society and retains a lingering mistrust of what Edward VII would have described disdainfully as 'trade and commerce'. There are, however, other and perhaps more serious drawbacks to the theory of the constitutional monarchy as it developed during the reigns of George V and George VI.

In a book Jennings wrote in 1943, he observed: 'If England had remained a republic after 1658, or had become a republic in 1688, it would by now have acquired that aurora of sentiment which attaches to *la patrie* or the Constitution of the United States.'[5] That, of course, did not happen. Instead, patriotic sentiments were focused upon the monarch. All very fine while the sovereign had some power and was part of the government, but after the death of George III the powers of the monarch were gradually eroded until they became entirely formal. This meant that the sovereign was transformed into a symbol of both loyalty and powerlessness. Politics, whatever else it may be, is about power and loyalty to a political entity – represented, for example, by an executive president, as in the United States – is a commitment to power. In Britain, thanks to the constitutional monarchy, the opposite is true. Allegiance to the monarch is a commitment to powerlessness. This, it is argued, is how it should be, because an elected president is transient and can be got rid of whereas a dynastic sovereign is permanent and cannot be voted out of office. That is nonsense. Kings have been disposed of and dynasties toppled. It is no easier to oust an elected president before his time if he chooses not to go than it is to overthrow an hereditary monarch. Furthermore, the English concept leads to an assumption that change is the enemy of power and thus of politics: things must remain basically the same if the governance of the nation is not to be upset. In the United States, change is viewed as the engine of power and therefore the business of politics. In the rapidly changing world of the twentieth century, it is not difficult to see which of those two perceptions is likely to produce the more successful nation and the most enterprising people.

Judging by the present intense popular interest in and obsessive publicity for the activities of the royal family in both their public and private lives, it appears that the monarchy has become more a branch of the entertainment industry than a necessary constitutional device in a country without a written constitution. Indeed, it may seem that rather than being a symbol of national pride and unity, the royal family functions as a diversion of public attention away from national decline, division and malaise. The pomp and circumstance remain, the ceremonial is if anything more splendid than ever, bearing in mind the need to satisfy television audiences, but the real purpose of maintaining the monarchy grows more obscure as the welter of words and the parade of pictures increase in volume. There is no doubt that the British monarchy has survived, when so many others have fallen, largely because it has understood the nature and importance of popular appeal. It may have made an error, however, in assuming that popularity is the only substitute for power available to an unelected head of state in the twentieth century. A high place in popular regard inevitably carries with it the risk of exposure to public criticism and disrespect.

The two Georges of the twentieth century clearly perceived the threats to the survival of the monarchy in an age of revolutionary change. They sought to meet those threats by, in some ways, lowering the tone of the monarchy. While its rituals and such constitutional rights as were left to it were retained, much of the ancient mystery and dignity of the monarchy was sacrificed in an effort to bring it closer to the people upon whom its continuation appeared to depend. But George V and George VI were both rather ordinary men who found themselves in an extraordinary situation, and in their anxiety to do what seemed to be expected of them, they may have failed to see dangers inherent in their course. Some people believe the monarchy is now more firmly established than ever; others regard it as an empty show, or worse – the playwright John Osborne once described it as 'the gold filling in the mouth of decay'. What appears to be incontrovertible is that the royal family is perceived today very much as public property. The implications of that for the future of the monarchy, whether in fact it has a future at all, are matters to be considered at the end of this book. First it is necessary to look back briefly to the reign of Queen Victoria, during which both George V and George VI were born, in order to set in context the monarchy that the two Georges inherited and to understand the effect their reigns would have upon it.

PART 1

'A System Unique in the World'

1

Albert's Memorial

Three days after the death of King George V in 1935, the Prime Minister, Stanley Baldwin, told members of the House of Commons that, 'The great achievement of the last century, culminating, perhaps, in the reign of George V, was the coming to terms of democracy and of monarchy, and the system under which we live today, a system unique in the world, was evolved.' That system, Baldwin said, had come about 'owing to the character of those who held that great position, the throne, in the last hundred years – Queen Victoria, King Edward VII and King George V'. What he did not say, and indeed could not have said, considering the context, was that George V, in coming to symbolise what was and is still considered to be the modern 'democratic' style of monarchy in Britain, owed rather less to Queen Victoria and King Edward VII than to Victoria's consort, Prince Albert.

It had been the Prince Consort who had realised, twenty years before the future George V had been born, that the development of the monarchy, even its very survival, depended upon its being perceived as espousing the essential virtues of the then burgeoning bourgeoisie. If the pragmatic approach of Prince Albert had been continued through-out the nineteenth century, the 'unique system' might have developed in quite a different way. However, on Saturday, December 14th, 1861 – 'this dreadful day,' as Queen Victoria called it – the Prince died of typhoid at Windsor Castle. His death at the early age of forty-two was not only a severe personal blow to the Queen, affecting her deeply both privately and in her public role, but it also served as a catalyst in an extraordinary process that would transform the way in which the people of Britain viewed their royal family.

Albert's contribution to the development of the monarchy had been crucial. Queen Victoria had inherited a throne stripped of most of its direct power and much public esteem. Her three immediate predecessors had been, according to one of her biographers, Sir Sidney Lee, 'an imbecile, a profligate and a buffoon'. Though the eccentric King William IV had restored to the throne some of the popularity it had forfeited during the reign of George IV, he had at the same time presided over the sweeping transfer of authority from sovereign to Parliament enshrined in the Reform Act of 1832 – indeed, William had had the distinction of being the last British monarch with the power personally to dismiss a government. The new Queen was a formidable character, but without the addition of Prince Albert's intelligence, capacity for detached observation and political awareness, it is doubtful whether her reign could ever have achieved the magnificent proportions it has assumed in retrospect.

The received image of Queen Victoria is of a revered monarch who symbolised all that was great in Great Britain at the height of its power and influence. Yet within three years of her accession Victoria had made herself something of an object of scorn among the public and had become thoroughly unpopular with a large section of the governing class. Later on, in the middle of her reign, Britain experienced what was probably its greatest upsurge of republican sentiment since the Civil War, again largely because of the behaviour of the Queen. The ineffably regal figure of postage stamps, statuary and modern popular perception is, like so much else about the age to which Victoria gave her name, mythical to a considerable extent. The myth, as we shall see, was created quite deliberately, though not by the Queen herself: one of the difficulties of constitutional monarchs is their vulnerability to exploitation for political purposes.

When William IV died early on the morning of June 20th, 1837, and the eighteen-year-old Victoria succeeded to the throne, the political leaders of the day – Wellington, Palmerston, Melbourne, Peel – assumed that they would have no difficulty in exerting influence over a sovereign little educated in the ways of the world. An idea of their patronising attitudes may be gained from some of the comments that followed Victoria's first Privy Council, when Peel praised her diffidence and dignity while the old Duke of Wellington said he could not have wished for better deportment from his own daughter. Before long, however, the politicians began to notice that the young Queen could display a strong will of her own, 'slight signs of a peremptory disposition'[1] and the ability to freeze with a mere glance even the most worldly-wise of men. She might, as she herself said, be inexperienced in many things, but she knew perfectly well what it meant to be a monarch and she relished the prospect before her.

At first, she relied heavily on the advice and political skills of her uncle, King Leopold of the Belgians, and his unofficial ambassador, Baron Stockmar. Leopold told his niece that she must make up her own mind on matters of state and stick to her opinions, that she should be firm in allotting time in which ministers could see her and that she should always make them wait for an answer. ('I will think it over' became her stock reply to ministerial suggestions, according to Charles Greville, clerk of the Privy Council and an illuminating diarist of the period.) Guided by such counsel and bolstered by her own natural wilfulness and a strong, though rather vague, sense of duty, the young Queen Victoria rapidly made it clear that she intended to be no mere figurehead but to exercise to the full – and on occasion even to exceed – the prerogatives remaining to the sovereign.

Yet for all her strength of character and her determination, as she put it, to be 'good', she remained in many respects an over-emotional and impressionable girl, which made her susceptible to a certain kind of hero-worship. It was a weakness deftly exploited by her first prime minister, the handsome and worldly Lord Melbourne. Through a mixture of flattery, flirtation and easily digestible philosophy, Melbourne managed to establish himself as the Queen's mentor, part protector, part father-figure and part dream lover. Such was his success that the influence of King Leopold and Baron Stockmar soon began to wane significantly.

Unfortunately, Melbourne was quite the wrong sort of man to have the power to mould a character that would always be notable not only for its strength but also for its stubbornness, vindictiveness and reliance on personal prejudice rather than well-informed judgment. Though intelligent, sophisticated, persuasive and witty, Melbourne was entirely cynical in outlook, and in place of any moral or genuine philosophical basis for his activities, he tended to fall back on a kind of careless scepticism. This is well illustrated by a story told about him at the time of the agitation over the Corn Laws. Presiding at a Cabinet meeting which was to decide to impose a fixed duty on imported corn, Melbourne is said to have put his back against the door and demanded: 'Now, is it to lower the price of bread or isn't it? It is not much matter which we say, but, mind, we must all say the same.'[2] Furthermore, despite his leadership of a Whig administration, Melbourne was deeply conservative by nature, assuming that change could never be for the better and completely dissociating himself from the reforming zeal of the Radicals in his own party. Thus while he taught Queen Victoria to mistrust Tories, he gave her a quite false impression of what Liberals stood for and at the same time, through his rather cold-blooded approach to life, he blunted the more generous and sympathetic aspects of her personality.

One early and particularly sad reflection of the Queen's less attractive propensities, as encouraged by Melbourne, was the infamous affair of Lady Flora Hastings, which was to lead to the spectacle of crowds hissing at the Queen when she appeared in public. Lady Flora, a lady-in-waiting to Victoria's mother, the Duchess of Kent, sought treatment from the Queen's physician in January 1839 for abdominal pain and swelling. Victoria immediately concluded that the woman, aged thirty-two and unmarried, was 'to use plain words – *with child*!!' and that the man responsible was the rather unsavoury Sir John Conroy, comptroller to the Duchess of Kent. Conroy was loathed and feared by the Queen because of his high-Toryism (which Melbourne had taught her to hate) and as a result of his continual plotting to establish some power over her: 'the Monster & demon Incarnate,' she called him in her journal.

Melbourne's response to what was no more than vicious gossip was to advise the Queen to wait and see how matters developed. That was his customary response in a crisis, a form of masterly inactivity, but it now served merely to inflame the Queen. Never one to display much patience, she took the Prime Minister's caution as proof of her suspicions and, filled with self-righteous indignation, she conferred with her ladies-in-waiting and decided on a course of action. The royal physician, Sir James Clark, was despatched to inform Lady Flora that she must be married in haste and in secret. When the unfortunate woman protested her innocence, she was banished from the Court and, in order to clear her name, underwent the indignity of a second medical examination, which established that her virginity was intact. The Queen was filled with remorse and quickly reinstated Lady Flora at Court, writing to her personally to express her regrets.

But the wagging tongues refused to be silent, and the Queen was only too ready to listen to them. Always unwilling to change her mind without a struggle, she was soon writing rather hysterically to the Duchess of Kent that the gynaecologist who had examined Lady Flora 'said that though she is a virgin still that it might be possible and one could not tell if such things could not happen. That there was an enlargement in the womb like a child. . . .'

In fact, the abdominal swelling was caused by cancer of the liver, which killed Lady Flora a few months later. After her death, the scandal was broadcast by the publication in the *Morning Post* of letters she had written to her uncle, the Marquess of Hastings, and to Melbourne. It began to be said that she had really died of a broken heart and among her family and friends there was no doubt as to who had been responsible for that. There followed a chorus of hostile comment in the press and the popularity of the Queen sank so low that Victoria was moved to congratulate herself in her journal on a particular public appearance that passed off 'without one hiss'.

However, it was not only the Flora Hastings scandal that made the Queen unpopular. In the midst of the personal crisis arising from her mishandling of the matter, Victoria also made a serious political misjudgment. Melbourne's administration had been at best precarious, and in the spring of 1839 it was brought down by determined opposition to the Jamaica Bill, which sought to impose labour reforms on sugar planters in the colony. On May 7th Melbourne resigned and handed the Queen a note offering her advice as to how she should approach the incoming Tory government. Victoria, who had once confided to Melbourne that she thought the royal family ought always to be Whig, was appalled at the prospect, particularly because the new prime minister was likely to be Sir Robert Peel. She had learnt to mistrust and dislike Peel, not simply because he was a Tory – though Melbourne's indoctrination had made that enough of an excuse – but also because she was intensely irritated by his stiff, humourless style and rather prissy manner. The Queen resolved to do whatever she could to place obstacles in the way of the new administration, entirely ignoring the constitutional requirements.

Her first tactic, on the advice of Melbourne, was to invite the Duke of Wellington to form a government, something which (as Melbourne must have known) was impossible. Apart from his advanced age and increasing deafness, the Duke had made himself unpopular with both his party and the public during his previous terms as prime minister and had stepped aside in favour of Peel in 1834. As he explained patiently in a twenty-minute audience at Buckingham Palace, Peel was the official leader of the Tory Party and as such it was he who must form the government. Very well, the Queen countered – again at Melbourne's prompting – if Wellington would not be prime minister, would he undertake to become foreign secretary in Peel's government? The Duke was startled by this apparent display of constitutional ignorance. Only the prime minister could decide on the composition of his Cabinet, he pointed out. The Queen must talk to Peel.

Suppressing as best she could her feelings of distaste, Victoria sent for the leader of the Opposition. Peel, briefed by Wellington on the royal attempt to circumvent his assumption of power, remained coldly determined in the face of the Queen's disapproval of the prospective Cabinet members he named; he also refused to promise that he would not insist on a dissolution of Parliament. (Melbourne had told the Queen that the Whigs would lose heavily in the event of a general election, which was why he had resigned rather than appeal to the voters.) But if Peel left the Palace feeling that he had had the better of the encounter, he reckoned without the willingness of the Queen, encouraged by Melbourne, to flout constitutional practice in an outrageous manner in order to prevent the Tories from forming a government.

There followed what became known as the Bedchamber Plot. Constitutional tradition demanded that the royal household be changed to reflect the political complexion of the new government, but the Queen, under Melbourne's coaching, demanded that changes made by Peel should be restricted to gentlemen of the household who were also Members of Parliament and should not affect the women, such as the ladies of the bedchamber, upon whom the Queen relied, even if their husbands or families were Whigs. To justify this position, Melbourne had told the Queen, she was to cite constitutional precedent, though in fact the argument was entirely spurious since for the previous century and a half the monarchs had all been men, so there had been no question of interfering with the households of queens. Nevertheless, Victoria told Peel at a second audience that because no previous queen had been required to change her Court ladies, she did not intend to do so. Not one of them.

Peel and Wellington tried to reason with her, explaining that there was an enormous difference between the position of a queen regnant and that of a queen consort, and pointing out that the whole process of government had been quite different during the reign of the last female sovereign, Queen Anne, who had died in 1714. The Queen was immovable, ignoring appeals for the customary display of royal confidence in a new administration, and when Melbourne persuaded the Whigs to agree to support her position, Peel knew he was beaten. He could hardly go to the country on the issue of who should be ladies of the bedchamber and he could not allow himself, as prospective prime minister, to be dictated to by a constitutional monarch. His only course was to decline to form an administration. The Queen delightedly recalled Melbourne, and a weak, unpopular government was artificially maintained in office for a further two years.

The fury of the Tories was matched by that in sections of the press, which accused the Queen of childish behaviour and of capriciously interfering with national institutions. Her earlier mentor, Baron Stockmar, offered the opinion that she must be as insane as poor George III had been. But the influence of Stockmar and his master were soon to be felt again. One newspaper had commented that what the Queen needed was a husband to restrain her, and King Leopold had identified the ideal man. By the time Sir Robert Peel did take office in 1841, the outline of a new style of constitutional monarchy was beginning to be discernible as Queen Victoria's new husband, Prince Albert of Saxe-Coburg-Gotha, brought his keen intelligence to bear. This German prince, according to Walter Bagehot, the inimitable nineteenth-century interpreter of the English constitution, 'had a scholar's caution and a scholar's courage' combined with 'the rare gifts of a constitutional monarch'. He it was who would take the first steps towards presenting the crown to the nation.

Prince Albert, whom Queen Victoria married on February 10th, 1840, brought an entirely new dimension to the British royal house. The legitimacy of the throne at that time depended – as it still does today – on the mystic perception of its labyrinthine line of descent from early tribal roots. The sovereign, in other words, has if not exactly a divine right to his or her position, then at least a right hallowed by history. Nothing else, not military prowess, not even special skill in statecraft, is demanded so long as the requirement that the monarch be Protestant is fulfilled. (The Hanoverians, from whom Queen Victoria was descended, came to the throne not primarily because of the lineal right of George I, which was at best distant, but because of a legal right conferred by the Act of Settlement, which barred the Catholic descendants of James II.) These simple require-ments, of course, account for the widely varying degrees of competence – or pure incompetence in some cases – displayed by monarchs down the ages and constitute the main argument against the principle of inherited power: There is absolutely no reason for supposing that the heir of a successful and talented leader will be equally gifted, as history has demonstrated many times. The societies to which the principle first applied had very straightforward means of dealing with bad or incompetent rulers, but it is some time since kings were expected to prove themselves by force of arms. The background of Prince Albert, however, was very different from the absolutism of the English theory of monarchy, and his effect on the institution was to be remarkable.

Germany, apart from the dominant Prussians, possessed thirty-eight more or less royal houses. Though the Saxe-Coburgs traced their line back to the Middle Ages and it encompassed some of the great figures of German history, this position depended less on heredity (indeed, they had lost the kingdom of Saxony, to which they were entitled by birth) than on merit, political acumen and diplomatic skills. With so many potential rivals always seeking to increase their power, influence and wealth, the Coburgs could not simply rely for their survival on the fact that they were descended from John the Constant or the romantic Frederick the Bitten. Moreover, the German royal houses of the nineteenth century were obliged to represent in some measure at least the aspirations of their subjects, for if they did not there was likely to be some neighbouring ruler who would. It was a system which, if less 'democratic' than that of England, was at the same time more symbiotic, with kings having more real power than English monarchs but also assuming rather more direct responsibility for the people they ruled. In Britain, the crown had become isolated from the currents of 'ordinary' life while the parliamentary government, where the actual power resided, had thus far failed to acknowledge and even to understand its responsibilities towards the people as a whole. The country had entered a constitutional watershed and for the monarchy the danger was that it would become irrelevant as the polity of the nation moved towards the final stages of development in the direction of participatory democracy.

Prince Albert grew up against a background of royal houses which in a sense remained at an earlier stage of evolution. The idea of a monarch exercising real power, whether directly or through various forms of influence, therefore came naturally to him. Any tendency towards despotism this might have produced, however, was mitigated by the wide, liberal education designed for him by his wise, sophisticated and politically aware Uncle Leopold, King of the Belgians. Albert's studies were supervised by the King's counsellor, Baron Stockmar, whose shrewd, almost Machiavellian brain foresaw the challenges that the modern world would present to the ancient institution of monarchy. As a result of this careful grooming (undertaken with the firm intention on the part of the Coburg family that the Prince should marry the future Queen Victoria), Albert, when he became Prince Consort, was able to endow the British monarchy with an awareness of political necessities and a new appreciation of its symbolic role under the constitution, rather than the narrowly practical and ceremonial functions with which both crown and government seemed to be excessively concerned.

The Prince Consort understood that if it was to play a full part in national life, rather than merely in the business of government, the monarchy had to identify itself with the finest instincts of the national will, to represent its subjects in emotional terms. The institution must maintain what Bagehot was later to characterise as the 'dignified' aspect of the constitution while leaving the 'efficient' part largely to the politicians (though still, of course, exercising the royal prerogative to be consulted, to encourage and to warn). At the same time, however, the monarchy should symbolise all that was best in Britain, the ideals which, if they could not always be upheld by the nation as a whole, could at least be aspired to. Free from the pressure of parliamentary expediency, the monarchy could be political in the widest sense of the word, standing above partisan considerations and in a sense speaking directly to the people over the heads of the politicians, whose view of what was best for the country would almost inevitably be coloured by ideology or party allegiance.

Queen Victoria alone could never have achieved such a position for the throne. She was too headstrong, too emotional, too much given to prejudice and too stubborn. She was also too susceptible to manipulation by attractive men, such as Lord Melbourne and, in her widowhood, Disraeli. Though intelligent, shrewd and quite well-educated, the Queen displayed a lack of self-control and an erratic nature that would have been serious obstacles to success as a constitutional monarch, had she been left to herself. Prince Albert, however, was a man attractive above all others in Victoria's eyes and, as such, his influence became paramount. The sober, high-minded, earnest and hard-working Prince Consort was able to remodel in his own image the unpredictable and often violent-tempered Queen. Long after his death she clung tenaciously – and sometimes, it must be said, inappropriately – to the principles he had so conscientiously taught her. While he lived, though, it was Albert rather than the Queen herself who assumed the mantle of the constitutional monarch. As the diarist Greville put it, 'He is become so identified with her that they are one person, and as he likes, and she dislikes, business, it is obvious that while she has the title, he is really discharging the function of the Sovereign. He is King to all intents and purposes.'

Brimming with nervous energy, Albert worked ceaselessly at his self-imposed task of making the monarchy the partner of government, rather than its opponent or its puppet. He was always by the Queen's side during audiences with ministers and sometimes he saw political leaders and foreign heads of state by himself. He dealt with state papers and wrote detailed memoranda on virtually everything connected with government. He held levees as if he were king and took a hand in the formation of ministries – indeed, he may be said to have personally formed the government of Lord Aberdeen in 1852, having presented the prospective prime minister with 'a list of the possible distribution of offices' in the Cabinet. When Albert died, Disraeli wrote: 'This German Prince has governed England for twenty-one years with a wisdom and energy such as none of our Kings has ever shown.'

Not everyone shared Disraeli's somewhat exaggerated enthusiasm, however. Apart from those, ranging from revolutionary Radicals to diehard Tories, who resented the fact that 'one man, and he not an Englishman by birth, should be at once Foreign Secretary, Commander-in-Chief and Prime Minister under all administrations,'[3] many influential politicians were concerned that a Prince Consort, German or otherwise, should pursue the line that the sovereign had a moral duty to share in government and 'the pre-paratory arrangement of party organisation' so that potential candidates for the premiership or Cabinet office could be excluded if they were unacceptable to the Palace. This was a definition of constitutional monarchy that went too far, certainly for the more aristocratic elements in Parliament, especially the Whigs, who saw any strengthening of the monarch's position as a threat to their concept of liberty.

But the days of Whig ascendancy were coming to a close, and along with them the tradition of aristocratic rule. The Industrial Revolution had spawned a new and aggressive middle class, who considered that political power was theirs by right because of the contribution they made to the national economy and, in consequence, to Britain's growing dominance in world trade and affairs. Serious, hard-working, proud of their common sense and respectability, the members of this new class saw merit as the yardstick by which a man should be measured and moderation as the cornerstone of stability and progress. Briefly, their philosophy was that a man should succeed by his own efforts, should not indulge himself to excess in any form and should care for those less fortunate (that is, less worthy) as much as was deemed good for them without impairing their ability to look after themselves through work and prudence. This class, in its earliest flowering, was represented in politics by Sir Robert Peel – worthy, steady, unemotional, sentimental and essentially rather dull – and in principle by Prince Albert.

According to his brother, Albert was contemptuous of mankind in general. He had a special disdain for the English leisured classes, sharing the German view reported by Greville in 1840 that 'the state of society in England and the character of its aristocracy was to the last degree profligate and unprincipled'. To the Prince Consort's disciplined Teutonic mind, the average English aristocrat was ill-educated, dissolute and self-indulgent and had little or nothing to contribute to the national interest. When Lord Derby briefly became prime minister in 1852, the Prince was appalled to discover that the people selected for positions at Court were 'the Dandies and Roués of London and the Turf' and promptly submitted his own list of names. This royal perception of the nobility was shared by the leaders of the new middle class, who envied the social superiority of the aristocracy, resented the fact that it was conferred by birth alone and sought to equal it through the acquisition of wealth, while at the same time pretending to superiority themselves by virtue of usefulness and moral rectitude. The underlying reasons may have been different, but the attitudes were the same: under Prince Albert's influence, the royal family became associated with middle-class ideals of probity and respectability.

There were other areas, too, in which the natural inclination of Prince Albert coincided with the emerging philosophy of the new middle class. He' was an enthusiastic supporter of free trade and enterprise. He subscribed to the doctrines of scientific rationalism and encouraged the development and application of new technologies and industrial processes. He understood the threat to stability and order that could arise from an exploited and disaffected under-class and took a lead in improving the conditions of the growing numbers of urbanised industrial workers, reasoning that the paternalistic provision of welfare, which was to become one of the hallmarks of the Victorian age, served not only to minimise class envy but also to keep the proletariat firmly in its place. (Both the Queen and the Prince Consort were terrified of the Chartist movement, which between 1838 and 1848 organised marches and demonstrations on behalf of the working classes that sometimes led to rioting.) At a more personal level, Albert embodied the other view most closely associated with Victorian England: that the path to happiness and fulfilment lay in the sanctity of home and family. In sum – despite the royal presumption of superiority and the arrogance that many who encountered him found offensive – the Prince Consort, king in all but name, was the essential bourgeois.

But while Albert was clearly the creator of the philosophical, social, ideological and political tradition of the modern British monarchy, inherited and developed in the twentieth century by George V and George VI, he also contributed indirectly to another, equally important, aspect of royalty which was to be exploited with great success by the heirs of Queen Victoria. The phenomenon was perceived by H. G. Wells when he wrote of the 'mystical awe' with which the royal family had come to be regarded by 'the ignorant and foolish'.[4] This new and spurious mystique surrounding the monarchy – a curious throwback, in an age of rationalism, to the magical and superstitious view of kingship held by our tribal forebears – did not arise by accident,

[23]

and the event that had most bearing on it was the premature death of the Prince Consort in 1861.

Queen Victoria was devastated by the loss of her 'ideal Being' and her reaction was to become a virtual recluse. For three years after Albert's death she refused to appear publicly in London, and when she did finally emerge it was only to be driven in her carriage to Paddington railway station. It was five years before she presided at the opening of Parliament, and then did so only with a good deal of ill-will. She tried in vain to prevent ministers from seeing her in person, but had more success in declining to receive visitors in state, limiting her participation to private audiences. 'To speak in rude and general terms,' complained Gladstone, the Liberal leader, 'the Queen is invisible.'[5] The credit of the monarch, he added, having been 'augmented by good husbandry in the early and middle part of this reign', was now diminishing.

Public discontent soon became obvious. There were critical comments and cartoons in the press and political agitators began to suggest that if Britain had a Queen whom nobody saw and who appeared to ignore what was expected of her, then there was little point in having a monarch at all. To demands that working men be given the franchise was added the thought that the nation might be better off with an elected head of state. Throughout the 1860s republicanism spread until there were more than fifty anti-monarchy societies scattered about the country. The Queen herself began to take the pessimistic view that the monarchy would not outlive her. Buckingham Palace was the target of mischievous posters declaring, 'These commanding premises to be let or sold, in consequence of the late occupant's declining business.' It began to look as if Prince Albert, who had done so much to enhance the position of the monarchy, was involuntarily to have a hand in destroying it through dying at the wrong moment.

But in this drama of an inconsolable Queen wallowing in self-pity, one actor had yet to appear. He made his triumphant entrance on February 27th, 1868: Benjamin Disraeli, summoned to the presence of the sovereign as prime minister. No one knew better than he how to manipulate, and from the start he set out to confound the republicans and the agitators by uniting the great mass of the people behind the person and the symbol of the Queen. He won over Victoria by extravagant flattery and pandering; he won over the people by creating the figure of a Queen who represented in her person all that was great and good in the nation, and by giving the masses the pomp and ceremony such greatness was considered to deserve.

A master of illusion, as might be expected of a romantic novelist and a highly skilled politician, Disraeli accomplished a remarkable double bluff. He actually diminished the political power of the sovereign, fought for by Prince Albert, while convincing the Queen that she had never enjoyed firmer control. He also persuaded the British people that in some mystical way the Queen was their supragovernmental representative whose presence cast a brilliant light over the grim shadows of nineteenth-century hypocrisy, injustice and complacency. Though his first term of office was brief, he continued to fawn to the Queen and, by the time the Conservatives were returned to power in 1874, the period of royal seclusion was history. Two years earlier, Victoria had been carried in splendour through the London streets – waving, nodding and smiling to cheering multitudes – to attend a service of thanksgiving at St Paul's Cathedral marking the recovery of her son, the Prince of Wales, from an attack of typhoid. Six years later, in April 1880, the Queen drove to a splendid state opening of Parliament in a new coach specially designed to give the public a better view of their sovereign than ever before.

By that time, Victoria had become Queen-Empress, as befitted the head of state of the greatest imperial power the world had ever seen, and Disraeli had been created Earl of Beaconsfield. Between them they had established the mythology of the modern British monarchy.

Yet neither Queen nor country would ever forget the precepts of Prince Albert, so that by the 1880s the monarchy had come to be perceived both as representing moderate, sensible, middle-class values and as deserving of the reverence accorded to a holy icon. Few people appeared to notice the paradox: indeed, the confusion of images became the foundation of the eccentric modern edifice known as the British constitution, the unwitting architect of which was Walter Bagehot, a journalist who in the late 1860s had written a series of articles outlining his personal vision of the governance of England – a treatise eagerly seized upon by the ambitious middle class, whose cause it espoused, and converted almost into immutable law. The contradiction inherent in the combination of Prince Albert's active, representative sovereign and Disraeli's surreal, quasi-religious symbol thus came to be accepted as the essential feature of constitutional monarchy. What has never been accepted is the fact that there *is* a contradiction, and this was to present difficulties to Queen Victoria's descendants.

King Edward VII, reacting wilfully against all Prince Albert stood for, preferred to ignore the disparity, embracing the mystical aspects of monarchy but not the middle-class philosophy. His grandson, Edward VIII, tended towards the opposite view, and foundered because of his fundamental misunderstanding of what middle-class attitudes were in the mid-1930s. It fell to George V and George VI to try to fashion some sort of working model of monarchy out of parts that did not really fit together. But, as second sons, neither had grown up with the prospect of kingship before him; neither had much experience of or objective interest in politics; neither had the astuteness, intelligence or acute instincts of a Prince Albert; neither appreciated the conflicting nature of the demands made upon him. It is hardly surprising that, in spite of their earnest intent and their best efforts, their reigns served mainly to increase the confusion and misunderstanding that surrounds the interrelationship of the monarchy, the government and the people in modern Britain.

2

'Peculiar to Himself'

The future King George V was born on June 3rd, 1865, at Marlborough House, the London home of his parents, the Prince and Princess of Wales. There were the customary artillery salutes at St James's Park and the Tower of London, but otherwise the birth of the Waleses' second son attracted little attention. Prince George was only third in line to the throne – the heir presumptive, after his father, was Prince Albert Victor, born eighteen months before George – and, in any case, the popularity of the royal family had fallen. Queen Victoria remained in seclusion following the death of her husband and public interest had turned towards the great politicians of the day in search of heroes. As the novels of Anthony Trollope show so vividly, politics in the second half of the nineteenth century was both a spectator and participatory sport. The comfortable classes found themselves diverted by parliamentary battles and manoeuvrings, while many intellectuals fashioned hazy visions of a new kind of liberty based on republicanism, and the disaffected members of the proletariat sought escape from the excesses of the Industrial Revolution through the Radical movement. The monarchy seemed at best irrelevant and at worst distasteful, the latter view reinforced by the behaviour of the Prince of Wales and his racy 'Marlborough House Set'. Even so firm a supporter of the monarchical concept as Walter Bagehot admitted that the crown appeared to be represented by 'a retired widow and an unemployed youth'.

The Prince of Wales was the antithesis of his father's exemplary ideals. Prince Albert, with his customary thoroughness and attention to detail, had designed for his eldest son a system of education which was described by the Bishop of Oxford as intended to make the heir of the throne 'the most perfect man that ever lived'. The effects of this education on its recipient, however, were almost entirely negative. Not only did the Prince of Wales lack his father's keen intelligence and self-discipline, but his personality was more attuned to an earlier, more liberal tradition than to Prince Albert's steady respectability and earnest industry. The strict regime imposed on the boy by his father, while well-intentioned and no doubt technically sound, left no room for the young Prince Bertie's passionate and loving nature, for the softer, more romantic side of his character, or for much in the way of childish fun. From the start it was a disastrous failure. Bertie showed no aptitude for and precious little interest in his studies and began to display a violent temper and a rebellious streak.

As a result, Prince Albert became increasingly disappointed in his son, but his own arrogance and self-righteousness could not admit of a fault in his thinking and he sought reasons elsewhere for this failure of rationality. After consulting a leading phrenologist, who commented on the feeble quality of Bertie's brain, Albert reached the conclusion that his son's weaknesses must have been inherited from what he considered to be the feckless Stuart line of the English royal family. The phrenologist, on the other hand, took the view that the mad Hanoverian king, George III, was responsible and recommended a programme of teaching that would not place too much strain on Bertie's mind. Whatever the scientific merits or otherwise of phrenology, it is interesting to note that the practitioner consulted by Prince Albert was remarkably accurate in his assessment of Bertie's character: obstinate, sometimes destructive, puffed up with self-esteem, but truthful, loyal and straightforward. So he was as a boy, as a man and as a king.

The Prince Consort, however, rejected the advice of his phrenologist, as he did the counsel of most of the tutors who tried to deal with Bertie over the years. The regime was not relaxed, but instead became so harsh and demanding that one must infer its aim was to break the boy's spirit. Orders were given that he must go to bed exhausted each evening and, as he grew older, he was denied the company of boys of his own age, lest they exploit his perceived weaknesses and lead him astray. It is odd that Albert, who appears to have understood so well the psychology of his wife, should have been so blind when considering the personality of his son, yet it is a fact that all the father's efforts produced in the heir to the throne effects that were the very opposite of those intended. Bertie's natural strengths became almost completely obscured by his weaknesses, which were indulged most freely once his father's restraining influence had been removed.

The consequences of this parental mismanagement were to be far-reaching, affecting not only relations between Bertie and Queen Victoria but also the way in which the Prince of Wales raised his own children, a significant factor in the course taken by the monarchy under King George V. In the first place, there was a serious and damaging conflict between Queen Victoria and her heir as to what the official role of the Prince of Wales should be. The Queen, of course, accepted her husband's judgment on Bertie as she did on all other matters. She had agreed early on that her eldest son could not be trusted to take part in the business of state until he had shown himself to be more responsible, and after Albert's death she saw no reason to change her mind. Indeed, she tended to hold Bertie partly to blame for his father's fatal illness on account of the young Prince's scandalous entanglement in 1861 with the actress Nellie Clifden, which had caused as much pain and anxiety to his parents as it had promoted mirth among high society in London and other European capitals. Furthermore, the refusal of the Prince of Wales to indulge in the same prolonged orgy of grief as his mother indicated to the Queen that he had not profited from his father's example and she began to suspect that the heir to the throne was less than fit for his calling. Generous and kind-hearted he might be – and relations between mother and son were rarely less than affectionate – but Bertie was lacking in tact and discretion, was inclined to act carelessly and selfishly and seemed to have little sense of duty. The Queen concluded that the Prince of Wales must be excluded from the conduct of affairs.

It is not clear what Victoria hoped to achieve through this policy. Presumably it was intended to demonstrate to the Prince that he could not expect to assume his proper role in royal and national life until he gave some sign of having acquired a sense of responsibility, of being 'ready' to take up the great burden which his saintly father had carried so manfully. The Queen apparently failed to understand that by refusing to allow Bertie any part in matters of state she was denying him the very opportunity he needed to show her that, in spite of his shortcomings, her suspicions about his fitness for the task were ill-founded. She was also robbing him of the experience necessary for him ever to carry out properly the functions that he would inevitably inherit one day and, perhaps more cruelly, she was leaving him with nothing to do but kick his heels and indulge in the pursuit of idle pleasure to which he naturally inclined.

What was really required for the Prince was not discipline but

direction, an outlet for his restless energy. Bertie, though not endowed
with great mental gifts, understood this himself, and so did a number
of politicians who pleaded with the Queen to give the Prince something
definite to do. Flexibility, however, was not one of Victoria's attributes.
Once she had made up her mind, it was well nigh impossible to move
her, added to which was the fact that the opinions of Prince Albert
had, with his death, assumed the quality of commandments in the
Queen's consciousness. If Albert had said Bertie could not be trusted
with state papers, then that was the end of the matter. All requests
for the involvement of the Prince in the business of the monarchy
were refused. On his part, Bertie reasoned that if the emptiness of
his existence was not to be relieved by some worthwhile endeavour,
then he might as well at least enjoy himself. The results of the Queen's
blindness and obstinacy were, in the end, bad for her relations with
her son, bad for Bertie himself, bad for his long-suffering wife and,
ultimately, bad for the monarchy.

In a way, Bertie was a throwback to an earlier notion of royalty,
having more in common with the Prince Regent than with the Prince
Consort. The sense of self-esteem noted by Prince Albert's phrenologist manifested itself in an attitude that noble birth was an excuse
for almost everything, a belief that the old idea of *le roi le veult* (or in
this case 'the *prince* wishes it') ought to be sufficient for it to be so.
Bertie's desire to take a hand in government was probably prompted
less by the urge to serve than by the notion that active membership
of the ruling class was nothing more or less than his birthright. In his
scheme of things, however, the ruling class was the aristocracy, a view
that did not find favour with the Queen, who regularly criticised the
Prince of Wales for his association with the more self-indulgent
members of the titled classes. Victoria firmly believed that the frivolity,
idleness and scandalous behaviour of certain sections of the aristocracy
– the 'fast' set – were the prime cause of unrest among the working
classes and the growth of republican movements. The excesses of 'the
Higher Classes', she told Bertie, brought to mind the period before
the French Revolution and she warned him that 'in the twinkling of
an eye' the highest in the land might easily find themselves at the
mercy of those they regarded as their inferiors.

The Prince would have none of it. He admitted, in a letter to his
mother, that there was growing distaste for and opposition to the
monarchy in certain quarters, but he did not believe this had anything
to do with the way he and his friends conducted themselves. The
trouble was that the lower classes already had too much power, more,
indeed, than they had any idea of. If this power was allowed to grow,

and if the people became aware of its extent, then they would become unmanageable and 'it will cause bloodshed'. As for the aristocracy, a great proportion would be 'idle and fond of amusement' – that had always been so. But the Prince thought the higher classes in England occupied themselves more fruitfully than their counterparts in other countries. England had always been an aristocratic country, he said, and he hoped it would always remain so, for the aristocracy was the mainstay of the nation. All these demonstrations by workers and all this republican talk, the Prince believed, should be prevented by the government, otherwise 'democratic feeling' would only increase.[1]

The Queen despaired. Her second daughter, Princess Alice, noted that 'she thinks the monarchy will last her time and it is no use thinking what will come after if the principal person himself does not, and so she lets the torrent come on'. The principal person himself certainly gave no appearance of caring about the future as his name was dragged through the courts in a series of scandals, including sensational divorce cases, and his love affairs became subjects of gossip that spread far beyond the Court and the great houses upon which Bertie would regularly descend and demand to be entertained in suitably royal style. Among his circle he came to be known irreverently as 'Tum-Tum' (although one drunken baronet who used the nickname to the Prince's face was summarily ejected from the royal country residence at Sandringham). In the popular press he was reviled, one newspaper expressing anxiety 'as to whether the Queen's successor will have the tact and talent to keep royalty upon its legs and out of the gutter'. To sections of the public the Prince was both a figure of fun and a target for abuse, greeted with hissing and catcalls and attacked in Radical pamphlets, one of which ventured to hope that he would 'never dishonour his country by becoming its King'.

At the time of an infamous divorce case in which Sir Charles Mordaunt sought to prove that his wife had committed adultery with the Prince of Wales, among others, the Prince found himself in the witness-box. A popular verse gives some idea of the esteem in which people held their future sovereign:

> This lady's appetite
> It really is enormous,
> But whether right or wrong,
> The papers will inform us.
> She is fond of veal and ham,

To feed she is a glutton.
She got tired of Charley's lamb
And longed for royal mutton.

This sort of thing, as the Queen rightly pointed out at the time, was hardly likely to enhance the image of the Prince among 'the lower and middle classes' who, Prince Albert had taught her, were the real mainstays of the country. But in doubting whether Bertie would ever succeed to the throne, or if he did whether he could ever be respected, she overlooked four significant factors that would influence public opinion.

First, among the supporters of the monarchy – who remained very much in the majority in spite of all the republican agitation in the 1860s – there was a great deal of sympathy for the Prince of Wales as an heir to the throne who was being prevented from learning his job. The newspaper editor W. T. Stead summed up the attitude of many shrewd politicians and observers when he said that 'if the Prince of Wales had been saddled with his father's duties, he might have developed somewhat more of his father's virtues'. The idea that the devil makes work for idle hands was a significant part of middle-class philosophy in Victorian England, as it is in our own day, and the scandalous behaviour of the Prince could be explained away, if not exactly excused, by the fact that he had no useful and worthwhile work to do. By excluding Bertie from serious constitutional duties, Queen Victoria was in effect creating for him a store of credit among those who would be disposed towards overlooking his peccadilloes once he became king. He had not been to blame, people would say: it had been the fault of the Queen for keeping him in enforced idleness.

The second thing the Queen did not consider when she expressed doubts about Bertie's fitness to reign was the depth of hypocrisy in the society over which she reigned. Although moral rectitude, hard work and self-help were the watchwords of the respectable classes, there remained in many apparently worthy minds both an envy of the leisured aristocracy and a sneaking desire for the fun and freedom of the libertarian eighteenth century. Beneath its cloak of pious earnestness, Victorian society seethed with vice and corruption which were characterised by their furtiveness. Pornography and prostitution flourished. And there is plenty of evidence to show that in many cases the degree of righteousness displayed was in direct proportion to the depth of lust felt, just as pride of position often increased in direct proportion to the corruption which produced that position. There were many people, therefore, who criticised the Prince of Wales for his philandering or his extravagance yet at the same time wished that they could emulate him (or even did so in their own small ways) and admired him for 'getting away with it'. Thus Bertie was not really as unpopular as he might have seemed to the Queen.

Thirdly, the Prince of Wales was, if not constitutionally useful, then at least visible. While the Queen remained in seclusion, it was Bertie who carried out the minor tasks that were coming to be expected of the royal personage – opening public buildings, laying foundation-stones, visiting institutions, attending official luncheons and dinners, presiding at charity functions, serving on committees, providing patronage for organisations and so on. He was also frequently seen enjoying himself at the races, so that he was a familiar figure to large numbers of people, whereas the Queen was remote and inaccessible. It was no accident that people came to view the Queen with awe and the Prince of Wales with affection.

Finally, the Queen also failed to understand that although there was opposition to the monarchy among some Radicals, and although 'respectable' people might imagine themselves scandalised by the association of the heir to the throne with the more raffish elements of the higher classes, the Prince of Wales was generally regarded as a relatively harmless figure, a lightweight in metaphorical if not in physical terms. The pursuit of pleasure in which the Prince and his friends indulged, and their thoughtless extravagance, might be condemned by Radicals as examples of social injustice and deplored by the industrious middle classes as empty and useless, but such behaviour could be tolerated because it presented no threat to what were seen as the main elements of national life. While Bertie and the Marlborough House Set ate, drank, danced, gambled and carried on their amorous intrigues, they were in no sense interfering with the more serious concerns of others, whether those concerns involved economic advancement, political reform or cultural development. Indeed, the Marlborough House Set had very little interest in such matters. One of the Prince's mistresses, Lady Warwick, summed up their attitude in a succinct comment: 'As a class, we did not like brains.' Although recognising that the country had to be governed, the law administered, books written and pictures painted, the members of the Prince's group assumed there were less elevated sections of society to whom these things could safely be delegated: upholding the ancient privilege of the leisured classes to enjoy themselves left little time or energy for anything else.

In short, the Prince of Wales and his aristocratic circle were irrelevant to the great march of progress that was the well-spring of nineteenth-century endeavour. Their attitudes and activities were quaint reminders of an old order which, everyone but the most blinkered could see, was rapidly disappearing. They were, in modern jargon, members of an endangered species who could be allowed to survive, suitably restricted, for the sake of curiosity and nostalgia, provided their survival offered no threat to the new order. Where was the harm in retaining a monarchy that was at least decorative and, unlike the Austrian Habsburgs, the German Hohenzollerns and the Russian Romanovs, was in no real sense oppressive? What was wrong with keeping a landed aristocracy that provided a living link with a glorious past, just so long as it was firmly disabused of any idea that it still ruled the country? The frivolous and well-publicised antics of the Marlborough House Set, because of their very superficiality and lack of connection with 'real' life, served to facilitate social change rather than to impede it. They helped to perpetuate the impression that the foundations of the British way of life remained the same, whereas in fact the last quarter of the nineteenth century and the first decade of the twentieth saw the making of a revolution as far-reaching in its own quiet way as the bloody upheaval that was to sweep Russia in 1917. The last British prime minister to govern from the House of Lords took office in 1895 and the first true constitutional monarch in the modern sense of the term, King George V, came to the throne in 1910.

Of course, none of this was apparent to Queen Victoria, who would no doubt have been surprised at the depth of affection inspired by the Prince of Wales when he eventually became king in his sixtieth year. Disraeli, however, who had transformed the Queen into the great imperial figurehead we now remember, would probably have smiled with satisfaction. He had seen that the rise of the middle-class, meritocratic elite was inevitable and had understood that, as far as Europe was concerned, the nineteenth century, which witnessed progress far more rapid and excited aspirations far higher than in any previous age, was a furnace heating up the raw materials of nationalism and pride of statehood into a fusion that would unite whole populations in a way never seen before. Disraeli also realised that this new sense of pride and loyalty could best be harnessed to the national good if it found expression through a powerful, familiar and harmless symbol – and England possessed just such a symbol in its monarchy. Despite the materialism and scientific rationalism of his day, he helped to create round the person of Queen Victoria an aura, a mystique with an emotional power as great as, if not greater than, that of the Church in the superstitious Middle Ages. So potent was this image, transcending the personalities even of those to whom it was applied, that it passed directly and immediately to King Edward VII when he was crowned at Westminster Abbey on August 9th, 1902.

Like his mother, King Edward bequeathed his name to an epoch, but his is a time viewed by history very much as an interregnum. The Edwardian age looks now like a period of relative calm before the great storms that have scarred the twentieth century, a breathing-space, a shuddering pause during which the old order managed to slow down for a time the monstrous engines of destruction which it had carelessly constructed in the name of progress and by which it would finally be overwhelmed. It was Edward's misfortune, perhaps, to become king in the twilight not only of his own life but also of the old world, and yet in a way the man and the times were in fitting conjunction. He was not a great king. In the words of Edward Grey, who was at the Foreign Office during Victoria's last years and throughout Edward's reign, his gifts as sovereign were no more than 'the intangible qualities of a personality peculiar to himself'. But those qualities matched perfectly the demands of the day and the characteristics required of the first inheritor of the new mystique of the monarchy.

Grey (later Sir Edward and finally Viscount Grey of Fallodon) noted approvingly that the King had 'in a very high degree the gift, proper and valuable in a Sovereign, for ceremonial. No one knew so well as he how ceremony should be arranged, ordered and carried through in the manner most effective and impressive.' This ceremonial function, so useful in the maintenance of empire, could only be performed by the monarch, Grey pointed out, but it was only a small part of what was expected of him.

> Unless there be something else, people are left satisfied but cold: they may even come to resent the pomp and the display. King Edward had a rare, if not a unique, power of combining bonhomie and dignity. The bonhomie was warm and spontaneous, but it never impaired the dignity. His bearing was a perfect example of tact, ease and dignity, and to this was added good sense and judgment that not only avoided mistakes, but perceived the thing that should be said to suit the occasion and please the individual.

All this makes the King sound like a public relations man, and indeed that is what he was to some extent. The mystique having been created, it was necessary for the monarch to live up to the image, to be what people now expected a king to be. Just what those expectations were Grey outlined concisely in his memoirs. The sovereign, he said, must maintain 'complete aloofness from rivalry and controversy. . . . He must, in his person, embody the traditions of the past as well as the practices of the present.' Such things came quite naturally to King Edward. He had a fine sense of his own superiority and the petty squabbles of lesser men were nothing to him. As for controversy, Grey was speaking in the political sense and politics was of little interest to the King, except where it interfered with his pleasures or prevented him from making one of the visits abroad which he so enjoyed. Upholding the traditions of the past was a way of life with him – again, so long as it suited his personal plans – and, as far as he was concerned, the practices of the present were what he himself did. He was perfectly prepared to do almost everything that was asked of him constitutionally, but his was a self-centred existence in which his comforts and his pleasures were paramount, so that there was also a certain air of detachment which, combined with his commanding presence and forceful personality, added lustre to the mythology of the monarchy. He was clearly a man apart, but one who because of his warm and unaffected good nature could also add glamour to ordinary life by appearing to take part in it. Margot Asquith, the wife of the leader of the Liberal Party, commented: 'He subscribes to his cripples, rewards his sailors, reviews his soldiers, and opens bridges, bazaars, hospitals and railway tunnels with enviable sweetness.' Far from perfect as a man, he was very much the ideal monarch for the England of his time.

Certainly, from the point of view of the politicians Edward could hardly have been a more suitable king, one who took notice of what 'his' government was doing but who for the most part did not interfere. Grey, who became Foreign Secretary in 1905, firmly dispelled the popular legend that the King, in his frequent visits to the Continent, was directing British foreign policy. Grey wrote:

> He not only accepted the constitutional practice that policy must be that of his Ministers, but he preferred that it be so. . . . He read all the important papers, and now and then a despatch would come back with some short marginal comment approving of something contained in it; but comment of any sort was rare, and I do not remember criticism or suggestion.

Not that the King was indifferent in the matter of foreign policy, but 'he did not care for long and sustained discussion' about its larger aspects.

On the other hand, he was extremely useful to the government on an international stage dominated by the imperial powers of Europe. As a king-emperor himself, albeit without the power of his royal relatives in Germany and Russia, he met the Kaiser and the Tsar on equal terms and his contacts with them naturally contained a strong personal element which took diplomacy to levels unattainable by ministers and ambassadors. A visit by him to Berlin or St Petersburg could be used as a cover for diplomatic activity while at the same time reassuring the Germans or the Russians that Britain remained close to them, even if, say, the governments in London and Paris were engaged in negotiations that might be unwelcome to the other powers. In the atmosphere of rivalry and suspicion that infected Europe during the early years of this century, such outward displays of goodwill could help to heal rifts at the political level or, if required, serve as a warning to governments not so honoured by a royal visit that they must work harder to earn Britain's support. For example, the republican French took offence when it was arranged that Kaiser Wilhelm should visit King Edward in London in 1907. 'That could not he helped,' the Foreign Secretary noted. 'There was no reason why our relations with France should stand in the way of good relations with Germany; it would have been still more unreasonable to suppose that King Edward and the Emperor were not to meet and to be as intimate as they chose.' As a concession to the French, however, the visit took place at Windsor rather than in London. Subsequently the King 'visited the Tsar at Reval and . . . in the course of his stay abroad, he saw the Austrian Emperor at Ischl,' which made the Germans 'as sensitive as anyone'. It was a sort of royal Punch and Judy show with the politicians pulling the strings.

The King himself cared little for such manoeuvrings. Edward Grey wrote:

> It was my impression that [he] enjoyed these visits, and he certainly had no desire to spoil his own part in them by going into deep political waters. He desired to have someone with him to whom he could refer any Sovereign or Foreign Minister who wished to have serious political discussions.

Nevertheless, the King could take a certain mischievous pleasure in the arrangement of his visits, particularly when they might tend to annoy the Kaiser. 'The King simply dislikes the Emperor,' the Princess of Pless (formerly Daisy Cornwallis-West) wrote in her diary towards the end of 1907 after a conversation with the Kaiser about the attitudes towards Germany in her native land. 'I am sure he has no real and dangerous intentions towards Germany; but he just shows his teeth when a German approaches him.' Edward was more at home in France, which he visited as often as he could, and he enthusiastically supported the development of the *entente cordiale*, no matter what the Germans might think about it.

Since the King's public interests were conditioned largely by his private desires, chief among them the urge to travel abroad, domestic policy meant little to him, except where it touched upon his own position and that of the old ruling class. He resented the power of the government to ignore the advice he was constitutionally permitted to offer and he frequently came into conflict with ministers, a situation not improved by his quick temper and obstinacy. One member of his staff, Sir Frederick Ponsonby, confessed that at times he was surprised by the King's smallness of mind: 'He would be almost childish in his views, and would obstinately refuse to understand the question at issue.' This attitude of the King's led some political leaders merely to ignore him, particularly the Conservative Prime Minister, Arthur Balfour, who took office in 1902. Balfour, a favourite of Queen Victoria during his days as a Cabinet minister, was 'of all men least able to bring his intellect down to what he no doubt conceived the low level of the King's,' wrote his friend Sir Lionel Cust, the art historian and surveyor of the King's pictures. 'The King to Balfour was at first just one of those irritating factors in general politics, which you cannot ignore, and which you must treat with dismal and fictitious solemnity.' By the end of Balfour's premiership in 1906 the King had virtually ceased seeing ministers in formal audience. He was more comfortable dealing with them at arm's length through intermediaries or conversing casually with them at social gatherings: they took so little notice of what he said that there seemed no point in making the effort any more.

Change was anathema to him, especially changes that suggested a greater degree of democracy. At the end of the South African War he complained bitterly at the government's decision to summon a royal commission to review the prosecution of the war – he could not see why 'dirty linen' should be washed in public merely to satisfy a few 'unimportant' Members of Parliament. He was appalled at the prospect of prominent Indians serving on the Viceroy's Council: 'clever Natives' would only cause trouble for the Empire. But, as he put it himself, no member of his 'precious government!' seemed to care what he said.

Like most of his aristocratic friends, the King was too concerned with himself to understand what was happening beyond the walls of palaces and stately homes, too little in touch with reality to see that the world was rapidly moving on and leaving his sort behind, too proud to admit that there might be serious flaws in the structure he was trying to protect. As a force in shaping the British monarchy, he may be discounted: indeed, the first serious demands of the new order, which came with the reforming Liberal administration of 1908, seem to have been too much for the King to bear. The Princess of Pless wrote to the Prime Minister, Herbert Asquith, in May 1910 saying she believed that 'on top of the King's serious illness in Biarritz, to come back to be dragged into the middle of a political struggle verging on Socialism and to see his country falling towards the blind pit of darkness . . . was quite enough to give him a shocking fit and so to kill him'.

His popularity as king and the deep sense of national loss felt at his death on May 6th, 1910, resulted from the largeness of his character and his all too human qualities, rather than from any great gifts as a constitutional monarch. His beliefs, even when they were wrong or outdated, were always honestly held and, as Lord Granville had said of him when he had still been Prince of Wales, he had 'all the faults of which the Englishman is accused'. If he was unfortunate in having had to wait so long to come into his inheritance, he was lucky to do so at a time when Britain was at the peak of its imperial power and could smile tolerantly and affectionately at his faults. Had he been more intelligent and more politically aware, he might easily have been mistrusted and unpopular. As it was, in the words of his friend Lord Fisher, the First Lord of the Admiralty, 'he wasn't clever, but he always did the right thing, which is better than brains'. That was certainly true at the time, but while it continued to be the case that intelligence was the last thing required of a British monarch, the idea of what was the right thing to do was beginning to change. The next king, George V, would be expected to play a role very different from that of his father – a part which he never quite understood, but for which, by the curious conjunction of history and his own personality, he proved to be perfectly cast. Yet in the very success with which George V is generally credited can be found the beginnings of a process that subverted Prince Albert's ideal of a constitutional monarchy and reduced it to a mere constitutional ornament.

3

The Education
of Princes

King George V was a month short of his forty-fifth birthday when he came to the throne, fifteen years younger than his father had been at his accession and, on the surface at least, considerably better prepared. True, in his early youth George had looked forward to nothing more than a career in the Royal Navy, rejoicing in the fact that he was not the heir to the throne after his father: 'My brother has to take all the kow-towing and gets a rotten time,' Prince George had once said, 'while I lark about and enjoy myself.' All that changed, however, when the elder brother, Prince Albert Victor, Duke of Clarence, died of pneumonia in January 1892, aged twenty-seven. George became heir presumptive and in the spring of 1893 was created Duke of York, Earl of Inverness and Baron Killarney. Although it was to be 1898 before he left the Navy for good, his real career – if such it may be called – during the intervening five years had already become that of a king-in-waiting. His father, bitterly aware of the disadvantage under which he was placed as Prince of Wales by Queen Victoria's stubborn refusal to initiate him into the mysteries of the business of state, resolved that his own heir should be given every opportunity to make himself ready for kingship when his time should come.

The fact that it was Prince George rather than Prince Eddy (as the Duke of Clarence was always called by his family, the diminutive of his fourth and final forename) who had to be educated for the throne must in a sense have been something of a relief to the Prince of Wales. While he and the Princess were devastated by Eddy's sudden death, they could hardly have failed to be aware that as a future king the Duke of Clarence had presented peculiar problems. He was not very bright and, as he grew older, his dissolute tastes became wellknown.

He was a notorious drinker, his name was linked to an unsavoury scandal surrounding a high-class homosexual brothel and there was also much gossip about his love affairs with women, some high-born and others definitely not so. There were widespread rumours that his lack of intelligence, unhealthy appearance and unstable nature were the result of softening of the brain brought on by syphilis and in 1888 it was even whispered in some quarters, including certain sections of the London police force, that Eddy was responsible for the terrible 'Jack the Ripper' murders of prostitutes in the East End. The evidence was entirely circumstantial and no open accusation was ever made, but a century later there are still those who harbour suspicions.[1]

During the year before Eddy's death, his behaviour had become so erratic and his parents' anxieties so great that there had been plans to send him on an extended tour of the Colonies and perhaps of Europe, too, so that he should be hidden from the gaze of the British public and kept out of the way of temptation for as long as possible. His early death, therefore, provided a solution for the royal family and the government to a very difficult situation, which could have become unmanageable had Eddy lived. The grand young Duke of York, who never seemed to put a foot wrong, was an altogether better prospect as a future occupant of the throne.

George, though he was almost eighteen months younger than Eddy, had always appeared to be the elder brother in physical and other respects. He was a healthy and high-spirited child and, while very far from being intellectually gifted, he possessed a sharp, practical intelligence allied to an open, friendly manner and some sense of propriety. Eddy, on the other hand, was sickly, immature, introverted, shy and noticeably slow-witted. Both in physique and in character Eddy was unattractive and his generally awkward manner sometimes gave way to behaviour that bordered on the vicious. Nevertheless, while he lived Eddy was the heir presumptive and, though his parents could not ignore his weaknesses, appearances had to be maintained and the fiction preserved that all was as it should be. One of the drawbacks of strictly hereditary monarchy is that there is no way of ensuring that the succession passes to the most suitable person.

The age difference of less than two years between Eddy and George suggests that there would have been no hint of the problems to come with the elder boy at the time of the second son's birth. Yet immediately after George was born it was noted, and reported to Queen Victoria, that the new baby was 'much larger than little Albert Victor and nice and plump'.[2] The Prince of Wales, the Queen told King Leopold of the Belgians, was very pleased with his second-born. The Queen herself, though, was less than pleased with the selection of the names George Frederick Ernest Albert for the new prince. She would have preferred some 'fine old name', she said, instead of George, which was merely a Hanoverian import of the previous century. Frederick she did not care for at all.[3] But the Prince and Princess of Wales, having been forced by the Queen to name their first child Albert Victor, were determined to have their own way in naming the second. Victoria had to be content with the fact that they had at least continued to respect her wish that the beloved name of Albert should be given to all the male descendants of the house of Saxe-Coburg.

The Prince of Wales was equally set on going his own way in the matter of his sons' upbringing, though again, like so much he did, it was to bring him into conflict with the Queen. He remembered with horror his own restricted youth, his father's almost obsessive concern with hard work and self-improvement, and he made up his mind that *his* children should have a much better time of it. His sense of deprivation led him to regard childhood in excessively romantic, even mystical terms. It was a time not to be endured, as he had experienced it, but to be enjoyed, and for as long as possible. Like many a parent, he sought to compensate for a perceived deficiency in his own life by remedying it in the lives of his offspring, without regard to whether it was good or desirable for them. In his efforts to ensure a happy childhood for his sons he was entirely supported by his wife, though from quite a different point of view. Princess Alexandra looked back with warm nostalgia to her happy early years in Denmark in the midst of an affectionate, united family of doting parents and devoted children and wished to recreate that atmosphere in her own household. But there was another reason for the abundance of maternal affection and indulgence she displayed, particularly towards Prince George, who was probably the most responsive of her children. It was the Princess's way of maintaining the security of love about her as the realisation grew that she had a husband who was at best egocentric and at worst uncaring, who increasingly devoted himself to selfish pleasures that did not require the presence of a wife, and who, easily bored, began to seek the constant stimuli he needed by dallying with other women. Perhaps in a sense, for the Princess of Wales, the open-hearted, affectionate and sentimental young Prince George became a partial surrogate for the preoccupied and philandering husband.

Of course, such a Freudian connection would have played no part in the conscious emotions of the Princess. So far as she was concerned, her children, again George in particular, never really grew up. 'I hate letting you out of my sight even for a week,' she wrote in 1879, the year when her two sons, aged sixteen and fifteen respectively, began their naval careers in earnest with two long cruises, the second of which was to take them round the world and last for two years. She told 'my little Georgie', whom she would always find 'quite the same and unchanged in every respect', that every evening she expected to see him coming in to her room after tea and 'every morning on awaking I can *almost* fancy your two little voices squeaking into my ear but instead it is only the two white kittens which [your] sisters are putting on my pillow'. (One would hope that the boys' voices had in fact broken by that time!) During the second of the two cruises, the Princess wrote to George: 'I am longing to hear from my dear little sprat. . . . How I miss you and long to see your dear little turn-up snout again.' Ten years or so later the tone had not changed at all. The Prince was twenty-five and commanding a gunboat when he received a letter from his mother that ended with 'a great big kiss for your lovely little face'.

For his part, the Prince, fond as he became of the rugged camaraderie and the salty humour of the wardroom, was quite un-abashed to find himself responding to his mother in terms that might have been thought rather less than manly: 'I wonder who will have that sweet little room of mine? You must go and see it sometimes and imagine that your Georgie dear is living in it.' He seems to have been quite content with the role of the boy who never grew up, sometimes even displaying a childlike selfishness in his relations with 'Mother-dear'. In 1909, less than a year before his accession, he received a letter from the then Queen Alexandra written during her summer holiday at Balmoral:

> I do miss you my darling boy so dreadfully at times. . . . Really on board the yacht at Cowes seems the only time we ever sleep under the same roof which makes me quite low and unhappy when thinking of how formerly we were so much together and to each other. Of course I know it can't be helped but that does not make it better. If I had not my darling Toria [Princess Victoria] with me I should indeed be quite miserable and lonely as Papa is always so much away now from home.

The Prince, then aged forty-four and with a family of his own, told his wife Mary: 'I have actually had a long letter from Motherdear at Balmoral. She writes in rather a sad frame of mind and says she feels so lonely that none of us are there, but she doesn't understand of course about the shooting, grouse are always shot in August.' Staying

[43]

with the Duke of Devonshire at Bolton Abbey for the opening of the grouse season, he was too absorbed in his 'play' to heed his mother's call.

A certain lack of maturity in the characters of Eddy and George, arising from their mother's refusal to let go of their childhood, was in one way balanced by the attitude of the Prince of Wales but in another way actually encouraged. As Victorian fathers went, the Prince displayed more than ordinary affection towards his sons, but he did it in the rough, gruff way that at the time was perceived as being pleasantly masculine: they were fellows, after all, and it would not do to have them growing up soft. While, as the Prince put it, 'a child is always best looked after under its mother's eye,' it was a father's job to endow his sons with the attributes of manliness, such as courage, physical prowess and a sense of honour and fair play. Outdoor pursuits and games involving bodily contact were approved of, while paternal affection most often took the form of that good-humoured but some-times hurtful teasing known as 'chaffing' and, in its physical manifes-tation, a rough-and-tumble. 'The Royal Highnesses like nothing so much as a romp,' reported Constance de Rothschild, later Lady Battersea, during a visit to Sandringham. 'They would not hear of our going before the Romps. We are to have blind man's buff, tapping hands, snap-dragon etc. . . .' The emphasis was on the more animalistic aspects of boyhood, the child as man-cub. It has been said that certain of the Princes' young relatives dreaded their visits to Sandringham, anticipating the unbridled high spirits and innocent violence that awaited them.[4] But at least Eddy and George were tough, independent and self-assured – real little men, rather than the mummy's boys that the Princess's indulgence might have made them. In that sense they developed quickly.

However, another part of a father's duties was to instil and impose a sense of discipline, and here the Prince of Wales was somewhat ambivalent. On the one hand, as he pointedly told Queen Victoria, 'if children are too strictly or, perhaps, too severely treated, they get shy and only fear those whom they ought to love'. On the other hand, though, His Royal Highness had both an innate capacity for inspiring respect and a short, savage temper that provoked actual fear, which must have affected the little Princes no less than it did anyone else with whom he came into more than brief contact. It seems obvious, then, that the limits on behaviour would have been arbitrary and the parental signals contradictory, with the boys not required to show self-control (almost the reverse, in fact) and subject only to external discipline in a peremptory fashion at the farthest margin of patience.

Evidence from those who watched the children grow up supports this view.

'They are such ill-bred, ill-trained children, I can't fancy them at all,' Queen Victoria complained when Eddy and George were aged eight and seven respectively. They were 'wild as hawks'. Many others judged that the boys were spoilt and one, Lady Geraldine Somerset, described them as 'past all management' and even their sisters – the Princesses Louise, Maud and Victoria – as 'rampaging'. The Princess of Wales herself acknowledged that her children were 'dreadfully wild', but her lack of concern at and, indeed, tacit approval of this may be judged from her remark that 'I was just as bad.' The lack of discipline from their father and the excess of maternal indulgence meant that the Princes remained childlike, in their different ways, longer than they perhaps should have done and, in some respects, for the rest of their lives.

Nowhere was their late development more noticeable than in their education. Prince Eddy was certainly backward and Prince George was no better endowed with intellectual equipment than his father had been, but the real problem was that very little effort was made to inspire the boys to realise such potential as they had. True, educational fashion had moved away from classical rigour towards an emphasis on character-building and the inculcation of moral and religious principles: Dr Arnold of Rugby once dismissed 'mere intellectual acuteness' as 'more revolting than the most helpless imbecility'. It was not until late in the nineteenth century that the pursuit of academic excellence became the ideal. Even allowing for this, though, the Princes' academic standards fell far short of those of their contemporaries, and it is not difficult to see in the attitude of the Prince of Wales towards their education a reaction against the sort of unremitting schoolroom toil to which his father had subjected him. Prince Albert's excessive attention to the virtues of study had been counter-productive in the case of the Prince of Wales, and it led him to make few demands on the minds of his own sons. His vision of a happy, healthy, active childhood – no doubt the one he would have wished for himself – did not include a great deal in the way of scholastic achievement. Indeed, it is not hard to imagine that if Prince George had been an intense, studious, bookish type, considerable energy would have been devoted towards changing him. As I have pointed out, the Prince of Wales and his 'set' disliked cleverness and mistrusted education. Some basic schooling was necessary, of course, but anything more was of little use to a member of the royal family whose way of life was already laid out for him. There was no point in requiring standards higher than those essential to a comfortable, orderly, civilised life. Character, the attributes of what Dr Arnold called 'a Christian gentleman', were what mattered, and it was with this in mind that the Prince of Wales chose the boys' tutor.

John Neale Dalton was a man of unimpeachable character, conscientious, determined, responsible, with a fine sense of duty and morality. He was also well-educated, but he was perhaps not a natural educator, certainly in the academic sense. His first-class honours degree from Cambridge was in theology and at the time of his royal appointment, when he was thirty-two, he was curate of the parish of Whippingham, Isle of Wight, in which Queen Victoria's summer home, Osborne House, was situated. While there is no doubt that Dalton was, in many ways, an ideal guide and mentor for the young Princes, he was keenly aware of the honour conferred upon him through his selection as their tutor and this led him to place too much emphasis on his role as a royal servant. To be sure, while he was habitually deferential, he was never servile and his opinions of the Princes' progress were always frank, even if they were not what he knew the Prince of Wales or Queen Victoria wanted to hear. Nevertheless, he seems to have found it difficult to step outside the role of the retainer and to apply academic standards rather higher than those demanded by the system of education envisaged by the Prince of Wales. Following his own instincts, Dalton coaxed and encouraged and tried to lead, but he did not push, so that his young charges received only the education they were prepared to accept, rather than the schooling their tutor knew they required. For example, Dalton tried to interest Eddy and George in art and architecture, but when they did not respond he appears to have been quite content instead to let them pursue their own inclinations and to caper about the grounds of Sandringham pretending to be a deer while the Princes shot at him with bows and arrows. Sir Arthur Bryant summed it up when he noted of Prince George, 'Neither then nor at any other time did he show much enthusiasm for books,' adding with unwarranted complacency: 'Then as always he preferred life to art.'[5]

Given the educational philosophy of the period, the requirements of the Prince of Wales and the distinct lack of interest in learning shown by Eddy and George, it is not surprising that Dalton's weekly record of his pupils' development should have been weighted much more towards their personalities than their academic achievements. Of Prince George, for instance, Dalton noted:

Much troubled by silly fretfulness of temper and general spirit of contradiction. . . . Too fretful; and inclined to be lazy and silly this week. . . . Self-approbation enormously strong, becoming almost the only motive power. . . . The slightest difficulty discourages him and when he frets he finds it hard to subdue himself. . . . Prince George wants application, steady application. . . .

The Prince was aged eleven at the time.

The curriculum covered English, mathematics, history, geography, Latin, French, drawing and Bible studies, but in accordance with the desires of the Prince of Wales, and contemporary theories concerning a healthy upbringing, plenty of time was set aside for games and sports. Prince George was taught to shoot at an early age and there was also coaching in football, cricket, tennis and croquet. At Sandringham there was riding for pleasure and in London more rigorous equestrian training with the Household Cavalry, bearing in mind the importance of the horse in royal ceremonial. An army drill sergeant attended the boys when they were at Marlborough House, where they also took fencing lessons and practised gymnastics. Physically, no doubt, the Princes – especially George – could match any boy of their age in agility and prowess, but as far as their minds were concerned the effect of the educational system laid down by the Prince of Wales and carried out by Dalton was notable more for its negative than its positive features. When Prince George was ten, an age at which even in those days a reasonably intelligent boy might be expected to read fluently, Dalton was sending him a report of the Charge of Balaclava 'for Mr Tower *to read to you*'. That same year, 1875, the Prince of Wales, away on a grand tour of India, felt obliged to upbraid both his sons mildly for poor writing and spelling in their letters to him. (Significantly, his letter to them imparts no information about India, merely concentrating on his exploits with a gun – 'I shot a crane' – and at pig-sticking.) Two years later, Dalton was writing to Prince George that 'there were several words spelt wrong in your last letter' (*carm* instead of calm, for example). It was to be some years before George mastered the mysteries of spelling, and even in middle age he wrote letters in a large, childish hand.

As an adult, George's knowledge of history was patchy and his appreciation of the arts almost non-existent: 'Went to Covent Garden and saw *Fidelio*, and damned dull it was,' runs a diary note from the 1920s. His reading list extended not much farther than light fiction and his theatrical interests revolved round undemanding comedy, musicals and variety. He spoke French, but never as fluently as his father did and always with an English accent, and German hardly at all. In spite of the fact that his naval career was to make him the most widely travelled monarch in British history up to that time, he knew and cared little about the rest of the world, apart from the Empire. Such was the intellectual legacy of the Prince of Wales and Mr Dalton.

The curious thing is that many biographers of King George V have tended either to make light of his limited intellectual abilities and interests or to view them almost as a point in his favour. Thus John Gore, in his personal memoir of George V written in the 1930s, made much of the King's sensible, simple English upbringing', claiming – as if it was something to be proud of – that the raising of the children of Edward VII was 'in no vital detail differing from that of the children of the upper class'. It seems not to have occurred to Gore that the nation might reasonably expect rather more from its royal family. He wrote: 'They were English children, Norfolk-bred, and that usually implies sturdy, independent, busy, frank children, with a fund of animal spirits and a sound knowledge of country lore, a love of sport ingrained and a love of the sea, of Norfolk and England assured.' Fair enough, no doubt, for the progeny of the eighteenth- or even the nineteenth-century squirearchy, but hardly, one might think, much of a recommendation for the future guardians of an institution considered so important to the British way of life as the crown. If such was the ideal background for kingship, it is small wonder that Queen Victoria came to believe that the monarchy would not survive beyond 1930.

But, as John Buchan put it in his 1935 tribute, *The King's Grace*, the duty of the British sovereign 'is not to act but to *be*, to represent the ultimate sanctities of the land which endure behind passing fevers and bewilderments'. In his lack of education, his limited intellectual powers, his conservatism, his love of neatness, order and respectability, his mistrust of foreigners and his faith in things British above all else, George V was just like the great mass of his subjects. Nor was that the only perceived advantage that George, as king, derived from his education and upbringing. Paradoxically, many of the features of his background that tended to limit the development of the man were crucial to what was later judged to be the success of the monarch. His childlike relationship with his mother, coupled with his devotion to and respect for his father, imbued him with that touching simplicity, even innocence, which is lost to people with more complex personalities and can confound those with more sophisticated and therefore more detached modes of thinking. Furthermore, those close ties with his parents gave him a firm sense of the importance of the family in sustaining an individual through the vicissitudes of fortune (though that would ultimately lead to difficulties with his own children). Then, John Dalton – whatever his failings as an educator in the academic sense – taught a brand of uncompromising, muscular Christianity which, added to the example of Princess Alexandra's simple piety, endowed Prince George with unshakeable religious faith, high moral values and a clear understanding of duty and responsibility.

In addition to all this, Prince George saw in his father natural dignity, generosity and a capacity for enjoying life. From his mother he learnt something that Queen Victoria had noted with approval, 'great simplicity and absence of pride': there was a difference between the public figure and the private person, and the deference accorded to the former as of right must not be allowed to corrupt the latter.

It was the virtues I have described – and virtues they undoubtedly were, no matter what the limitations that inevitably accompanied them – that made King George V so popular. He was the embodiment of the values to which the middle classes, whose dominance was assured by the time of his accession, subscribed, or at least aspired. He was, indeed, the kind of monarch the new ruling class would have elected, had that been the system. And yet this conjunction was quite accidental. It has to be remembered that Prince George had been destined not for the throne but for the Royal Navy. As it happened, it was the Navy that provided the final layer of the not very complicated character which would come to symbolise the British ideal – vague, confused, contradictory and ultimately unsatisfactory – of constitutional monarchy.

The Prince of Wales was firmly of the opinion that the Royal Navy 'affords the very best possible training for any boy'. But Queen Victoria, recognising that Prince Eddy and Prince George were not just any boys, had other ideas about training them. She wanted them to go to a public school, Wellington College. 'The very rough sort of life to which boys are exposed on board ship', the Queen wrote, 'is the very thing not calculated to make a refined and amiable Prince. . . .' Then, with a perspicacity perhaps unexpected in one who had come to personify British imperialism and ideas of superiority, she added:

> Will a nautical education not engender and encourage national prejudices and make them think that their own Country is superior to any other? With the greatest love for the pride of one's own Country, a Prince, and especially one who is some day to be its Ruler, should not be imbued with the prejudices and peculiarities of his own Country. . . .

(Perhaps such an enlightened view reflected the influence of Prince Albert, or King Leopold.) At any rate, the Queen thought Wellington would be much more suitable. The Princes could live in a house of their own near the school and thus be protected from 'the mischief done by bad boys and the things they may hear and learn from them', while they could mix with 'good boys, of whatever birth,' so as to 'prevent the early notions of pride and superiority of position which is detrimental to young Princes, especially in these days. . . .'[6]

There were three obstacles in the way of the Queen's proposal. The first was that the Prince of Wales was determined that his second son should have a naval career and therefore considered that the sooner it began the better. (The Queen had no quarrel with the career: she simply wanted Prince George to spend eighteen months at Wellington first.) The second difficulty was that, in the opinion of both the Prince of Wales and Dalton, Prince Eddy and Prince George needed to remain together. 'Prince Albert Victor', as Dalton was careful to call him in a memorandum to the Queen, 'requires the stimulus of Prince George's company to induce him to work at all. . . . Difficult as the education of Prince Albert Victor is now, it would be doubly or trebly so if Prince George were to leave him. . . .' If George was to enter the Royal Navy, then Eddy must, too, for the time being, even though the Queen's argument that different things were demanded of the heir to the throne was accepted. Finally, and most significantly, neither boy, as Dalton was obliged to point out, had reached the educational standard normally required of boys of their age at public school, though that standard was not particularly high. If they were to go to Wellington, therefore, they would begin with a serious disadvantage.

The Queen was not entirely convinced, but in spite of her misgivings she acquiesced in the naval 'experiment', which was how the Prince of Wales put it to her, and in September 1877 Eddy and George joined the training ship HMS *Britannia* at Dartmouth in Devon. Dalton accompanied them to continue their tuition in non-naval subjects and generally to keep an eye on them.

Britannia was a warship of Nelsonian vintage, so her comforts were few and life aboard was hard, though wholesome and healthy according to the conventional wisdom of the day. The only privilege accorded to the young royals was a cabin of their own under the poop, but there they still had to sleep in hammocks like the other two hundred or so cadets, and in other respects, as King George recalled many years later, 'It never did me any good to be a Prince, I can tell you. . . .' There was a good deal of fighting among the cadets and since George was both younger and smaller than the other boys, he often took a beating. But he enjoyed handling boats and soon became proficient at it, as he also did in mathematics. He learnt the discipline that had been lacking at home and the very orderliness of naval life suited his simple, practical nature. As one of his *Britannia* contemporaries put it half a century later, 'In my humble opinion the training . . . in the Royal Navy, and the strict discipline to which he was subject, were tremendous factors in forming the character of the great and lovable man, and wise king he afterwards became. . . .'[7]

Yet in this aspect of his upbringing, too, there were negative factors that would prove to be as significant subsequently as the positive ones. 'In order to understand his character,' Harold Nicolson wrote in his official biography of King George V, 'it is important to realise that, in all essentials, it crystallised in early adolescence.' In other words, those first years in the Navy put the finishing touches on his development. 'The great events which happened to him in later life', Nicolson concluded, 'served only to deepen and widen furrows which had been traced in his boyhood years. Not being an intellectual, he was never variable: he remained uniform throughout his life. . . .'

So while the Navy underpinned the qualities of courage, constancy and devotion to duty that would clearly mark the reign of King George V, it may well have also inhibited his ability to absorb later lessons. For a man not much given to reflection, except in a nostalgic way, the precepts of naval life offered simple answers to doubts and difficulties. To do one's duty, to follow the accepted rules and, for the rest, to trust in God – those were the principles that would continue to govern him and, as Nicolson said, it was 'the consistency of his principles and beliefs . . . which . . . enabled him to symbolise stability and to command universal confidence'. Yet it was the immutable quality of his beliefs that also caused problems. There is a certain irony in the fact that although George V was widely regarded by his subjects as a safe rock on which the nation could rest as it was battered by a turbulent sea of change, he was responsible for helping to push the monarchy towards one of the greatest crises in its history, the abdication of King Edward VIII in 1936. The refusal of George V to modernise the monarchy, his unwavering attachment to old ways and to concepts that were being rendered obsolete by rapid and sweeping social and political developments, were in part to blame for the damaging and dangerous overreaction of his heir. The frustration Edward VIII had felt as Prince of Wales, in the face of his father's unchanging nature, drove him to attempt within twelve months to bring about changes in the style of the monarchy that should have evolved gradually during the previous twenty-five years. Thus resistance to change on the part of George V would lead to fundamental alterations in both the style and the substance of the monarchy, and what was intended to strengthen it would ultimately serve to weaken it.

And the early naval training of Prince George was to have another effect noted by the shrewd Harold Nicolson:

> The intimacies of nautical life are . . . different from those forged by other associations. On the one hand, they are more physically proximate and thus more stark and less selective: on the other hand – in that, with a change of ship, the whole pattern of acquaintance has to be reformed – they are more adventitious and therefore less profound. The tendency thus arises to adopt a standardised pattern of comradeship, in which emotional relations are seldom involved. Friendliness becomes more common than friendship and general good fellowship more customary than exclusive individual affections. In the case of the two Princes, this general habit of impersonal intimacy was reinforced by the presence of Mr Dalton. Anxious as he was that they should be exposed to no influence other than his own, he discouraged any close familiarity, any partial preferences, any selective fraternisation.[8]

If one of the aims in sending the Princes to HMS *Britannia* was to compensate for the remoteness of their royal childhood (and that was one of the arguments put forward to counter the opposition of Queen Victoria), then it may be argued that the psychology was faulty. Certainly the Princes experienced the hardships and the joys of people less privileged than themselves and no doubt their time as cadets – together with a later career, in the case of Prince George – served to dispel 'early notions of pride and superiority of position'. But the very nature of naval life did little to remove the feelings of separation between royals and ordinary people, the impression still noticeable today that while royalty has a role to play in the everyday existence of the nation it somehow remains outside it.

As sovereign, George V was able to mix easily with kings and commoners, even to form relationships with people such as trade union leaders, and through this ease of contact to give the impression that he was close to the concerns of ordinary folk. He acquired a reputation as something of a 'man of the people' – an imperial democrat, modern commentators have called him, delighting in the juxtaposition. Yet in fact he remained aloof from and unknowable to the vast majority of his subjects, a remote figure more to be revered as an icon than loved and respected as a man. Though in a superficial way he was closer to the people than any monarch had ever been before, he had no idea of how his subjects saw him or felt about him – as he was to admit himself during the great national celebration of the twenty-fifth anniversary of his accession. His upbringing and naval career made that detachment, that lack of real contact, seem natural to him; the shortcomings of his education meant that his mind was not opened to other possibilities as, under the pressure of history, he set the tone of the constitutional monarchy. George VI, helped by his wife, would make significant changes. Elizabeth II would make more. But all those later developments depended upon an attitude towards the monarchy formed largely by the character and instincts of George V, an attitude that persists even in a world that would be unrecognisable to him. The simple sailor who became king unwittingly began a process that eventually produced the ambiguities and illusions – delusions, one might almost say – which so hamper the monarchy today and which might ultimately threaten its survival.

4

Bred to the Sea

Prince George and Prince Eddy spent two years in HMS *Britannia* learning the craft of seamanship and, with the ever-present Mr Dalton, engaging in other studies relevant to their royal future: history, politics, the British constitution and so on. In 1879, having successfully completed this first phase of naval training, they passed out as midshipmen. Prince George exercised the 'option' granted to him by his father and chose the Navy as his career. Matters were not so clear-cut in the case of Prince Eddy, who showed no particular aptitude and very little enthusiasm for doing anything. It was obvious that the life of a naval officer was not for him and in any case, as heir to the throne, he had to extend his range of interests and activities beyond the confines of a ship. Yet the fundamental problems had not changed as a result of his training in *Britannia*. He continued to require the company of his younger brother as both a stimulus and a form of protection against the adverse influences of character and society to which he was only too susceptible. Furthermore, Eddy remained in a category that a later epoch would describe as educationally subnormal; therefore, sending him to a public school was still quite out of the question.

The royal tutor's solution, which gained the approval of the Prince of Wales and Queen Victoria, was to continue playing for time and hoping that Eddy would improve with age. Prince George, as a putative naval officer, was to pursue his education by joining a sea-going training ship for a series of cruises: Dalton suggested that Eddy should go as well, along with himself, of course, and with the addition of two other instructors who would help in the attempt to raise the level of the Princes' academic performance. Accordingly, on September 17th,

1879, the Princes and their pedagogic retinue sailed from Spithead aboard the corvette HMS *Bacchante*, fully rigged but with auxiliary steam power in case of emergency, and with a complement of officers apparently selected from *Debrett's*.

The royal voyages of *Bacchante* lasted three years in all. The first cruise, of a little more than seven months, took the Princes to the Mediterranean and then to Barbados, Grenada, Martinique, Jamaica and Bermuda. After a short break in the summer of 1880, the vessel joined the Channel Fleet to sail in less exotic waters, visiting Bantry Bay in south-west Ireland and then crossing to Vigo on the Atlantic coast of Spain. Finally, in September 1880, *Bacchante* became part of a squadron that meandered round the world with imperial licence for the better part of two years, taking its princely midshipmen across the Atlantic to South America and back again to South Africa, then via the Indian Ocean to Australia, into the Pacific for a visit to Japan, and back home by way of China, Singapore, the Suez Canal and the Mediterranean. It was an epic journey for the young Princes and Dalton ensured that they made the most of it, though he himself made rather too much of it when he published a 750,000-word account of the voyage, supposedly extracted from journals kept by George and Eddy. The alleged diary entries display such dazzling scholarship and detailed observation that the Princes would have had to have spent by far the greater part of their time composing them, whereas – so far as we can judge from Prince George's actual diaries of the time (which were as mundane, matter-of-fact and unscholarly as any of the journals he kept during his life) – the boys were kept fully occupied with naval matters and their lessons. Such spare time as they did have at sea was spent in mindless pursuits like killing sharks and albatrosses. That apart, the references and reflections that abound in the three volumes of *The Cruise of HMS Bacchante* betray an authorial intelligence far more developed and sophisticated than the minds of the two under-educated teenage Princes.[1]

But if the voyage did little in the way of broadening the minds of the young royals, or of stimulating their imaginations, it was, certainly in the case of Prince George, a useful exercise in character-building. As in *Britannia*, the Princes had their own cabin, but it was hardly luxurious, and while Eddy spent much of his time studying with Dalton, George was required to play his full part as a midshipman, with the exceptions of standing watch at night and taking his turn at boat service in rough weather. As one of his shipmates recalled many years later, the Prince had not yet reached the age of fifteen when he went to sea, but:

even at this early age he had, when in charge of one of the ship's cutters, for instance, to accept full responsibility for the lives of men. He also had to endure all the discomforts and all the hardships which were the inevitable and common lot of anyone who went to sea in those days ... weeks and weeks at sea, sometimes very monotonous weeks, living on food that was more than monotonous, and also exceedingly nasty. Mostly salt pork and ship's biscuits.[2]

The experience toughened him and gave him a sense of responsibility beyond his years. It also taught him to control, when required to, the volatile temper that was so much a part of his personality. His mess-mate remembered:

> One got rather bored at always seeing the same old faces round the same old table, and tempers at times were apt to get a little frayed and irritable. Yet . . . I never remember Prince George losing his temper. . . . Unselfish, kindly, good-tempered, he was an ideal shipmate.[3]

The Prince was developing the attributes of a naval officer, but they were characteristics that would be of use to him in his other, then quite unexpected, career. As king, he would face repeated tests of his courage and nerve and he would shoulder daunting responsibilities. Also, as he covered what would become an ever more monotonous round of royal engagements, he would have to appear, in public at least, always calm, interested and good-humoured, no matter how bored, irritable or even nervous he might feel. There was a sense in which the Prince of Wales had been right: in some respects the Navy did offer good training.

There was yet another aspect of that long final cruise in *Bacchante* which helped to fit Prince George for the role he would later be called upon to fill. Queen Victoria had stipulated that the boys should not be received in foreign ports with the honours ordinarily due to royalty, but – disagreeing with her as he so often did – the Prince of Wales believed that since they were princes they should be treated as such by local dignitaries. It fell to the captain of the *Bacchante*, Lord Charles Scott, to arbitrate in the matter as the voyage progressed, with the result that in some places George and Eddy were accorded the welcome given to any visiting naval officers, but elsewhere they were greeted with ceremony befitting their station. The contrast between the exaggerated formality of official functions and the humdrum realities of life and relationships aboard ship cannot have been lost on

Prince George, the more so because most of the attention was focused upon his brother, the heir presumptive, and George was to some extent an observer. It made him aware that beyond the confines of palace walls was another existence, less comfortable but equally demanding in its own way, so that when he became king he was able to look outside the privileged, protected world of courtiers and politicians, many of whom had no idea how ordinary people lived. At the same time, there was instilled in the impressionable young Prince a sense of his own 'ordinariness' and even a sort of delight in it. While he would always take seriously the constitutional and ceremonial duties of kingship, and its attendant honours and protocols, at heart he remained, in many respects, a retired naval officer, enjoying all the pleasures and prejudices of the upper-middle class. He embraced the values of Christianity, home and family, respectability and keeping up appearances; he was suspicious of intellectuals, seeking stimulation in entertainment of the music-hall variety or on the sporting field; he accepted the doctrine of progress, but favoured moderation and gradualism, adapting to change with reluctance. In short, he represented perfectly the desires and doubts, the strengths and shortcomings of the new ruling class, raised to maturity under Victoria and Edward and coming into its inheritance as King George V came into his.

But as *Bacchante* returned home in August 1882, there was no sign of the inheritance that was to come to Prince George. He and his brother were to be separated for the first time, Eddy to continue his education as the heir to the throne, George, with no defined role in royal life, to pursue the conventional course of the future naval officer. The brothers spent six months together in Switzerland learning French (a language with which, as I have said, George was never comfortable, though he could read and understand it reasonably well), then Eddy returned to Sandringham, where a group of tutors attempted to compensate for the deficiencies in his schooling and to prepare him for Cambridge University. George joined HMS *Canada* as a midshipman and became a small component in the fighting machine that was the Royal Navy's West Indian and North American Squadron. Now he was entirely on his own: no tutor, no manservant, no brother. No private cabin, either, and no discretion allowed to his captain regarding his treatment in foreign ports of call. The Prince of Wales, for once supporting and supported by Queen Victoria, made it clear that his second son was not to be accorded royal honours when ashore, even in British colonies, and that there were to be no state receptions for him. 'His Royal Highness will be treated in all respects and on all occasions ... in the same manner as the other officers of his own rank. ...'[4]

Quite what the purpose of all this was supposed to be is not clear, but there were probably two basic strands to the policy governing the youth of Prince George, one constitutional and the other more personal. First, it is necessary for any monarchy to maintain strong links with the military, for both historical reasons and simple self-preservation. Western tradition does not deify its tribal rulers, and supremacy in our violent past most often depended upon force of arms, so the king was placed firmly at the head of his fighting men. More recently, the growth of democracy and the establishment of the standing army changed the ground rules, so that while the monarch was no longer required to fight himself, it was important both for his security and for the stability of the state he symbolised that he retained the allegiance of the armed forces. Even today, Britain's servicemen swear allegiance to their sovereign, not to their country or to the civil power that has effective control of them – which could lead to an interesting situation if ever a British government were to decide the time had come to abolish the monarchy. The shrewd royal family, therefore, does well to win the sympathy of the armed services by offering them sons it cannot usefully employ elsewhere; and at the same time it wins the admiration of the populace by demonstrating so directly its commitment to the defence of the realm.

The commitment need be no more than a token one, as in the case of the present Prince of Wales, Prince Charles, who as heir to the throne must restrict his military activities and direct his real energies elsewhere. But for Prince George, as for Prince Andrew now, service in the Royal Navy was intended to be a longer-term prospect, and in the establishment of that tradition I think we may detect the hand of Prince Albert. The Prince Consort, with his Teutonic thoroughness and abhorrence of idleness, laid careful plans for the education of his children. His eldest son, Bertie, was of course to be groomed for kingship; his second son, Prince Alfred, Duke of Edinburgh – born in 1844 and known as 'Affie' – was destined to become Duke of Coburg in succession to Albert's elder brother, should no heir appear in the meantime. There were, however, two problems. The first was that the boys showed neither the enthusiasm nor the aptitude for the system of primary education that Albert designed for them; the second problem was what should be done with them to make them useful until such time as their future roles became vacant.

The brothers were very close and proved to be an extremely troublesome pair, encouraging each other in mischief and rebellious-

ness, so they were separated (much to Bertie's chagrin) as soon as it
was practicable, and by the age of fourteen Affie, who had expressed
an interest in the sea, was undergoing naval training. In his case,
therefore, the two problems were solved at a stroke. He became a
captain at the age of twenty-two and went on to be Admiral of the
Fleet. Thus he was usefully employed until 1893, when Duke Ernest
II of Saxe-Coburg-Gotha obligingly died without issue and Prince
Alfred went to spend the rest of his days reigning over a Ruritanian
backwater, where he died of throat cancer in 1900. (He was invited
to take the throne of Greece in 1862, but Queen Victoria refused it
on his behalf, saying he was too young and in any case she could not
afford to lose a prince: it would not, of course, have fitted in with
Prince Albert's plan.)

The Prince of Wales, then, had a precedent when it came to the
future of his own second son. What the ultimate parental ambition
for Prince George might have been is unknown, but he seemed to
take to the Navy and it provided him with an occupation for the time
being. The tradition continued with George's own second son, later
King George VI, and is carried on today by Queen Elizabeth's second
son, Prince Andrew, who like his grandfather and great-grandfather
bears the title of Duke of York. During the intervening century it
seems not to have occurred to anybody that the second son of the
sovereign might become an artist or an architect, a merchant banker
or a musician, a writer or a research scientist. Admittedly, it is many
a year since the British royal family has been noted for its intellectual
qualities, but the time has also long passed when the armed forces
and the priesthood were considered the only respectable refuges for
the second sons of the nobility. It is odd, surely, towards the end of
the 1980s in a country ruled by a materialistic mediocracy and reigned
over by a monarchy that itself has become essentially middle class in
appearance and outlook, that when the Queen's third son, Prince
Edward, decided life in the Royal Marines was not for him, there
should be newspaper headlines asking, with a note of despair, 'What
will he do now?'

In Prince George's day there was more excuse. Britain was the
greatest military power on earth and there was general acceptance of
the view that making war belonged, as the Prussian theorist Karl von
Clausewitz put it, 'to the province of social life . . . the continuation of
politics by other means'. It was a source of both pride and reassurance
among the people that a prince of the royal house should play a
practical role in policing the empire over which that dynasty presided
and upon which Britain's supremacy depended. At the same time,

because the monarchy was relatively more remote and less public than it is now, military service not only represented one of the few ways in which a member of the royal family could gain some insight into the experience of life outside the narrow circles of the Court and the aristocracy, but also provided a worthy and disciplined occupation for princes with comparatively few demands on their time and attention. While the less senior royals did have certain roles to play, the monarchy of Victoria and Edward VII was by no means the 'family firm' – to borrow the phrase of King George VI – that it would later become.

And so, while painstaking but vain efforts continued to prepare Prince Eddy for what was assumed to be his future station in life, Prince George progressed in his more mundane career. After the best part of a year at sea with the North American Squadron, he graduated to the rank of sub-lieutenant in the summer of 1884 and, after a holiday with his family, continued his theoretical studies at the Royal Naval College, Greenwich, where he was commended for his sound and honest work. The following spring found him at Portsmouth, taking a gunnery course in HMS *Excellent*. His commanding officer, Captain J. A. Fisher, noted the Prince's 'pleasant and unassuming manner' and praised 'his aptitude for the practical work of his profession', tactfully pointing out to Queen Victoria that 'Your Majesty may perhaps consider that this is the chief point, as it will not probably fall to his lot to write learned reports or to make mathematical investigations'. The Prince gained first-class honours in gunnery, torpedo practice and seamanship, but could only manage a second in piloting. Still, his abilities, in the view of the First Lord of the Admiralty, were of an unusually high standard and in October 1885 he was promoted lieutenant.

Throughout Prince George's naval training, as we have seen, the Prince of Wales and Queen Victoria placed much emphasis on their desire that he should be treated just like any other junior officer, and in many respects, no doubt, he was. But a prince is a prince whatever he does, and any of his superiors who forgot that fact would have been foolish indeed, given the constant supervision of George's father and grandmother. Similarly, no chances were taken in the matter of selecting a ship for the young royal lieutenant. In December 1885 the private secretary to the Prince of Wales, Sir Francis Knollys, wrote to Captain Henry Stephenson of HMS *Thunderer* to inform him that the Admiralty had agreed that Prince George should join his ship the following February. Stephenson was a nephew of Admiral of the Fleet Sir Henry Keppel, one of the royal family's closest friends, and since 1878 he had served as an equerry to the Prince of Wales. He therefore had the complete confidence of the Prince and, of course, George had known Stephenson 'ever since I can remember anybody'. Sir Henry Keppel was in fact a guest at Sandringham that winter and no doubt it had been at his suggestion that one of *Thunderer*'s lieutenants had been transferred to another ship so that 'Prince George can therefore have his cabin', not to mention the benefit of a sympathetic captain with strong royal connections.

There was a further good reason for choosing *Thunderer* as Prince George's home away from home. The ship was attached to the Mediterranean Fleet, which was at that time under the command of none other than the young lieutenant's seagoing royal predecessor, Prince Alfred, Duke of Edinburgh. Affie could thus not only keep an avuncular eye on the progress of George's naval career but also mitigate the homesickness that afflicted the Prince throughout his time in the service – and indeed grew worse as promotions took him away from the company of his family. Within days of joining the *Thunderer*, George was writing to his father that he missed him every minute of the day and that he was relieved to be under the care of Captain Stephenson when he was separated from all he loved and all his friends. Affie and his wife Marie, the only daughter of Tsar Alexander II of Russia, provided a surrogate family to which George was genuinely attached. He was very fond of the Duchess of Edinburgh and became close to her eldest daughter, 'Missy' (later Queen Marie of Romania). Also, it is said to have been Affie who introduced Prince George to philately, which became a lifelong interest and hobby.

If life at the San Antonio Palace in Malta became boring, there was more familial support not far away in Athens, with one of the Prince's other uncles, King George I of Greece (brother of the Princess of Wales) and his wife Queen Olga, who was more like a mother than an aunt to Prince George and called him her little sunbeam. It is clear that the Edinburghs and the royal family of the Hellenes were almost in competition with each other for the favour of Prince George's presence and the sentimental young Prince was always greatly affected by visits to and partings from such warm-hearted relatives who did so much to lessen the loneliness and sense of isolation that life at sea induced in one whose chief pleasures were those of home.

The Mediterranean station, however, was not without its disadvantages, at least so far as the Prince of Wales was concerned. He was constantly writing to Captain Stephenson at the Fleet's base in Malta suggesting that the *Thunderer* put to sea for a cruise or to undertake manoeuvres. He claimed that the Maltese climate presented health risks of particular relevance to his family, who had shown congenital vulnerability to fevers of certain kinds: because of the heat, Prince George should not eat too much meat or smoke too much and when ashore he should be encouraged to take part in sports and active games. The reasons for such solicitousness, though, were not entirely hygienic, except, perhaps, in one specific area. Malta, like any large naval base, was well-equipped with those pleasures sailors traditionally seek as a release from the frustrations of solely male companionship. If Prince George was to be treated at sea exactly like his brother officers, there was every reason to suppose that, left to himself, he would see it as natural to share in their activities on shore as well. Venereal disease was the AIDS of the nineteenth century, with syphilis especially feared because of its ability to affect succeeding generations: in 1899, Prince Alfred's eldest son would shoot himself rather than die slowly of tuberculosis complicated by VD. The Prince of Wales knew that his son had to be protected. Captain Stephenson was instructed to be strict with him and not to let him 'kick his heels' during the generous shore leave officers were granted in peacetime.

Nor were prostitutes the only problem. It is often forgotten that what might be called 'social' sexual promiscuity did not begin with the self-styled permissive society in the 1960s. The Victorians were simply more discreet – and certainly more hypocritical – about it. The women of the leisured classes had little to do with their time and even less to relieve the boredom of their existence, while the men tended to make distinctions between women they married and those they wanted merely for sexual gratification. A place such as Malta offered plenty of opportunities for *les liaisons dangereuses*, particularly to a handsome, emotional and somewhat immature young royal. Twenty-five years earlier, Prince Alfred himself had entered into a compromising relationship with a woman in Malta, causing much distress to Queen Victoria. That was one precedent the Prince of Wales did not want his son to follow.

Captain Stephenson transferred from *Thunderer* to HMS *Dreadnought* and, naturally, Prince George went with him. Towards the end of 1887, however, a problem arose when Stephenson was recalled to London as part of the promotion process. (He went on to become an admiral, to receive a knighthood and finally to command the Channel Fleet.) The Prince of Wales wrote the captain a 'most private and confidential' letter enquiring anxiously about George's future. The Duke of Edinburgh had apparently suggested that his nephew should join him in his flagship, HMS *Alexandra*, but the Prince of Wales was opposed to this idea because in the nature of things the flagship was likely to spend more time in port than the other vessels of the fleet –

and that, of course, meant Malta, which the Prince thought really would not do. On the other hand, Affie might be deeply offended if consent to George's transfer to *Alexandra* was withheld. What, the Prince of Wales asked Stephenson, was to be done?

The captain must have been a wise and shrewd individual, and not without influence where it mattered. Prince George, he counselled, should remain in *Dreadnought* for the time being, under the command of Captain Noel Digby, who, the Prince of Wales was assured, was a splendid fellow in every respect and would keep up the good work as far as George was concerned. So it came to pass, and without sending Affie, touchy as he was, into a fit of the sulks. Under the Stephenson plan, the excuse for George's staying with *Dreadnought* was that the King and Queen of the Hellenes expected the Prince, and therefore his ship, in Athens for the Greek Christmas celebrations, which would coincide nicely with a series of torpedo exercises to be undertaken by *Dreadnought* in the Bay of Salamis. Then, in March, Prince George would be required to return to England on leave for the silver wedding anniversary of his parents, so there would be no point in his changing ships before that time. Following that leave, however, he could join HMS *Alexandra*, which, coincidentally, would be preparing to leave Malta for an extended summer cruise. Thus the arrangements suited everybody.

Everybody, that is, except Prince George, who was even more chagrined than his father at the departure of Stephenson. On Christmas Eve 1887, the Prince wrote a wistful little letter to the captain – who was at Sandringham for Christmas – saying how miserable he felt after seeing him leave Malta. It was horrible aboard *Dreadnought*, surrounded by new faces and with nobody to talk to or seek advice from; everything was at sixes and sevens as the new captain made his presence felt; a change in station for the Prince himself (in charge of machine-gun crews), which he did not like; and finally the inevitable touch of homesickness – lucky Captain Stephenson to be back in 'dear old England' and seeing all his friends again. As it was with the young lieutenant, so it would be with the king; change had to be accepted, of course, but it was usually for the worse, and the greatest treasures were those to be found at home.

Still, duty had to be done, and done it would be, with as brave and cheerful a face as possible. Yet one can imagine the joy in the Prince's heart when, in November 1888, the end of his term of service with the Mediterranean Fleet appeared in sight and he set off for home, to spend his first Christmas with the family at Sandringham for three years.

He was now aged twenty-three and, like his father, he had taken to wearing a full beard, in spite of reservations on the part of Prince Eddy, who had become something of a 'masher', the 1880s version of the elegant man-about-town. But the beard was not the only sign of George's growing maturity. He dared to criticise (though only to his mother) Queen Victoria for voicing reservations about the amount of time he had been spending with his Greek relatives, and he ventured to express his own opinion that Prince Eddy, for whom marriage plans would soon have to be considered, should be found an English bride, rather than some German princess, as the Queen and the Prince of Wales seemed to think desirable. Being away from home, he told Princess Alexandra, had prompted him to think more about such things than he had previously done.[5]

What was mostly on his mind at Sandringham that winter, however, was sport. He shared his father's almost fanatical passion for shooting and had become expert with a gun, recording his achievements with pride. On December 31st, 1888, he noted in his diary that the day marked the first time he had brought down one hundred pheasants at a single stand.

The middle of February found him at sea again, feeling horribly homesick of course, on his way to join HMS *Northumberland*, part of the Channel Fleet, for a cruise from Gibraltar to North Africa and Spain. By April, though, he was home again and the following month he went to HMS *Excellent* at Portsmouth – for a final torpedo course before receiving his first command – which allowed him to spend a good deal of leave in London. He was given the freedom of the City in June and, awfully nervous at this first important ceremonial occasion of his own, he made two speeches.

An event of more significance at the time, however, occurred on July 18th, 1889, when Prince George took command of Torpedo Boat No. 79. She was small, only one hundred and twenty-five feet long and weighing seventy-five tons; she was uncomfortable and notorious for her erratic behaviour in all but the calmest seas, which did nothing to relieve Prince George of the seasickness he suffered throughout his career. But the Prince was her skipper and proud of it: he had made the grade as a naval officer, and he continued to impress his superiors with his practical, seamanlike skills as he guided his little ship through fleet exercises at Spithead in honour of his cousin, the German Kaiser, Wilhelm II, and later as he rescued another torpedo boat in a difficult and sometimes risky operation off the west coast of Ireland. In May 1890 his abilities were recognised with the command of a larger ship, the gunboat HMS *Thrush*, which he took to join the

West Indies and North American Squadron operating out of Bermuda and Halifax, Nova Scotia.

That same year, Prince George received military recognition of quite a different kind, too. During a state visit to Berlin with his father (Prince Eddy, whose performance had improved little, having been sent on a tour of India), George found himself being invested with the Prussian order of the Black Eagle and honorary command of a German regiment. His relationship with Kaiser Wilhelm, and the Ango-German royal practice of awarding honours to each other, would become a source of acute embarrassment to the future King George V, and of suspicion among a large number of his subjects, when he and the Prussian grandson of Queen Victoria presided over the bloody conflict that was to bring to an end the world as they had known it. Princess Alexandra, whose bitter resentment of Germany did not lessen with the passing of time, offered an unconscious presentiment of the future when she wrote of her horror that her Georgie boy should have become a 'filthy bluecoated Pickelhaube German soldier!!!'[6]

Meanwhile the necessary dynastic processes were at work under the watchful eye and direction of Queen Victoria. As Prince George received his first naval command, Prince Eddy was created Duke of Clarence and Avondale and, since he had reached the age of twenty-five, the search began in earnest for a bride suitably qualified to become a future queen consort of England. Familial ties notwithstanding, there were no really promising and willing young women among the German royal houses – and, in any case, the unification of Germany under the 'protection' of Prussia had reduced once-independent kingdoms to mere puppets. The best prospect in 1890 was the second daughter of the Comte de Paris; Princess Hélène was not only beautiful but she had also, apparently, been in love with Prince Eddy for two years and her pedigree was impeccable. Her father, though exiled from republican France in 1886, was the grandson of King Louis-Philippe, had been recognised in the 1840s as the heir apparent to the French throne, and remained the unchallenged head of the Bourbon family. They were Roman Catholics, of course, which would mean that Princess Hélène would have to change her religion in order to marry the future King of England, who was and is forbidden by the Act of Settlement to be or to take as his wife a Roman Catholic. Queen Victoria and the Prince of Wales appeared to see no difficulty in this, despite the suspicion and mistrust it would almost certainly have aroused in many of the Queen's subjects, and Princess Hélène herself expressed her willingness to renounce Rome. But the Comte de Paris would not entertain the idea that his daughter should abandon her religion; indeed, he insisted that she must obtain a papal dispensation to prevent her excommunication as a result of marrying a Protestant. So desperate was the Prince of Wales to see his heir safely married that he canvassed the opinion of the Prime Minister, Lord Salisbury, as to whether Parliament would accept a Catholic as a prospective queen consort if she entered into a solemn undertaking that her children should be brought up in the Anglican faith.

In the event, Salisbury decided that the proposed match was unthinkable and so did the Pope: Leo XIII was known as an enlightened pontiff, but there were limits to his tolerance where Protestantism was concerned, such limits, in fact, that a few years later he would officially declare Anglican orders invalid. Eddy became bored with the tortuous process of negotiation and transferred his fickle affections to Lady Sybil St Clair Erskine, though she was never a serious candidate as a bride for him. Princess Hélène was left to find a suitable Catholic husband, which she did four years later when she married an Italian duke. (It is interesting to note, in this connection, that before the present Prince of Wales became engaged to Lady Diana Spencer, there were 'scare' stories in the press suggesting that he might cause a constitutional crisis by marrying a Roman Catholic, given the current world shortage of available princesses. However liberal our society might consider itself today, there are some things that seem not to change.)

There have been suggestions in recent years that the Princess Hélène affair was seen in some quarters, perhaps within the royal family itself, as an opportunity to remove Prince Eddy from the line of succession to the throne, which considering his disabilities might well have been a consummation devoutly to be wished. It is said that there were discussions about the prospect of Eddy's relinquishing his succession right in order to marry a woman he loved, and that there was encouragement for such a course of action. The outcome, however, seems to indicate that if the subject of renunciation was ever broached it was not taken seriously.

Amid all this feverish nuptial negotiation, Prince George was not immune from the matchmaking propensities of his grandmother. Queen Victoria had her eye on the Prince's cousin and companion from his days in Malta, Princess Marie, as a possible bride for him, even though 'Missy' was not yet sixteen. Princess Alexandra objected strongly, however; the girl's father, Prince Alfred, was, after all, heir to the dukedom of Saxe-Coburg-Gotha and altogether too close to the Germans, and Alexandra did not want her son mixed up with that side of the family. As it happened, her opposition was mirrored on the other side. 'Missy' had a German governess who hated the English and used her influence to discourage any thought of betrothal to George. Crown Prince Ferdinand of Romania was a much more acceptable suitor, and Princess Marie married him a few months after her eighteenth birthday.

In their own minds, neither the Duke of Clarence nor Prince George saw marriage as a priority. They were quite content sowing their wild oats. At one point they shared a mistress who lived in St John's Wood in London (she was a 'ripper' according to Prince George) and the dashing young naval officer was also in the habit of bedding a girl in Southsea, conveniently near the Portsmouth naval base.[7] George wrote to Queen Victoria in February 1891 saying that he understood her desire to see her grandsons married but expressing the opinion that marrying too young was a bad thing. Of course, Eddy *was* twenty-seven, which could hardly be called too young, he conceded, but as for himself, he offered the tragic example of Crown Prince Rudolf of Austria-Hungary, who only a couple of years earlier had brought shame on the house of Habsburg and the most terrible sorrow to his wife by shooting his mistress and then himself at the hunting-lodge at Mayerling. That was the sort of thing which could result from marriage at too early an age, the Prince warned his grandmother. He also made it clear that he would resist any attempt at an arranged marriage for him, such as was being considered for the Duke of Clarence when the match with Princess Hélène had to be abandoned. The one thing he could never do, George told Queen Victoria, was marry someone who did not care for him – that would make him unhappy for the rest of his life.

Perhaps this thought was prompted by the fact that there was someone who cared for him, and for whom he cared very much. Julie Stonor – 'my darling Julie', Prince George called her in his diary – was almost part of the family at Sandringham. She and her brother Harry were the children of one of the first ladies-in-waiting of the Princess of Wales, but their mother had died at a relatively early age in 1883. They were almost of an age with Eddy and George and, taken under the maternal wing of Princess Alexandra after their own mother's death, they spent a good deal of time with the two young Princes. As they grew older, a sexual attraction developed between George and Julie, though there is no evidence that it was ever consummated. The Prince, when serving abroad with the Navy, saw Julie regularly during his periods of home leave and sometimes she and her brother accompanied the Wales family when they went on holiday to the South of France. Letters between George and Julie were full of affection and, as time went by, it became clear that they were in love. Either the Prince and Princess of Wales did not realise what was happening, or they simply assumed that the growing bond between their son and Julie Stonor resembled love of the brother-and-sister variety and would not develop into anything really serious. Yet the emphasis through the upbringing of Prince George, at the insistence of the Prince of Wales and Queen Victoria, had been on treating him as far as possible just like the other people with whom he had come into contact. That such people had been carefully vetted, so as to avoid undesirable influences and the possibility of future pressures, probably did not occur to George himself. Julie had been part of his life for many years, came from a 'good' family and, as far as George could see, had been regarded as an equal. It was perfectly natural that the Prince should have been unaware of any reason why, if he loved the girl and she loved him, they should not marry.

But reasons there were. Not only was Julie Stonor a commoner, and therefore an unacceptable bride, according to the precepts of the time, for a man who was third in line to the throne, but she was also a Roman Catholic; even if she had possessed royal blood, there would have been the same difficulty that had prevented a match between Eddy and Princess Hélène.

The reaction of the Prince of Wales to his son's suggestion that he might marry Julie Stonor may easily be imagined. As a father he was neither insensitive nor stern (rather the reverse, if anything), but he would have immediately dismissed the idea as being quite out of the question, whatever Prince George's feelings. Fortunately, matters emotional were, in the view of the Prince of Wales, part of a mother's domain, and it was left to Princess Alexandra to deal with the problem. It was a delicate situation for a mother determined not to cause pain to a son she still regarded as a child and a girl of whom, in common with the rest of the family, she was extremely fond. The Princess understood the nature of love and was concerned not to shatter George's romantic dream, while pointing out to him that in this case it could never be more than a dream. 'I only wish you could marry and be happy,' she told her son, 'but, alas, I fear it cannot be.' It was, she thought, 'rather a sad case ... for you both, my two poor children!'[8]

It was inconceivable that Prince George should act against the wishes of his parents, particularly when it was pointed out to him where his duty lay. That he accepted the judgment without bitterness, though, says much for the warmth and tact of Princess Alexandra.

Nor was the relationship between the Wales family and the Stonors damaged in any way. Julie married a French nobleman in 1891, but she remained George's close friend for the rest of his life and, when he became king, was the only commoner allowed to address him simply by his Christian name. Her brother Harry, appointed gentleman-usher to Queen Victoria in 1882, went on to perform the same function for Edward VII, George himself when he came to the throne, and George's sons Edward VIII and George VI.

While Julie Stonor was getting married, Prince George of Wales was being promoted to the rank of commander in the Royal Navy. His active naval career, however, was about to come to an end. When he left HMS *Thrush* on August 23rd, 1891, he was to have one more brief period commanding a ship and thereafter his Navy promotions were to be purely honorary.

5

Grand New Duke of York

There is some evidence to suggest that after fourteen years Prince George had had enough of the sea. In later life he would reminisce about his naval days, and until he died he would retain many of the habits he had learnt aboard ship, but nostalgia for past youth has a happy knack of making it seem better than it really was and it is not difficult to persuade oneself that something was enjoyable when one no longer has to do it. As he looked back, George might well have preferred to forget that when, in July 1892, he took part in fleet manoeuvres as the commander of the cruiser HMS *Melampus*, he wrote that he hated the whole thing and hoped he would never have to take part in such exercises again. His 'choice' of the Navy had been subject to strong parental influence and, although he showed considerable aptitude for the craft of seamanship and for taking the responsibilities of command, he was throughout his naval career prone to bouts of seasickness, which made life uncomfortable, and he continued to suffer the pangs of homesickness I have described, which made him depressed. In letters he often expressed regret that he was not present for family events, holidays and so on, and he would find himself feeling twinges of envy towards those who were able to be, say, at Sandringham for Christmas. Perhaps he resented the fact that his brother was closer to home than he himself was; possibly the romance with Julie Stonor served to sharpen a sense that there was a large part of life from which he was separated by the sea. There must be a suspicion that, having proved his manhood and succeeded in his profession to the extent of achieving the rank of commander, the young man who so needed the support of home and family would have been looking towards more freedom to develop in new directions, towards a more settled and less circumscribed existence, towards leaving the Navy.

That, however, must remain in the realm of what might have been. By the summer of 1892, everything had changed. The pattern of Prince George's future had been set as a result of circumstances beyond his or anyone's control.

The crisis began in the second half of 1891. The Prince of Wales's philandering had become very much an open secret in Society and his lack of discretion in his current affair with Daisy Brooke, wife of the good-natured heir to the Earl of Warwick and former mistress of the Prince's friend, Lord Charles Beresford, so distressed Princess Alexandra that she escaped abroad on the pretext of visiting her far-flung relatives. The Prince had been attacked in the press as a 'wastrel and whoremonger' when details of the private lives of himself and his circle had emerged during the infamous Tranby Croft libel case, in which a wealthy army officer, Sir William Gordon Cumming, brought an ultimately unsuccessful action against the Prince of Wales and others who, having accused Sir William of cheating at baccarat during a house party at Tranby Croft in Yorkshire, had forced him to sign an undertaking that he would never play cards again in return for their silence on the matter. It was widely suspected that the Prince of Wales had broken the accusers' side of the bargain by telling the story to Daisy, whose penchant for repeating gossip may be judged from the nickname given to her by the hacks of the less reputable newspapers of the day – 'the Babbling Brooke'.

Sir William claimed that the affair of the signed undertaking had been an attempt to protect the heir to the throne from public scandal, and the Prince of Wales was forced to appear as a witness in court, where he gave a very poor account of himself.[1] Public sympathy was on Sir William's side and when, after what seemed a biased summing-up by the judge, the verdict went against him, reaction was violent. Crowds at Ascot races, which took place shortly after the trial, booed the Prince of Wales and Queen Victoria complained that people were alarmed and shocked not by this particular case but by the Prince's way of life in general: he was setting a bad example and lowering the tone of the monarchy, the Queen thought.[2]

Prince George was as aware as anyone else of the Tranby Croft case and the criticism of his father it occasioned, but his filial devotion remained unshakeable – newspaper reports of the baccarat *scandel*, as he called it in a note, were a lot of rot in his opinion.[3] How much he knew about the extramarital activities of the Prince of Wales and the reasons for Princess Alexandra's absence in the autumn of 1891 remains a matter for speculation. Probably he knew little at this stage other than that his father was away from home for much of the time and that his mother sometimes appeared anxious and unhappy: it seems certain that Princess Alexandra would not have discussed her difficulties with her son, even though she expressed them by keeping him as close to her as she could. Yet there was bound to be an atmosphere of tension in the Wales household and it must have seemed odd to Prince George that his mother should see fit to absent herself from the celebrations at Sandringham that November marking the fiftieth birthday of the Prince of Wales, an absence which Sir Sidney Lee, in his biography of Edward VII published in the 1920s, ascribed to 'domestic reasons'. And even if the young Prince did know or suspect what was going on, he would not have allowed it to detract from his respect and admiration for his father. Men, after all, were men, as he had learnt in the Navy.

But it was at Sandringham on November 12th, just three days after the birthday of the Prince of Wales, that more acute domestic trouble struck the family. Prince George developed a fever and became so ill that he was taken to London, where doctors diagnosed typhoid. Princess Alexandra, who with her two unmarried daughters was staying with the Tsar of Russia in the Crimea, hurried home to watch over her son during an illness of peculiar dread to the royal family since it had killed Prince Albert and had almost done the same to the Prince of Wales in 1871. The Princess reached London on November 22nd, just as Prince George's disease entered its critical phase. Within a few days, however, the worst was over and the Prince began to recover, though he was very weak and had to remain in bed for a further month.

After all they had been through in 1891, it must have been a tremendous relief to the Wales family to be able to announce in December that Prince Eddy, that weakest of links to the future of the British crown, had become engaged to the eminently suitable Princess Mary of Teck, whose mother, as a granddaughter of King George III, was Queen Victoria's cousin. With the turn of the year, though, came the most severe blow of all. A mere month after the announcement of his betrothal, Prince Eddy caught influenza at Sandringham. Less than a week later, he had what the doctors said was pneumonia and by the morning of January 14th, 1892, he was dead. The eager discussion of plans for his wedding, which was to have taken place in February, was now transformed into the gloomy task of arranging his funeral.

Prince George was distraught. After the first shock of grief at the loss of Eddy – and as he told Queen Victoria, he was sure that no two brothers could have been closer – came sneaking feelings of guilt, not only the normal ones involving past quarrels and lapses of affection but also a kind of remorse that he should have survived a dangerous illness while Eddy did not. He was in any case low in strength and spirits as a result of the typhoid fever and the realisation that he must now assume the responsibilities of the heir presumptive served to make his mental condition worse. He might well have wished to leave the Navy, but his reason for doing so would not have been to exchange one set of restrictions for another. Furthermore, he did not consider himself at all prepared for the course that lay ahead of him. His was not a particularly enquiring mind and, as a naval officer, he had never found cause to take much interest in politics and current affairs or time to involve himself greatly in the everyday public duties of royalty. At the age of twenty-six he would in some ways have to begin his education all over again.

But not quite yet. After Eddy's funeral at Windsor, with George still too frail from his illness to join the procession, the family spent a little time in Eastbourne and then went to the French Riviera, where George passed a month or so in idleness and bouts of depression, to the disgust of at least one member of the household, who felt that the Prince was being allowed to wallow in his grief far more than was good for him.[4] As George recovered his physical strength, however, his spiritual resources revived. In May his new position was confirmed when the Queen created him Duke of York, Earl of Inverness and Baron Killarney, and the following month his father and the Duke of Connaught introduced him into the House of Lords. The heir to the throne was dead, long live the heir to the throne.

The death of Prince Eddy has been the subject of much speculation and rumour. He was not the only member of the family to catch influenza that winter, but he was the only one to die as a result of it. There are certain doubts about the diagnosis of pneumonia: some of the Prince's symptoms did not accord with that condition. Furthermore, the arrival of two royal physicians, Dr Francis Laking and Dr W. H. Broadbent, coincided with a dramatic decline in their patient, leading the sort of people who subscribe to conspiracy theories to suspect that the Prince's end might have been hastened by medical intervention. Such suspicions have been heightened by the recent revelation that King George V was 'assisted' in death by his physician, Lord Dawson of Penn.[5]

For two important reasons, however, the conspiracy theorists are on shaky ground. First, there is a world of difference between the case of George V, who was in his seventy-fourth year, and that of Prince Eddy, who was just twenty-eight. Lord Dawson knew that the King was dying anyway and his action in giving a large dose of morphia was intended to minimise suffering, as he made clear in his diary. If the suspicion that Prince Eddy's doctors, without the knowledge of the royal family, administered poison to him were well-founded, we would be talking about premeditated murder. At the very least we should have to consider the possibility that medical attention was withheld from the Prince in the knowledge, or at least the hope, that without it he would not survive. These are serious matters indeed.

Second, the idea that the royal doctors were involved in a plot to rid the monarchy of what everyone knew could be a serious problem rests on the fact that the heir to the throne was patently incapable of being a king, and that influential courtiers and officials feared irreparable damage to the crown if his erratic and unstable personality was exposed to public scrutiny, as it certainly would have been if the succession had proceeded in the normal way – and once he was on the throne, it would have been difficult (though not impossible) to have deposed him. But this argument ignores one vital factor. The British constitution, being founded on custom and practice and not being written, is infinitely flexible: in other words, it can quickly be revised to suit a particular set of circumstances. Although in most cases the heir apparent does actually succeed to the throne, this process is not necessarily automatic. It would have been unusual, certainly, but nevertheless perfectly possible for Eddy to have been bypassed in favour of Prince George: the Duke of Clarence could, for example, have been prevailed upon to renounce his claim to the throne on grounds of poor health, without any constitutional crisis arising. It would, to be sure, have been an extreme course of action, but by no means as extreme as either killing him off or allowing him to die through neglect. Nearly half a century later, there was some discussion as to whether, following the abdication of King Edward VIII, the crown should pass to the next in line, his younger brother, who did in fact subsequently become King George VI. The circumstances were entirely different, of course, but the very existence of the idea that the then Duke of York, whose health was uncertain and whose children were girls, might step aside and pass the crown to the third son of George V, the Duke of Kent, does indicate a degree of latitude in the succession process, given co-operation on the part of the natural heir.[6]

With the benefit of hindsight, it seems clear that the proposed marriage of Prince Eddy to Princess Mary was a last attempt to bring him under control and prepare him for kingship. If that had failed, some constitutional way would have been found to prevent what would otherwise undoubtedly have been a disastrous, and probably brief, reign. In the event, nothing of the sort was necessary. Poor Prince Eddy did the crown the favour of dying young.

To Eddy's fiancée, Princess Mary of Teck, shocked and upset though she was by the sudden death of her husband-to-be, it must have seemed on reflection to have been something of a blessing. In spite of the impression given to the public that her betrothal to the Duke of Clarence was the result of an affection stretching back to childhood, it was nothing of the sort. The Princess had in fact been coerced into accepting a proposal of marriage that Eddy had been more or less forced to make to her, and she looked forward with deep misgivings to her future with this most unprepossessing of princes – though the prospect of being Queen did much to mitigate her fears.

Princess Mary, known in the family as May, was the daughter of a minor and indeed suspect German royal, Prince Franz, Duke of Teck. His father had forfeited his right to inherit the throne of the kingdom of Württemberg through a morganatic marriage to a Hungarian countess, and his son, therefore, had to make his own way in the world, which he did not do very well, having expensive tastes but lacking the wherewithal to indulge them. As a young man he served in the Austro-Hungarian army, then in 1864 he had what appeared to be a stroke of good fortune when he met the Prince of Wales, who invited him to England. There Franz met the daughter of Adolphus, Duke of Cambridge (one of George III's sons), Princess Mary Adelaide, and married her – only to discover that she had no money either and equally extravagant habits. Fortunately, Queen Victoria had a soft spot for Mary Adelaide, who was, of course, her cousin, and over the years was extremely generous to the Tecks. First she allowed them to live in her childhood home, the south wing of Kensington Palace, where May was born on May 26th, 1867; then, after mounting debts and the threat of the bailiffs forced them to flee to Florence, the Queen brought them back to England and granted them the use of White Lodge in Richmond Park, where she kept them out of financial trouble with large handouts. This naturally led to resentment in other branches of England's multifarious royal family, and the reputation of the Tecks did nothing to improve the marriage prospects of their first-born. When May 'came out' into Society in 1886, not a single prospective husband emerged and her future looked unpromising until, in November 1891, May and her parents were summoned to Balmoral by the Queen, who had indicated to the Tecks that the Princess had been chosen as a bride for Prince Eddy.

The romantic fiction of long devotion between the couple, concocted by the royal family and its advisers, concealed a determinedly arranged marriage for which the only real enthusiasm lay with the respective sets of parents, supported by the Queen.

From Eddy's point of view, May was no great beauty and certainly did not stir his heart as Princess Hélène had done. Marrying May, however, was a considerably more attractive proposition than the alternative offered by his father: the Prince of Wales had made it clear that if Eddy did not marry soon, he would be shipped off abroad for a long period so that he could not indulge his dissolute tastes, or if he did the British public would not know about it. May, for her part, could hardly view Eddy as an ideal partner. He looked, not to put too fine a point on it, a mess; he was decadent, drunken and boorish – she had known him from childhood, when she had suffered from his bullying ways, and she had not liked him much then. The passage of time had made his personality and his behaviour if anything even less appealing.

None of this mattered to Eddy's parents or the Tecks. The former had a dynasty to protect and the latter a future to secure. Both were quite cold and calculating about how to achieve their aims. It was Princess Alexandra who saw marriage to May as the most satisfactory solution to the Eddy problem. She was perfectly well aware of her eldest son's faults, just as she was of those of her husband, and in each case her reaction was to accept them and to try to cover them up, carrying on as if everything was perfectly normal. Because part of her way of dealing with her husband's selfishness was to transfer an excess of affection to her sons, the Princess liked to keep them as close to her as she could, so she resisted the idea of the Prince of Wales that Eddy should undertake an extended tour of the Colonies. That he should marry instead was infinitely preferable and May seemed to be the ideal candidate: the Princess knew that she was a solid, sensible, practical young woman and she hoped that with May's help and under her influence, Eddy would settle down. The Prince of Wales accepted his wife's judgment. His priority seems to have been to get the embarrassing Eddy out of the way by any available means and, although his inclination was to pack him off abroad, he, too, felt that marriage to May might be equally effective in deflecting public attention from his son's unsavoury habits. Marriage, as the Prince of Wales well knew, could cover a multitude of sins.

Queen Victoria's role in the affair was that of an enforcer as far as

Princess May was concerned. Here at last, after all the failures and false starts, was an opportunity for the Queen to achieve her cherished ambition to see her grandson and successor-but-one safely and suitably wed. She well knew that for the Duke and Duchess of Teck the proposed match was an answer to their prayers. With their daughter confirmed as the future queen consort of England, they could no longer be scorned by their royal relatives and their financial base would be secure – no more fleeing from debt-collectors. Furthermore, the Queen's generosity towards the Tecks had left them in the palm of her hand: one squeeze would be sufficient to ensure that, if May proved to be reluctant, her parents would leave her in no doubt as to where her duty lay.

But Princess May of Teck was nothing if not a dutiful daughter and she offered no resistance to the arrangement 'Aunt Queen' sanctioned. Prince Eddy was in no position to resist either. The engagement was announced, the public informed that it was a 'love match'. Then, as now, the reporting of royal life in the newspapers, particularly at a personal level, was highly unreliable. 'Columns of *rot*,' was how Lady Geraldine Somerset, lady-in-waiting to May's grandmother, described the novelettish inventions published at the time of the engagement.

Indeed, the betrothal occasioned no family celebrations at Balmoral and as time went on, with feverish arrangments being made for the earliest possible wedding date, it became a source of some regret, almost panic, in the mind of the bride-to-be. May soon realised that, apart from her responsibility to bear children for the crown, she was expected to fulfil the combined roles of mother-substitute, nanny and secretary to the weak, slow-witted and idle Duke of Clarence. She began to wonder whether she could go through with it, but her mother made it absolutely clear that there was no turning back. Loyal daughter that she was, May gritted her teeth and looked forward to a life that must have seemed to her in some ways like a prison sentence. If, in the midst of the trauma and grief of Eddy's unexpected demise, she allowed herself a small, secret sigh of relief, who could blame her?

On the other hand, the loss of her fiancé left her in an unenviable position. At the age of twenty-four she had been saved from what might well have been lifelong spinsterhood, only to be placed firmly back on the shelf a couple of months later. The Duke and Duchess of Teck were in despair, not only on behalf of their unfortunate daughter but also for themselves. Quite apart from their usual indebtedness, they had borrowed heavily against their future financial security as parents of the queen consort: another flight abroad seemed a distinct possibility. But Princess Mary Adelaide was not prepared to give up her glittering prize without a fight. If the crown passed to the next in line, there was no reason why the bride should not go with it.

The Duchess of Teck knew that Queen Victoria, fearful for the future of the monarchy when it passed into the care of the now ageing and, in the Queen's eyes, unreliable Prince of Wales, was desperately keen to establish public confidence in the generation that would succeed him, and there was no better way of doing that than to make a popular match for the new heir presumptive, Prince George. May, though not remarkable for her looks, had captured the public's heart after the announcement of her engagement to Eddy and, though some might think it odd that she should be 'passed on', so to speak, to Eddy's successor, there was every chance that the majority of people would welcome her as George's bride-to-be.

Thus it came about that the Queen and her cousin conspired to make it happen. Within weeks of Eddy's death Victoria was consulting with her ministers about the prospects of a bride for George, while Princess Mary Adelaide arranged for the Tecks to turn up in the South of France only a couple of miles from Cap Martin, where the Wales family had settled to recover from their bereavement. The Prince of Wales was aware of the plot being hatched between his mother and Princess Mary Adelaide and was appalled – not because he had anything against Princess May but because of what he considered the indecent haste of the whole thing. Princess Alexandra was not happy about it either: having just lost one son through death, she had no desire soon to lose another as a result of marriage. The Prince of Wales, therefore, put pressure on Mary Adelaide's brother, George, Duke of Cambridge, to persuade the Tecks to change their plans.

The Duke was no more in favour of his sister's machinations than was his nephew: it would be indecent, he thought, for May to be passed from hand to hand in such a fashion. Cambridge prevailed upon the Duchess of Teck to modify her plans and take a villa in Cannes, which is nearly a hundred miles from Cap Martin. The requirements of seemly behaviour were thereby satisfied.

Whether George and May knew what was going on is an open question, but if they did it is unlikely that they would have had any objection. Even in childhood, May had preferred the company of Prince George to that of his elder brother. He was not a great deal cleverer, but he had more zest for life and a kinder, more generous nature. Her recent experience of the late Duke of Clarence made George seem almost saintlike, and she had grown fond of him during her all too brief period of closeness to the Wales family she had been expected to join. The Prince was fond of May, too, though he had never thought of her as more than a cousin and his future sister-in-law. In the aftermath of Eddy's death, however, they had grown closer together, supporting each other in their loss – though it was mostly George depending on May, who understood the importance to him of his family and the nature of his grief. The Duchess of Teck had noted this deepening attachment and encouraged May to accompany the Wales family to Osborne after Eddy's funeral and later to join them in their sojourn at Eastbourne. There, May and George spent a good deal of time together and drew ever closer, though May was by nature extremely shy and reserved, while the Prince was not the most demonstrative of men and was still very much in thrall to his mother, who reminded him that nobody could come between them and that, since she had lost Eddy, George must love her for both himself and his brother.

So far, so good, in the eyes of the Duchess of Teck as she transported her family to the South of France, where after what the Prince of Wales considered a decent interval (though it must have seemed an age to Princess Mary Adelaide) there was an exchange of hospitality. Any reluctance on the part of the Prince and Princess of Wales was certainly not shared by Prince George as more and more of his attention was taken up by his 'dear Miss May'. At this point, however, May began to draw back a little: she knew that George would be a far better husband to her than Eddy would have been, even though there was between the couple a significant difference in both intelligence and education, but she doubted whether he could be wrested from the clutches of his mother. He was, as we have seen, remarkably immature and that left him easy prey to Princess Alexandra's rather dramatic appeals to his affections.

The matter was resolved, like so much else, by the intervention of Queen Victoria. She definitely made up her mind that George and May should marry and she warned the Prince of Wales that he had better not place obstacles in the way: that warning, of course, also applied to his wife. But this time the Queen was prepared to let events take their course. She did not particularly care whether George and May loved each other (she was well aware that May had not cared for Eddy), but it would obviously be better, in the circumstances, if affection between them grew naturally. Then, of course, the Court was still in mourning for the dead prince and for the moment there could be no question of an announcement that Eddy's former fiancée had become engaged to his brother.

Throughout 1892, then, George and May kept in touch by letter and saw each other when the other calls upon the Prince's time allowed. Apart from his naval excursion in *Melampus* and his introduction to the House of Lords as Duke of York, he was sent to Heidelberg in what proved to be a vain attempt to learn German and he also began to study the politics of the country over which he would one day be expected to reign. In December, the Duke of York spent time with his grandmother at Windsor and the Queen made it absolutely clear that she wanted him, expected him, to marry Princess May. The way was opened by the ending of the official mourning for Eddy on the first anniversary of his death (though Princess Alexandra continued to wear black for some time afterwards).

In May 1893, George was staying with his sister, Princess Louise, the Duchess of Fife, at her home in Surrey, and on the third of the month May was invited to lunch, which proved to be a formal and rather uncomfortable affair. The story goes that after lunch, Princess Louise prompted her brother to take Princess May into the garden on the pretext of showing her some frogs in the pond. At any rate, George made what must have been a somewhat halting proposal of marriage and the 'darling girl', as he told his parents, accepted. The consent of the Queen having been obtained, of course, rapidly and without difficulty, the official announcement was made on May 4th.

The Times welcomed the news, settling any doubts about the propriety of the engagement by delivering itself of the opinion that sufficient time had elapsed since Eddy's death to render it seemly and expressing the pious and somewhat eccentric hope that because it had been founded in tragedy, the forthcoming marriage might be even happier than it would have been in the ordinary way.

The wedding took place at the Chapel Royal in St James's Palace on July 6th, a blazing hot day that brought out spectators in their thousands to line the processional route from Buckingham Palace – rather than driving straight along The Mall, the coaches and landaus with their splendid military escorts followed a semi-circular course, turning left outside the Palace and proceeding up Constitution Hill to Hyde Park Corner and then along Piccadilly to approach the chapel from St James's Street. It was, said Lady Geraldine Somerset, 'the greatest success ever seen or heard of', and it foreshadowed the importance that would later be attached to royal weddings as public spectacles, beginning with that of the next generation's Duke of York.

George and May spent their honeymoon at Sandringham in what was to be their family home for the next thirty years or so, even after George, as king, had inherited 'the big house'. York Cottage, as it was renamed when the Prince of Wales gave it to his son as a wedding present, had begun life as a lodge known as Bachelors' Cottage, since its purpose was to accommodate male visitors during the shooting season. Harold Nicolson described it perfectly when he called it 'a glum little villa', with all the suburban images the noun evokes. It had been built in a corner of the Sandringham deer park, a hundred yards or so from the main house, from whose view Princess Alexandra had insisted that it be obscured by a thick hedge of laurel and rhododendron. The dense foliage threw the cottage into shadow, which was deepened even further by the enormous conifers of the surrounding park, but even if it had been entirely open to the light, most people who saw it agreed that the house would not have appeared much more attractive.[7] It was constructed of dull, brown Norfolk stone in Victorian Gothic style, though parts of it had been rendered and of these some had been disguised with white paint and mock-Tudor black beams.

The interior was hardly more appealing, featuring as it did the dark oak, Doulton tiles and coloured glass fanlights which, ironically, were favoured by the pretentious middle classes of the Victorian era, who sought to give their houses what they thought might be the appearance of the stately homes in which their social superiors lived. The accommodation was fairly extensive, though few of the rooms were very large, and certainly there was overall insufficient space for a royal couple, their children when they came along and their household. Most of the servants lived out (the Duke once joked that he assumed they slept in the trees) and to this inconvenience was added rather basic plumbing, with too few bathrooms, and inadequate heating.

But the Duke of York thought the cottage was charming and was never happier than when he was at home there, tending his garden, supervising the farm over which his father had given him management and, most of all, shooting. During the game season, his routine seldom varied: breakfast at nine-thirty, out with the guns at ten to cover up to twelve miles (he took a pedometer so that no detail should be missed in the record he kept of each day's shooting). In the evening, he would deal with whatever business the comptroller of his household brought to him, then, as his family grew, there would be a visit to the nursery. The periods immediately before and after dinner would be spent with his wife and his day would end with a game of billiards and an early bedtime.

Of course, there was a home in London, too, York House, a seventy-five-room wing of St James's Palace, but the Duke thought it 'beastly' and unhealthy while the Duchess was appalled that her husband had furnished it, without consulting her, in the latest style available from Maples department store – another middle-class touch from the man who would become known as 'the people's king'. In one sense at least he showed early a common touch that was unerring.

London in any case held few attractions for the Duke of York. He did not care to indulge in the pleasures of Society, neither entertaining nor being entertained, and the cultural delights of the capital did not appeal to a mind that had only a limited appreciation of them. Sandringham was his home, both practically and spiritually. There he could enjoy all the things he remembered from his rural childhood, surrounded by familiar scenes and objects, untroubled by the complexities of social life and with the added emotional security of a wife and, very soon, children of his own. The public demands on royalty were much fewer then than they are now, and when some ceremonial occasion or civic obligation intruded, he accepted it uncomplainingly with the discipline of a man trained by the Navy and the good grace of one satisfied by the knowledge that he was doing his duty. Such calls upon him were infrequent enough as the reign of Queen Victoria drew to a close and the main public functions of the crown fell to the lot of the Prince of Wales; they were a small price to pay for the comfort, privilege and order of his protected and self-indulgent life. He would have been curmudgeonly indeed had he not continually expressed, as he did in letters to family members and close friends, his pleasure in his good fortune.

For the Duchess of York, however, the early years of married life were somewhat less idyllic. Her husband was inured to the pervasive presence of Princess Alexandra – to the extent that, although he loved her deeply, when her desires interfered with his cherished pursuits, he had the knack of ignoring maternal influence – but May found it a strain, particularly at Sandringham, where the Princess of Wales developed the habit of dropping in at York Cottage unannounced and with dogs and spinster daughters in tow. Apart from that, Alexandra never really accepted her daughter-in-law: she was too possessive a mother to let her gratitude at the happiness May had brought to George entirely override her sense of rivalry towards the woman who had stolen the greater part of her only remaining son's affection.

The closeness of George's family in general was a problem for May. As in many a tightly-knit clan, beneath the surface warmth seethed a multitude of petty resentments and bitterness and, again as is so common, the repressed feelings of these internal grudges were turned against the newcomer. Princess Louise, rather snobbish and reserved almost to the point of reclusiveness, married to the strutting Duke of Fife, directed what may have been jealousy at May's popularity into disdain for the less-than-royal aspect of the Teck lineage.

George's beloved Toria (Princess Victoria, to whom, when he was king, he would telephone every day he did not see her) was envious of May simply because she was married; Victoria was kept as a sort of special handmaiden by Princess Alexandra, who used a bell to summon her, and she never married. The youngest sister, Princess Maud – who was to marry King Haakon VII of Norway in 1896 – was rather less hostile, but she joined the others in their pique at May's obvious advantage in intelligence and notably superior educational accomplishments, which they tended to dismiss to other people as 'dullness', presumably meaning that she was not empty-headed and frivolous.

Finally there was the problem of George himself. That he loved May deeply is beyond doubt, but having grown up in almost exclusively male company he seemed to consider it an affront to his manhood to tell her of his love other than in letters. When he wrote to her, he was full of passion and devotion, but when they were together he appeared unable to break down the bluff exterior of the naval officer. Furthermore, he had the same selfish streak that characterised his father; even an adored wife was not to come between him and his pleasures (though at least May could count herself fortunate that *her* husband's predilections were sporting rather than amorous).

Yet George's very homeliness was something of a disappointment, too. Here was May, Duchess of York and the third lady of the land after the Queen and the Princess of Wales, prevented from enjoying to the full the social privileges she felt were hers by right – and denied to her previously owing to the taint of her family – because her husband preferred to bury himself in the country and massacre birds. Nor was he on the same intellectual plane as she was, so that she found herself having to help to educate him as he struggled to come to grips with the constitutional aspects of his new role as heir presumptive. His devotion to her was assured, but it came very close to dependence. As he himself said, one of the reasons why he became increasingly reluctant to travel abroad was that he felt insecure when he was away from his wife. (The other reason was that, not being a linguist, he could not always understand what foreigners said.)

So the new Duchess of York possessed all the social position and prestige that any lady of her generation could have wished for, but she felt isolated and ill at ease. Her husband's family was suspicious of her and sniped at her; George himself was immature, inhibited with her and, certainly in the early years, not nearly as supportive as he might have been and far more dependent than he should have been. Always diffident and introspective, May found herself thrown back more and more on her own resources, which made her in turn increasingly inhibited and reserved.

She would later confess to her husband that she believed they had never really had the chance to learn to get to know each other properly, that in those early months and years, things were done which could not easily be undone. As May's best friend, Mabell, Countess of Airlie, put it, her shyness crystallised and a 'hard crust of inhibition' gradually encompassed her, obscuring what was in reality a warm and tender personality. However much they loved each other, there was from the start – even before they were married – a certain distance between George and May, an emotional gap widened by insensitivity and lack of consideration and never completely closed. Theirs would be seen as an ideal marriage, their life together as a model of respectability, but something was missing at the core and, as will become clear when their family life is explored in more detail, it was to play its part in causing serious difficulties for the monarchy.

6

Royal 'Regiment' of Wales

The death of Prince Albert Victor had left the succession to the throne of England in a somewhat parlous state. After the Prince of Wales, the Duke of York was the only man who stood between the crown and three women – the younger children of the Prince of Wales, the Princesses Louise, Victoria and Maud. That made Queen Victoria nervous, particularly since Prince George had given everyone a fright by contracting the disease that had robbed the monarchy of its strongest element, Prince Albert. There is, of course, no constitutional difficulty about the succession of a woman to the throne (indeed, the record of England's female monarchs has been on the whole a remarkably good one), but Queen Victoria knew perfectly well that none of the Wales girls was regal material. At the time of Eddy's death, Louise, next in line to Prince George, was the only married one, but her shyness, which bordered on neurosis, would have been a tremendous obstacle to the popularity of the monarchy had she ever been called upon to rule, while her husband, the Duke of Fife, was eminently unsuitable as the prospective consort of a queen of England.

It was largely because of the succession problem that Queen Victoria became obsessed with finding a bride for Prince George as quickly as possible: he had to have children so that the Wales girls could be relegated to the dynastic third division. If this seems heartless, even cynical, it should be remembered that there was a degree of urgency about the situation. The Queen was in her mid-seventies and the Prince of Wales already in his fifties. It was perfectly possible that neither would see out the century; the young Prince George, mean-while, had just survived a potentially fatal illness – he might not be so fortunate next time. In an epoch when radical thought was beginning to foreshadow social and political upheavals to come, the Queen was already fearful for the monarchy's prospects of survival: its future had to be placed in the safest possible hands. Such considerations no doubt influenced the Queen as she decided that the suitable consort found for the late heir presumptive should be married to his successor, Prince George.

The new Duchess of York was not to disappoint the Queen. By the summer of 1894, two weeks short of her first wedding anniversary, she had fulfilled one of her most important responsibilities, providing the royal family with its next heir – and a male one at that. The new prince was born at White Lodge, Richmond Park, on June 23rd, 1894. Queen Victoria expressed her delight and satisfaction when the birth provoked an outburst of public celebration and goodwill that emphasised both the nation's and the Empire's loyalty to the crown. 'The young Prince', *The Times* intoned, 'is heir to a noble inheritance, not only to a station of unequalled dignity, but more than all to the affection of a loyal people.' Those people, the Queen told the Duke of York in a letter, would expect the boy to be christened Albert in memory of one who had brought such blessings to the whole Empire. The Duke was not impressed by his grandmother's argument. Displaying that streak of stubbornness which was at once a strength and a weakness in his character, he responded by telling the Queen that he and May had long ago agreed that their first son should be named Edward, in honour of his dear departed brother. Victoria huffily pointed out that Eddy's first name had in fact been Albert, adding that she supposed the parents of the child must have their own way, but it was a pity that a future king of the Coburg dynasty should not rule under the name of its founder. (She was not to know, of course, that the Coburg name itself would later cause severe embarrassment to her grandson and his relatives.)[1]

So Edward it was, with Albert second: Edward Albert Christian George Andrew Patrick David, neatly incorporating the names of the patron saints of the four home countries. And with parental independence thus established, little Prince Edward became known ever afterwards among his family as David. The reason for this idiosyncrasy has never been clear, but perhaps the child's last name was preferred because the use of his first one – inevitably shortened to Eddy – would have aroused painful memories best left to lie undisturbed, considering the circumstances surrounding his parents' marriage. There may have been another reason, too. Prince George knew that a fortune-teller had prophesied to Queen Victoria that she would be followed by two kings whose reigns would be short, then a third who would match the glory of her own reign: the name of that third king would be David.[2]

Eighteen months after David's birth, the Duchess of York produced a second son, and her most important child as far as the long-term future of the dynasty was concerned. Her timing could not have been worse: the boy was born on Queen Victoria's 'dreadful day', December 14th, the date on which Prince Albert had died. It was now 1895, thirty-four years after the Queen's tragic loss, but the Yorks still feared she would be angry and would see the birth date as a bad omen. The Prince of Wales, however, suggested a way of turning an unfortunate accident into a happy event: the Queen should be told that this second prince would have Albert as his first name. The ploy worked. The 'new one', said the Queen, would be the more dear to her, in spite of his birth on such a sad day, because he would bear the name that was a byword for all that was great and good.[3] He was christened Albert Frederick Arthur George, his maternal grandmother, the Duchess of Teck, expressing the hope that some day his last name might supplant his less favoured first one. The Duchess's remark proved to be an unconscious prophecy, more accurate than the one given to Queen Victoria by the clairvoyant many years earlier. The second son was known as Prince Albert, Bertie to family and friends, but George was the name he chose to use when he was required to guide the monarchy out of the gravest crisis it had faced in more than two centuries.

There were to be four additions to the family during the next ten years. 'I shall soon have a regiment, not a family,' the Duke of York observed at one point.[4] In 1897 the Duchess gave birth to her only daughter, Princess Mary, who was to marry Viscount Lascelles (subsequently Earl of Harewood) and to become a very popular Princess Royal. Three years later the future Duke of Gloucester, Prince Henry, was born, then in 1901 the family's nomenclature changed. Queen Victoria died on January 22nd that year and Prince George's father was proclaimed King Edward VII. George was now heir apparent, and with his new status came the automatically devolved Duchy of Cornwall, so that he became known officially as the Duke of Cornwall and York. Then on November 9th, 1901, without ceremony, Edward VII passed on to his son his own former title as heir to the throne, Prince of Wales.

Thus it was as Prince and Princess of Wales that George and May had their fifth child in 1902, named George after his father and destined to become Duke of Kent. Their sixth and last child was born in 1905 and christened John, the second name of Princess Alexandra's last child who had died only a few days after his birth in 1871: the name proved to be a tragic inheritance. The baby suffered serious breathing problems as soon as he was born and later it was noticed that he seemed physically and mentally backward for his age. He began to have fits and, when he was four, epilepsy was diagnosed. During the next year, the seizures increased in both frequency and ferocity and poor Prince John was banished to Wood Farm, at Wolferton, on the Sandringham estate, to spend the rest of his short life in seclusion, for the most part ignored by his family, except Prince George and his grandmother, Queen Alexandra, both of whom visited him daily when they were at Sandringham. John was unable to attend his parents' coronation in 1911 and died eight years later, at the age of thirteen, after a violent seizure. It was, his mother noted, a blessed release for a restless soul.

As his family grew steadily, Prince George was in his element. At least until the death of Queen Victoria, royal duties lay lightly upon him and, freed from the limitations imposed in his younger days by his naval career, he could enjoy the leisurely life of a country gentleman. These years, according to his own diaries and letters, were supremely happy: he had a good wife and what he considered a comfortable home at York Cottage; he had his shooting and his stamp collecting; he could play the countryman in a very practical way through the Sandringham farm his father had given him to manage; and to the closeness of the family in which he had grown up, and which had always been of the greatest importance to him, was added the bonus of his own children. Apart from its exceptional luxury and privilege, its freedom from financial strain and the necessity of earning a living, and its various layers of cushioning against the vagaries of the world, this was a way of life to be found in countless British homes throughout the Victorian twilight and the rosy dawn of the Edwardian age.

In fact, the household of Prince George was less the ideal expressed by Walter Bagehot of a royal family bringing down 'the pride of sovereignty to the level of petty life' than an example of a royal family *living* a petty life. Sir Arthur Bryant recorded with pride and pleasure a reminiscence of 'the York Cottage children dressed in blue serge suits playing in the woods at Sandringham with rosy-cheeked nurse-maids – as natural, jolly and unspoilt as the boys and girls of any poor professional man', brought up 'in almost Spartan simplicity'. But, of course, these were not the children of a poor professional man. They were the future first family of the nation, young people who, without any effort on their part, without the requirement of any outstanding characteristics, would grow up to find themselves atop a dizzying pinnacle of wealth, privilege and status. Yet the focus of their rearing was on ordinariness. In terms of intellect, talent and ability, the children might be thought to have been ordinary enough, and perhaps even below a generally accepted standard of ordinariness. The effect of their upbringing was to make them more ordinary still: the eldest lacked the character and fortitude to maintain himself in the position that was his by birth; the second worried himself into an early grave when that exalted position passed to him; as for the rest, they became nothing more than spindly offshoots of a family tree.

So far, history has attempted to make excuses for them. The conventional wisdom is that King George V, good and revered monarch though he was, and Queen Mary, though remembered with awe as a splendid regal figure, so neglected, mismanaged or misunderstood their parental responsibilities as to place their children at a serious disadvantage when their turn came to don the mantle of monarchy. The abdication of King Edward VIII was regrettable, but understandable given the attitude of his parents towards him. The fact that the reign of King George VI only became as successful as it was because he happened to be married to a sensible, practical and strong-willed woman may be explained by the deprivations of his childhood. There are, however, other, simpler and perhaps fairer explanations.

For a start, history has fundamentally misunderstood and carelessly misrepresented the performance of George V and Queen Mary as parents. It is now taken for granted that Prince Edward (David) and Prince Albert (later George VI) – the two in whom history has quite naturally taken most interest – suffered dull, miserable, lonely and emotionally deprived childhoods, bullied by a tyrannical and irrational father and kept at arm's length by a mother who was reserved to the point of frigidity.

So firm is this conviction that one biographer, Frances Donaldson, in her generally excellent book about Edward VIII, did not shrink from making the astonishing claim that King George and Queen Mary were temperamentally unsuited to parenthood.[5] Leaving aside the large question of what does and does not constitute a 'temperament suited to parenthood', Lady Donaldson hedged her statement with qualifications and caveats to the extent of casting doubt upon it herself, yet it seems to have been largely accepted. As recently as 1982, for example, a study of George VI contained the catchy but rather less than entirely accurate chapter heading, 'A Royal, and Deprived, Childhood'.[6]

The legend of parental incompetence owes less to fact than to the chasm that separates modern attitudes from those prevalent at the turn of the century, when the children in question were actually growing up. It arises, too, from floundering attempts to identify the psychological factors that influenced the erratic behaviour of Edward VIII and the almost pathological shyness and constant anxiety of George VI. The popularisation of only dimly comprehended psycho-babble has led to a widespread belief that personality flaws and behavioural aberrations are never natural occurrences but must always have some identifiable and probably external cause. Such an explanation allows our society to evade responsibility for personal short-comings, and an easy way to justify the evasion is to blame one's defects and deficiencies on the way one was treated as a child. The fault, dear Brutus, lies not in our stars, or in ourselves, but in our parents.

Thus, the theory goes, the inability of Edward VIII to carry the weight of the crown stemmed not from a basic weakness of character but rather from a lack of confidence engendered by his domineering, absolutist father; his infatuation with the unsuitable Mrs Simpson was merely his search for a Freudian mother-substitute, since he felt rejected by his own mother. In the case of George VI, his unfortunate stammer, his continual stomach trouble and his nervous excitability are seen as the results of fear of his father and emotional neglect by his mother. All very neat in terms of popular psychology, yet these conclusions not only fail to accord with certain other aspects of the personalities of Edward VIII and George VI, but they also depend on the suppression of a number of facts. A more complete examination of the evidence available produces a rather different picture of the home life of the King and Queen.

The main case against George V and Queen Mary rests on evidence any objective judge would consider doubtful. Much of it is based on the testimony of King Edward VIII himself. In his book *A King's Story*, published in 1960, the then Duke of Windsor portrayed his father as a stubborn martinet who cared more for discipline, the niceties of appearance and the finer points of correct behaviour than for the developmental aspects of child-rearing, and as a man warm only in disapprobation. The Duke looked back over fifty years to the 'disconcerting' summons to the library for parental reproof or admonition and he recalled the multiplicity of rules, often relating to very minor concerns, that governed the lives of himself and his siblings.

His father, the Duke wrote,

had the Victorian's sense of probity, moral responsibility, and love of domesticity. He believed in God, in the invincibility of the Royal

Navy, and the essential rightness of whatever was British. . . . If through my family's position my childhood was spared the mundane struggle that is the common lot, I nevertheless had my full share of discipline. For the concept of duty was drilled into me, and I never had the sense that the days belonged to me alone.

These recollections have led many commentators to conclude that with such a background it should hardly be thought surprising that as Prince of Wales, and even more so as king, Edward should kick over the traces and oppose everything he believed his father stood for. If only George V had treated him with more understanding and the Queen had shown him more affection, what a splendid king he might have made . . .

Yet there are points about the Duke of Windsor's memoir that generally have been overlooked. For one thing, *A King's Story* was to a large extent an exercise in self-justification by an ex-king who abandoned his throne not only for love (as he would have us believe) but also because he simply could not have his own way, and who later felt that he had been shabbily treated by his family, apparently ignoring the fact that he had deserted them, wounded them deeply and might easily have brought them to ruin. Autobiography is seldom a model of objectivity and it can be argued that the Duke of Windsor had a larger axe to grind than most. The book betrays a degree of bitterness and is marked by the tone of immature irony, almost flippancy, that so characterised the attitudes of a prince who lacked both strength of will and a sense of purpose.

The second point to be made about the Duke's evidence is that even while he complained he failed to make a convincing case for the baleful effects of his upbringing. The punishments he remembered were not cruel or unusual, the rules under which he was obliged to live no more numerous or strict than was common in middle- and upper-class homes of the period. To be sure, King George was famous and feared for his outbursts of temper and notorious for his rather rough style of humour – the 'chaffing' which had been such a large part of his own father's idea of having fun with children. But parental traits such as these, while they may be alarming at first to small children, quickly become familiar, if tiresome, and the normal child develops resistance to them or at least the ability to accept them with equanimity.

Furthermore, in the Duke's autobiographical writings there is as much to suggest that the offspring of George V had a childhood that was happy, high-spirited and, for the most part, untroubled. One has the impression that the Duke of Windsor's view of his formative years varied according to his mood at the time of recall. He wrote: 'I find today that my diary during that period at Windsor is full of sunny and intimate details.' Sandringham, he remembered, 'possessed most of the ingredients for a boyhood idyll', and when his father, before he became king, roamed with his sons over the estate, 'he laughed and joked, and those "small days" at Sandringham provided some of my happiest memories of him'. Later on the Duke commented that 'affection was certainly not lacking in my upbringing', though he regretted that his father's accession to the throne in 1910 'inhibited the closer continuing intimacy of conventional family life'.

This last observation was undoubtedly true to some extent, but there is reason to believe that the demands of kingship were not entirely to blame for the estrangement that grew between George V and his eldest son. In September 1910, David Lloyd George, then Chancellor of the Exchequer in the Liberal government, visited the royal family at Balmoral and described a scene that does not suggest a particularly inhibited family life:

> Sat between the Queen and the Prince of Wales [David, then aged sixteen] at lunch. Quite a nice little fellow. After lunch when the cigars came on the Queen remained to smoke a cigarette, the boys began the game of blowing out the cigar lights – then little Princess Mary wanted to join in & got very excited over it – then the Queen & the rest of us all joined in & the noise was deafening until the little Princess set her lamp on fire. We thought then it was time to stop.[7]

The Duke of Windsor's testimony, then, is at best inconclusive and at worst unreliable because of its subjective nature. Treated selectively, it may be used to 'prove' either that George V was an impatient, nagging, unfeeling bully or that he was a jovial, concerned and loving father. What is clear is that relations between Prince Edward and the King did deteriorate seriously as the Prince grew older, but although the father was in some measure responsible for the deepening rift – in, for example, his refusal to accept that social behaviour had changed since his own young days – the faults were not all on one side. The Duke of Windsor's impression that family relationships suffered when his father became king might well have had less to do with the accession itself, and the changes it inevitably meant in the lives of his parents, than with the fact that at the time David was going through the most difficult period in the transition from boyhood to manhood.

Furthermore, the difficulties commonly experienced by teenage boys were in his case magnified by his abrupt acquisition not only of the title Prince of Wales but also, and more importantly, the traditional perquisite of the heir to the throne, the Duchy of Cornwall, with its substantial income. At the age of sixteen he was transformed from a naval cadet dependent on pocket-money of a shilling a week into one of the wealthiest young men in the kingdom. It must have done wonders for his self-esteem and sense of being grown-up, but it brought frustration, too, because in the eyes of others (not only his father) his immaturity was obvious and he was therefore prevented from enjoying to the full the independence his new position conferred. Until he was eighteen – the royal age of majority – there was nothing he could do about the restrictions placed on him, and the resentment he felt was stored away to burst forth quite dramatically later on.

The Duke of Windsor, however, is not the only source for the indictment against King George in his capacity as father. In 1959 Randolph Churchill published a biography of the seventeenth Earl of Derby in which the following passage appeared:

> Derby was distressed by the way King George bullied his children, and he ventured one day at Knowsley, when they were walking up and down the terrace, to raise the subject, justifying his remarks on the ground that he was the King's oldest friend. He said what delightful companions his own children had become when they grew up, and begged the King to realise that the royal children were on the verge of manhood and that he was missing very much in life by frightening them and continuing to treat them as if they were naughty schoolboys ... the King remained silent for some four minutes after this and then said: 'My father was frightened of his mother; I was frightened of my father; and I am damned well going to see to it that my children are frightened of me.'[8]

This is a most curious anecdote. Churchill gave his source as Harold Nicolson, yet in his own diaries, published some years after the Derby book, Nicolson rendered the story in a completely different way. 'At dinner', he wrote, 'I sit next to Cromer. He makes interesting points about George V. (1) He believed that Princes ought to be brought up in fear of their father: "I was always frightened of my father; they must be frightened of me." '[9] The alleged comment, then, appears to have been third-hand gossip when Churchill came across it – hardly a solid basis on which to make a judgment about the King's attitude towards his children.

But there are other, more telling reasons for doubting the accuracy of an apparently damning remark which had led some writers to conclude that George V was deliberately brutal to his sons. Lord Derby, though an exact contemporary of the King, was not exactly a close friend, and certainly not the closest friend George V had. Moreover, since the noble lord's extreme susceptibility and earnest desire to please caused him, in Douglas Haig's memorable description, to resemble a feather pillow, bearing the marks of the last person who sat on him, it is inconceivable that he would have dared to criticise the King's parental style, always assuming he knew what it was. It is even less likely that the often brusque and hot-tempered George V would have responded to such criticism, no matter how veiled, with a four-minute pause for thought: an explosion of royal wrath would have been the characteristic reaction.

Even if such obstacles as these could be overcome, the King's reported statement does not bear serious examination. He must have been aware that his father, while he was often at loggerheads with Queen Victoria, was quite definitely not afraid of her, often directly contravening her wishes and sometimes poking fun at the barrage of advice, injunction and complaint he had to endure from his mother even in his later years. The personality of Edward VII was large enough and strong enough not to be inhibited by fear. If he did on occasion tiptoe round his mother so as to avoid incurring her displeasure, it was not because she frightened him but because he knew that in dealing with her manipulation was better than confrontation and anyway her whims and fancies were deserving of respect simply because she was the Queen. The idea that Prince George was afraid of his father is also difficult to sustain. When Edward VII died, the then Prince of Wales wrote: 'I have lost my best friend & the best of fathers. . . . I am heartbroken.' For his part, Edward VII once wrote to his son: 'I have always tried to look upon you far more as a brother than a son, though I have never had occasion to blame you for any want of filial duty.' All the available evidence suggests that theirs was not a relationship based on fear. Indeed, as I have shown in an earlier chapter, the main effects on Prince George's personality arising from his relationship with his parents had more to do with a surfeit of affection and, on the son's part, excessive dependence rather than heavy-handed authoritarianism and the inspiration of fear by his father.

On the other hand, Edward VII was nothing if not awesome, and one of the elements of the awe with which he was regarded by almost everyone was a species of fear. The emotion is a complex one, however, and in the case of Prince George it seems to have taken the form of worship, as of a god. To him, his father was a fount of wisdom, an ideal of courage, of duty and of manliness. In short, he was a figure of heroic proportions, in spite of his manifest faults, and if he provoked apprehension in his heir, it had to do with Prince George's doubts as to whether he could match the exacting standards which, as his letters and diaries make clear, Edward VII had achieved in his son's estimation. George did not so much fear his father, in the ordinary sense of the word, as revere him, but to a mind unused to reflection and lacking in imagination, the feeling he experienced would have seemed akin to being afraid.

Still, a remark attributed to George V that was obviously widely enough known to be mentioned to Harold Nicolson at dinner deserves some consideration as to its provenance. It is not likely that Lord Cromer made it up, still less so that it was an invention of Lord Derby's. The conversation described by Randolph Churchill probably did take place, but rather than directly criticising the King, Derby would almost certainly have confined himself to remarks about his own relationship with his children. Perhaps he laid it on a bit thick, provoking the King to respond in his characteristically jocular but cutting manner. What George V thought of as humour often depended upon deadpan delivery, one example being the time when he told Prince Edward that his newborn brother had flown in through the window during the night and added, in response to the boy's question, that the baby's wings had been cut off.[10] The King would have regarded a joke about making his children afraid of him as a suitably damning riposte to what he would have regarded as Derby's sentimental nonsense – at least it would have had the effect of changing the subject.

What is clear is that the evidence cited to support the King's perceived parental failings is easy to refute. More important, however, is that it should not have been adduced at all. One of its great weaknesses, apart from its selective and unreliable nature, is that it attempts to prove the wrong case. The effects of the King's personality and behaviour upon his children, and especially on his two eldest sons, were more subtle and far-reaching than has generally been allowed: indeed, they played a crucial role in changing the nature and public perception of the monarchy in this country, as will become obvious.

Like most unenlightened fathers of his generation, George V demanded unquestioning respect, even reverence, from his sons, but he would never have wanted them to be afraid of him. Satisfied with his own upbringing and sustained by memories of what he always thought of as a happy childhood, he was committed to passing on to his children what he perceived as the benefits of his early life. That meant rough games and high spirits, a love of the countryside and its sporting pursuits; a not very demanding system of education and a close family life, insulated against unsettling or unsuitable outside influences. Therein, perhaps, lay his great error. As in so many other things, he looked backwards rather than forwards. Furthermore, he was not the man his father had been. Though he loved his children dearly, showed great pride in them and, when they were babies, boasted of how he did the honours at bath time, he lacked the open warmth and affection that was the corollary of Edward VII's explosive temper. He rarely embraced his sons, preferring a perfunctory hand-shake or a dutiful peck on the cheek at bedtime. The geniality of which he was capable with other children – and stories of such good humour are legion – was frequently missing when he dealt with his own because the emotion involved was too deep and therefore, to him, inexpressible. The excessive formality considered proper in parent–child relationships during the Victorian and Edwardian periods accorded perfectly with his own inclinations. As with his wife, he could only say on paper what was in his heart. This restraint was imposed on the boys, too: they addressed him as 'Papa' in letters but as 'Sir' to his face. But times were changing, and with them notions of child-rearing, so that in common with thousands of others who reached maturity in an age that allowed more room for emotion, the young Princes became aware that in their childhood they had been starved of paternal affection, and that awareness influenced their subsequent behaviour.

Two other factors governed the conduct of George V towards his children. One was his personality, which tended towards neurotic over-anxiety. Punctuality was an obsession with him and he was driven to placing undue emphasis on minor details of dress or behaviour. Having received one of the famous summonses to the library – which in truth contained rather more in the way of sporting guns than books – David and Bertie would be required to march into the room in line astern and 'stand easy' before the commanding officer. If, while he said what he had to say, they should so far forget where they were as to put their hands in their pockets, as small boys will when they are ill at ease, their nanny would be ordered to stitch up all their pockets so that the offence could not be repeated.

This obsessional and misdirected worrying was linked to the other factor influencing the raising of the Princes: the knowledge always foremost in their father's mind that they would grow up to inherit the responsibilities of royalty. That, in the eyes of George V, demanded of them standards of behaviour and concepts of duty beyond all reason, and his neurotic temperament led him to nag them constantly, as they failed to reach the impossible limits of perfection he set for them, and to harangue them continually as part of the discipline he believed they required. Had he known anything of the writings of Machiavelli, which is extremely doubtful, George V would have disagreed most strongly with the assertion that 'a prince who desires to maintain his position must learn to be not always good, but to be or not as needs may require'. To this most upright of monarchs, a prince had always to be better than good.

The guilt of George V as a father, if such it was, lay not in harshness or lack of parental concern, but rather in ignorance and insensitivity, a pathetic conviction that what had been right for him held good for his children, and a misguided desire to do his best to prepare them for what he saw as the burdens to come. His attitude, not an uncommon one for the times, as I have indicated, was no doubt unfortunate, but it only became tragic because of the personalities of the children it affected most. David had inherited some of the waywardness of his grandfather, while Bertie suffered from the same nervous excitability as his father. That these characteristics would be aggravated rather than mitigated by rigorous training never occurred to George V. He believed, like many an over-anxious father, that what he was doing was for the children's own good.

Ironically, Queen Mary, branded by so many as unmaternal and even unfeeling, did much to mitigate the effects of her husband's system of beliefs on their children. As with the myths about the harshness of George V, reservations need to be applied to the widely accepted view of Queen Mary's shortcomings as a mother. The main charge against her is that she was cold towards her children and unable to communicate with them on anything other than a formal level. Once again, some of the evidence is too subjective to be of much value and some has simply been carefully chosen to prove an argument decided in advance. It must be admitted, however, that the Queen's extremely reserved nature does present difficulties in reaching a balanced view.

One of the chief witnesses for the prosecution is the Empress Frederick of Prussia, Queen Victoria's eldest daughter, who died in the same year as her mother. Commenting on the then Princess May, the Empress wrote that she displayed 'something very cold and stiff, something distant in her manner: each time one sees her again one has to break the ice afresh'. She could not resist adding that the Princess was 'very unmaternal'.[11] On the first point, it is not surprising that Princess May should have been stiff and distant, considering the way in which she was treated by her royal relatives, partly because they resented her superior intelligence and partly on account of her 'tainted' morganatic blood; she was not, in their view, really 'royal'. The Empress Frederick, for all the 'rare tenderness' with which she was credited, was no more sympathetic than anyone else in this case and it never occurred to her that Princess May's reserve was merely her response to what all the great royal ladies were saying about her behind her back. Then, too, the Empress cannot have been very pleased that a girl of such flawed lineage, as she saw it, should have been chosen as her nephew's consort in preference to one of his eminently more suitable Hohenzollern cousins. The comment about the Princess's lack of maternal qualities was no doubt based on the observation of May's 'coldness', but it seems obvious that if the Empress did not consider May fit to marry the heir to the throne of England, she might seek to find fault with the way she brought up a new generation of royals. In any case, if one is to judge by results, the Empress Frederick's record as a mother is somewhat less impressive than Queen Mary's. The damage done by the abdication of Edward VIII can hardly be compared with the havoc wrought by the Empress's vain, spoilt son, Kaiser Wilhelm II, whose ambition and arrogance helped to bring about the deaths of millions of young men, the laying waste of large parts of Europe and ultimately the destruction of his country.

But if the Empress Frederick may be suspected of bias, and possibly also of not being best qualified to judge, no such accusation can be levelled against the other source most frequently cited by those who glibly prolong the legend of inadequacy in what is now called 'parenting'. Mabell, Countess of Airlie, a lady-in-waiting to Queen Mary and one of her oldest and most trusted friends, would have been more likely to have shown partiality in the Queen's favour, which seems to add weight to any note of apparent criticism Lady Airlie uttered. The fact is, though, that Lady Airlie's memoirs, which were published in 1962, are rather muddled in their opinions on the parental qualities of the King and Queen and are also greatly influenced by hindsight, as was probably inevitable.[12] On the one hand, she could write that 'the King . . . was proud of his sons but he was often harsh with them' and that the Queen 'remained tragically inhibited with her children', who 'with the exception of Princess Mary . . . were strangers to her emotionally'. Yet elsewhere Lady Airlie commented:

[98]

King George V and Queen Mary have often been depicted as stern and unloving parents, but this they most certainly were not. Remembering them in my early days at Sandringham before their family was even complete, I believe that they were more conscientious and more truly devoted to their children than the majority of parents in that era.

What are we to make of these apparent contradictions? Harsh and emotional strangers, but not stern and unloving. Either Lady Airlie was not quite sure what she meant or else she was hedging so as not to seem too critical. She went on: 'Princess Mary's attitude to parenthood I could well understand, for it was much the same as my own. Although she disliked the routine of childbearing, and had no interest in her children as babies, she grew to love them dearly when they were older.' That was normal among conventional privileged parents in an age of nannies and nurseries, governesses and tutors, and a complicated social life that did not leave much room for children. Only the modern mind, influenced by ideas of 'bonding' and child-development, would see a cause for blame in such an attitude, and the remainder of Lady Airlie's paragraph reflects the change of view that developed in the intervening years:

> But the difference between us was that while I, being a commoner, could keep in step with my children as they passed from babyhood into childhood and adolescence, she was prevented by her position and her public life from having this close contact with them. When they reached an interesting age, and began to develop personalities, her sons were taken away from her and delivered over to tutors. Her only opportunity of getting to know them as individuals was during the hour they spent with her in the evening, and that is not enough to create a happy relationship between child and parent.

Few Victorians or Edwardians would have agreed with that conclusion in their own day. Boys then were generally viewed rather like wild animals who had to be tamed, who were – in the words of Dr Arnold of Rugby – 'not susceptible of Christian principles in their full development and practice'. As I have already pointed out, character-building was the theme of the times and to this end the sons of Lady Airlie's class of commoners were, often at the age of eight or nine, taken away from their parents and delivered over to the tender mercies of the English public-school system, there to be turned into brave, helpful, truth-telling Englishmen, and gentlemen, and Christians, as

[99]

the father in the classic public-school novel *Tom Brown's Schooldays* put it. By contrast, the royal sons of the day actually remained closer to the family orbit since they were taught at home by tutors until the age of twelve, when they went as naval cadets to Osborne. An hour in the evenings – even if that was all it amounted to – offered Princess May a better chance of getting to know her children than was afforded to the mother who did not see her son from one school holiday to the next.

To be sure there was distance between mother and sons, but in those days the lives of children and parents in the privileged classes tended to overlap only by more or less formal arrangement and generally there was not the free and easy contact we now take for granted. Children, like everyone and everything else, had their place, and this was particularly true of royal life. The really telling part of Lady Airlie's remarks quoted above has to do with the children's reaching *an interesting age* and beginning *to develop personalities*. The concepts that children might be born with distinctive personalities and that every age of childhood might be interesting did not figure in the Victorian and Edwardian schemes of rearing the young. Infants were regarded rather as household pets, who needed to be fed, cared for and house-trained, and the job of nannies and nursemaids was to carry out those tasks so that the babies could be presented in a docile state to their parents for interludes of affection and admiration, much as one might cuddle a cat or pat a dog. It was only when children were able to behave like miniature adults that parents began to take an interest in them as people, to recognise individuality of character and to pay attention to their development as human beings. Hence Princess May could say of David, as a precocious two year old, 'I really believe he begins to like me at last, he is most civil to me.'[13]

Perhaps, also, she was beginning to like him at last. He was no longer an infant requiring the breastfeeding that was so distasteful to her, or emitting the odours she found so repellent, or making the wailing noises which, in the confines of York Cottage, got on her nerves (as they did with her husband, too, when he shouted to the nurse to do something to stop that damned crying). As her children grew older and became more acceptable companions, she relaxed more with them and in time her boudoir and sitting-room offered protection against the gales of their father's wrath when he was particularly overexcited.

When the family was at York Cottage, the children would take tea with their mother in the drawing-room at four o'clock, while their father disappeared into the Library to read *The Times*, write letters or review his stamp collection. With a lady-in-waiting at the piano, songs would be sung and then the children would return to the nursery quarters until an hour before their bedtime, when they would join their mother in her boudoir, where each had his or her own little chair beside the sofa on which May reclined before dressing for dinner. Assuming the children behaved themselves (and any who did not would be removed by a nursemaid), May would talk to them or read from Dickens or Kipling or Tennyson, or sometimes recite passages of Shakespeare from memory. While this was going on, the children would be encouraged to undertake a simple form of crochet, making things for one of the multifarious charities in which their mother took an interest.

Critics have made much of the apparently restricted nature of these habits, complaining that Queen Mary did not spend enough time with her offspring and suggesting that such behaviour was unusual, indicating a lack of maternal concern that damaged the children. Criticism of this sort is misplaced: when the family was at Sandringham, the children probably had more contact with their parents than most of their contemporaries did with theirs. The real problem concerning the upbringing of the children of George V and Queen Mary was not that their parents were peculiarly cold or forbidding, strict or neglectful, as we have been led to believe, but that they were depressingly devoted to the contemporary standards of conventional respectability. Sir Arthur Bryant noted with satisfaction that the King schooled his sons in 'the princely virtues of courtesy, industry and punctuality'.[14] It is hard to see what is particularly princely about such virtues: they are surely closer to the 'poor professional man' than to an ancient institution the survival of which, as the constitutional expert Sir Ivor Jennings pointed out, depends to a large extent on its retention of an aura of medieval 'romance'.

The limited vision, lack of self-confidence and essentially bourgeois outlook of a king who reigned in the shadow of an idolised father, bought his furniture at Maples and found his ideal of domestic bliss in what was, apart from its position, hardly distinguishable from the grander sort of suburban villa, had a profoundly deadening effect on the future representatives of the crown. Nor was the new generation helped by the insecurity of a mother who disguised her inner disappointments and doubts by developing an impervious shell of regal grace and grandeur and who, while recognising the faults and mistakes of her husband, had never been close enough to him in a real sense to attempt to change his ingrained attitudes. 'I have always to remember', Queen Mary once said rather sanctimoniously, 'that their father is also their king.' He was her king, too, and like any good Victorian wife she was not going to interfere in what were considered to be his concerns.

For the Princes David, Bertie, Harry and George, it was not so much a harsh or deprived childhood as a confusing one. (Princess Mary was less affected because she was a girl and her father's favourite and because, according to the thinking of the times, all that would be demanded of her would be that she made a good marriage.) As I have tried to show, their experience differed little from that of countless other boys of their generation who were handed over to the care of nannies and tutors. Their main difficulties arose from the fact that they were sent out to face a new world on the basis of a training that had hardly been suitable for the old one and without the mitigating factor of being able to depend on their parents as their father had done on his. Furthermore, while they realised from an early age that they were special people – and were treated as such by everyone outside their family circle – they were brought up to believe that for all practical purposes they must pretend to deny the very specialness, the fact of their birth, that set them apart from the rest of the world.

The already quoted remark of King George V, during the silver jubilee celebrations of 1935, that he was 'only a very ordinary sort of fellow', was sincerely felt and deeply rooted. His father's insistence that George be treated in his youth just like any other boy of his age had left its mark and had been reinforced by the monumental absence of ordinariness in Edward VII. The effect of that philosophy on the sons of George V was doubled by the towering personality of their grandfather and the fact that in the case of their father, there was nothing to distinguish him from the mass of humanity other than that a crown was placed on his head. How 'ordinary' is it possible for a prince or princess to be? Two generations later, we are beginning to find out, as the great-grandchildren of George V acquire the vain and insubstantial glamour of characters from a sort of Ruritanian soap opera.

7

An Honest Man's Conviction

In September 1910, a few months after the accession of George V, David Lloyd George wrote to his wife: 'The King is a very jolly chap but thank God there's not much in his head.' The Chancellor of the Exchequer was no great supporter of monarchy, but his words, written in Welsh, were not intended to be insulting. He was merely expressing in a somewhat elliptical way the view of many contemporary politicians that a sovereign with an active and enquiring mind might well be a dangerous animal if let loose on an elected government. The twentieth century had brought with it the consolidation of attitudes already forming in the nineteenth.

Queen Victoria, encouraged by the example of her manically industrious husband and in spite of her tendency to make hasty judgments based on prejudice or sometimes inadequate knowledge, had stoutly defended and on occasion exceeded the monarch's right to be consulted by ministers, to encourage them and to warn them. Her actual interference with the business of government was for the most part confined to matters in which, for whatever reason, she took a particular interest – foreign affairs, for example, or the armed forces, or appointments in the Church of England. The force of her personality, however, combined with the sheer length of her reign and the experience with which that had endowed her, had compelled successive prime ministers to take the Queen very much into account when formulating their policies. Under King Edward VII, all that had changed. Being the sort of man he was, Edward had been keenly aware of his prerogatives, and indeed he had paid scrupulous attention to his despatch boxes, but his lack of political education had allowed governments, both Tory and Liberal, to dismiss him as an ingénu and to treat his constitutional position with scant respect. Certainly, he was used at times as an instrument of foreign policy (a role he was happy to play, given his pleasure in travel abroad), but when he was consulted it was generally after the event, while his encouragement was rarely sought and his warnings heeded hardly at all.

Most important, perhaps, was the fact that the governance of Britain was changing. Never again would a prime minister sit in the House of Lords, and furthermore the Upper Chamber would be stripped of its most significant powers even as George V came to the throne. The mediocracy was making its hold on power unassailable, short of civil war or military coup. The middle classes, whose industry and probity had, during the nineteenth century, done most to secure for Britain the position of what would later be called a superpower, were claiming their reward. In political terms, the monarchy lost its identity and was absorbed into what is still referred to as the crown, an abstract amalgam of royal privilege and democratically conferred power which is in fact vested in the government of the day. In this ill-defined entity – and the British remain on the whole stubbornly and inexplicably proud of the idea that their constitution is so elusive that it is virtually immune from legal challenge – the sovereign was and is perceived as essential to the conduct of government but is in reality nothing more than an attractive backdrop to it. The Queen today speaks of 'my government' when she makes the speech from the throne at the State Opening of Parliament, but for all practical purposes the reverse is true: the possessive pronoun in the case of the Queen belongs to whichever political party has been voted into power. As Walter Bagehot put it even in Victoria's day, a republic had insinuated itself under the folds of a monarchy.

King George V was the first monarch obliged to confront this new situation directly. Queen Victoria had carried on almost as if nothing was changing. For the reasons I have outlined, and with the encouragement of Disraeli's Arthurian vision of the mystical monarchy, she was able to exercise to the limit and beyond the remaining royal prerogatives. Burdensome though this might have been to her prime ministers – who tended to see her as something like an extra department of state for which they were responsible – it also suited them because it added legitimacy to their actions in the sense that the Queen was perceived as representing the interests of the people as a whole, not just the faction that supported one or other of the political parties. The response of Edward VII, on the other hand, had been to float with the tide. He railed in private against the cavalier way in which prime ministers circumvented or simply ignored his constitutional rights, but he did nothing to arrest the process of erosion. Already elderly and growing tired when he came to the throne, he possessed neither the energy nor, indeed, the will to contemplate disrupting his generally comfortable position by engaging in a battle royal over its constitutional aspects. Towards the end of his reign, when his health was declining, he suffered periods of boredom (though that was never shown in public) and depression, to the extent that he even considered the possibility of abdication, and he could not bear to maintain the tradition of receiving ministers personally.[1] His son, in his mid-forties when he became king, enjoyed both the vigour of comparative youth, and the prospect of a reign sufficiently long to set the tone of the modern constitutional monarchy.

Lloyd George, as he would discover, was mistaken in saying that the King had nothing in his head. What was in his head, however, was – though undoubtedly well-meaning – muddled, imperfectly formed and subject to serious limitations. Intellectual power he certainly lacked; his mind, never extended by education, worked slowly; his thought processes might be classified as linear and he sometimes had difficulty in grasping a point or recognising a nuance of argument. He was highly excitable, often talked too much about matters of which he knew little, and had a distressing habit of taking things personally, which could lead to errors of judgment. He was also much too inclined to judge things by the standards of the past. 'There is nothing like a chip off the old block,' he said in a speech in New Zealand, which he visited as Duke of York in 1901. 'One knows that the old block was wood of good grain and sound to the core.' The possibility that old wood might be worm-eaten and rotten was not part of his thinking.

After his death, nostalgic commentators tended to turn his limitations into virtues. Sir Arthur Bryant wrote that in his speeches he 'seemed to prefer words of one syllable, and, though at the time clever men dismissed him as one only redeemed from mediocrity by his rank, we can see that preference now ... as something in keeping with his whole character and a piece of the profoundest wisdom'.[2] It is not a very convincing argument. Yet it is true that George V possessed an important redeeming feature often lacking in finer minds and those motivated by ideological commitment, something that the mass of Englishmen (and I use the national classification carefully) value perhaps more highly than any other mental attribute: common sense. During the General Strike of 1926, when the Earl of Durham referred to striking miners in his coalfields as 'a damn lot of revolutionaries', the King retorted sharply: 'Try living on their wages before

you judge them.' He also displayed rather more tolerance and awareness than his government when he warned it against taking measures
against the strikers that would have been excessive and possibly
illegal.[3] The Establishment won hands down anyway, but the popular
feeling that the King understood the problems of the common man
did much to establish him in public esteem.

He was also willing to learn, though his further education was a
very gradual process and the lessons presented were often not fully
absorbed. Common sense was of no great value in understanding
constitutional niceties or grappling with increasingly complex and
diverse political matters. Until the death of his elder brother, Prince
George had taken no interest in politics, but when he became heir
presumptive in 1892 his father – determined that his son should be
offered the serious preparation for kingship that he himself had been
denied by Queen Victoria owing to her stubborn doubts about his
fitness to reign and his discretion – encouraged George to acquaint
himself with some of the political issues and personalities of the day.
He dined with Gladstone, in his final term as prime minister, and
with Herbert Asquith, then Home Secretary. The Irish Question
(though Disraeli had complained that nobody could actually say
precisely what the question was) dominated the political stage during
the Liberal government of 1892–95 and Prince George discussed the
matter at length with the Chief Secretary for Ireland, John Morley,
as Gladstone prepared his controversial Home Rule Bill. Listening
to the start of the Home Rule debate in the House of Commons on
February 13th, 1893, the Prince, according to his diary, was chiefly
impressed by Gladstone's eloquent two-and-a-quarter-hour speech,
which he thought was a remarkable achievement for a man of eighty-
three. The resulting parliamentary row he found 'very amusing', as
one might describe a sideshow, which in a sense is what it was at the
time. A natural conservative, Prince George understood instinctively
that with Britain at the peak of its imperial power, home rule for its
nearest colonial possession was a non-starter in 1893. Almost forty
years later, though, older and wiser, and having witnessed much
misery and bloodshed, King George V found nothing amusing about
Ireland when he remarked with some bitterness: 'What fools we were
not to have accepted Gladstone's Home Rule Bill.'

The naïvety and detachment the young Prince George displayed
during his early forays into politics were not easily overcome. His wife
was appalled by not only his lack of accomplishment in English and
foreign languages but also his ignorance of constitutional history,
which she herself had studied before there had been any suggestion

that she might become a king's consort. The Prince, though he had succeeded his brother as heir to the throne, appeared not fully to have grasped what that meant. Queen Victoria's glorious reign continued undimmed, while the Prince of Wales represented the monarchy's public face in a round of official duties and appearances that was none too burdensome, and otherwise enjoyed the privileges of his position. To the newly created Duke of York the requirements of kingship must have seemed a very long way away and very much less important than his daily concerns and pleasures.

Harold Nicolson, while writing the official biography of George V, which was published in 1952, confessed to his diary:

> I fear that I'm getting a down on him. He may be all right as a gay young midshipman; he may be all right as a wise old king, but the intervening period, when he was Duke of York . . . is hard to swallow . . . he did nothing at all but kill animals and stick in stamps.[4]

Princess May did what she could to remedy the deficiencies in her husband's understanding of what lay before him. While he read novels to her, she tried to interest him in, among other things, history and constitutional practice, reading to him from books that were familiar to her and patiently expanding from her own knowledge on points that were difficult or obscure. On the rare occasions during these years when the Duke had to make a speech, May helped him to write it. As for the Duke's tuition in current affairs, that came mainly from the pages of *The Times*, upon which he was to rely heavily throughout his life. One of his private secretaries, Sir Clive Wigram, wrote to the editor of the paper in 1936:

> H.M. loved his *Times* and I don't think he felt happy at the end of the day if he had not studied his paper. More than once he said to me when I went to see him in the evening: 'Now hurry up with your work. I have been busy all day and have not yet had time to read my *Times*.'

Early in 1894, the efforts of the Duchess of York and *The Times* were supplemented by those of Professor J. R. Tanner, a constitutional historian from St John's College, Cambridge. If the Duchess had not done so already, Tanner introduced Prince George to Walter Bagehot's *The English Constitution* and persuaded him to study at least that part of it relating to the powers and responsibilities of the monarchy. The fruits of that study are preserved in the Royal Archives at Windsor Castle in the form of a school exercise-book in which the Duke of York noted what was presumably Tanner's analysis of the principles laid down for the conduct of kings by England's nineteenth-century version of Machiavelli. This analysis, in the Duke's slow, careful, almost childlike handwriting, was so important as a key to the strengths and weaknesses of the reign of George V that Harold Nicolson reproduced it in full in his biography, and it is worth some comment here.

Tanner's instruction cannot have been too clear, for after the heading 'Monarchy' the Duke plunged immediately into confusion by referring to the functions of 'the Crown', failing to distinguish between the monarchy itself and the conceptual coalition of sovereign and government that was in the process of becoming the crown. Bagehot, in outlining his scheme of things, was for the most part careful to refer to the uses and powers of 'the monarchy'. Where he wrote 'the Crown' when he meant the monarch, he was either exhibiting the journalist's dislike of using the same word too often or he may be excused on the ground that he was writing in 1867. Obvious changes in the electoral system and the style of government during the intervening twenty-seven years – changes that had begun to have an effect even as Bagehot had been writing – would leave no such excuse open to a constitutional expert: the problem was that Tanner was an historian and thus inclined perhaps to concentrate on past rather than contemporary developments. The analysis of monarchical functions he presented to the Duke of York, then, was essentially backward-looking.

Be that as it may, the Duke noted that in what Bagehot called its 'dignified' capacity, the monarchy made government intelligible and interesting to the masses and strengthened government through the religious tradition connected with the crown. In social terms, the monarchy protected the traditional English class system. The Duke copied out Bagehot's words: 'If the high social rank was to be scrambled for in the House of Commons, the number of social adventurers there would be incalculably more numerous & indefinitely more eager.' Morally speaking, the monarchy could set the tone of the nation, while its very existence served to disguise change and therefore to deprive it of the evil consequences of revolution.

The Duke then turned to what he called the crown in its 'business capacity', observing that although the monarchy lacked its actual power of former times, it retained 'unexhausted influence' that could be exercised in various ways: in the formation of ministries, especially in choosing between statesmen who had a claim to lead a party; in the continuance of ministries, through the sovereign's rights to be consulted, to encourage and to warn; at the break-up of ministries, through the powers to dissolve Parliament and to create new peers. 'This', the Duke noted mysteriously, 'can be treated best in connexion with the House of Lords.' He would find, when he came to the throne sixteen years later, that his power to create peers was very much a mixed blessing.

Finally, there was Bagehot's point that while heads of government, that is prime ministers, changed continually according to electoral preference, the head of state – the sovereign – held his office for life. 'He is independent of parties & therefore impartial,' the Duke wrote; 'his position ensures that his advice would be received with respect; & he is the only statesman in the country whose political experience is continuous.'

The cryptic notes in the Duke of York's exercise-book were to be the basis of the kingly creed of George V. Nicolson observed: 'His faith in the principle of Monarchy was simple, devout even; but selfless. All that he aspired to do was to serve that principle with rectitude; to represent all that was most straightforward in the national character; to give the world an example of personal probity; to advise, to encourage and to warn.' And the official biographer added with wicked irony: 'To few men has it been granted to fulfil their aspirations with such completeness.'

Whether the Duke of York studied the rest of *The English Consti-tution* is a matter for conjecture; Nicolson offers as an aside the information that the record of Professor Tanner's visits to York House, compared with those of a philatelist named Tilleard, shows that the Duke much preferred stamp-collecting to studying constitutional practice. Whether he fully understood the intent and implications of even Bagehot's chapter on the monarchy is questionable. For example, the Duke jotted down the thought that kingship on the English model 'is still a great political force & offers a splendid career to an able monarch'. The penultimate word is crucial. Bagehot wrote:

> If constitutional monarchs be ordinary men of restricted experi-ence and common capacity (and we have no right to suppose that *by miracle* they will be more), the judgment of the sovereign will often be worse than the judgment of the party, and he will be very subject to the chronic danger of preferring a respectful common-place man . . . to an independent first-rate man.

George V was just such a constitutional monarch of restricted experience and common capacity. Nor, according to Bagehot, should that have surprised anyone:

> A constitutional sovereign must in the common course of government be a man of but common ability. I am afraid, looking to the early acquired feebleness of hereditary dynasties, that we must expect him to be a man of inferior ability. Theory and experience both teach that the education of a prince can but be a poor education, and that a royal family will generally have less ability than other families. What right have we then to expect the perpetual entail on any family of an exquisite discretion, which if it be not a sort of genius, is at least as rare as genius?

At the outset, then, the model on which the future George V was to base his kingship contained a crucial contradiction. Bagehot argued that a constitutional monarchy offered a better system of government for Britain than one based on a presidency, but he made it clear that a really successful constitutional monarchy depended upon a sovereign with extraordinary gifts which, if the monarchy was based on the hereditary principle, he or she was unlikely to possess. The only way to resolve this contradiction was to have a constitutional monarch who did not interfere in the business of government but merely served as, on the one hand, an umpire in a political cricket match and, on the other hand, a rubber-stamp for the policies of whichever party held power – the sovereign as a sort of superior civil servant.

> The occupations of a constitutional monarch are grave, formal, important, but never exciting; they have nothing to stir eager blood, awaken high imagination, work off wild thoughts. . . . His career is not in the air; he labours in the world of sober fact . . . in the long run he will be neither clever nor stupid; he will be the simple, common man who plods the plain routine of life from the cradle to the grave.

Such was the course King George V accepted without question and decreed for his descendants. He chose to interpret Bagehot's precepts as meaning that the constitutional sovereign was little more than a slave to public duty.

That choice – indeed, the very adoption of the Bagehot model – was to have serious implications for the development of the monarchy, and continues to do so. The Duke of York, like Tanner and very many others who came after them, assumed that Bagehot's work was the nearest thing to a written constitution that existed in Britain and regarded it almost as holy writ, or a legal document. That view is fundamentally wrong, for a number of reasons.

First, Bagehot was not a constitutional lawyer; he was a political journalist, and like all good journalists he was a natural sceptic. Second, *The English Constitution* was not a scholarly dissertation or legalistic analysis, but a piece – admittedly brilliant – of reportage combined with sometimes irreverent editorialising, which appeared first as a series in *The Fortnightly* and then in book form in 1867. Bagehot himself would have been horrified to think that anyone might view his work as a definitive study of constitutional practice: he saw it as a lively commentary on the polity of England in the middle of the nineteenth century, a portrait of an age that was already passing when he wrote it because of the 1867 Reform Act that enfranchised a whole new class of people and changed the nature of parliamentary government. 'It describes the English Constitution as it stood in the years 1865 and 1866,' he wrote in 1872, when a new edition of the book was published. 'The change since 1865 is a change not in one point but in a thousand points; it is a change not of particular details but of pervading spirit. . . . A new world has arisen which is not as the old world. . . .' So the model of constitutional monarchy that the Duke of York drew for himself so assiduously in 1894 had been acknowledged as out of date by its author twenty years before. The sixteen further years that were to elapse before Prince George succeeded his father to the throne would see changes far greater than anything Bagehot could possibly have imagined, leaving the new king to grapple with them on the basis of theories and guidelines that simply could no longer be applied.

But the final and, from the point of view of the monarchy, perhaps the most damaging aspect of the unquestioning acceptance of the monarchic principles set out in *The English Constitution* lies in a failure to understand that it was very far from being an objective study even within the limits admitted by the author. Bagehot very definitely had an axe to grind, an axe that – as the late Dick Crossman, distinguished Labour Party chairman and Cabinet member, pointed out – was essentially anti-democratic.

Bagehot could never quite make up his mind whether he was a historian describing a process of development that had been going on since 1832, or whether it was his real purpose to recommend to the new middle-class rulers of the country a Machiavellian piece of social engineering. . . . I am pretty sure that he would have brushed aside the notion that, when he wrote *The English Constitution*, he was trying to organise an open conspiracy and equip its members with a new technique of government. . . . But he undoubtedly felt that the new middle class – unsure of itself and ignorant of the art of politics – needed to be shocked out of its complacency and confronted with the problems of power.[5]

Like many other people in the mid-nineteenth century, Bagehot was disturbed by the ripples of radicalism disfiguring the previously placid faces of the lower classes, for whom he had profound contempt. In 1866 Queen Victoria told Lord Derby, 'If the question of [electoral] reform be not taken up in earnest, very serious consequences might ensue.' A popular uprising did not seem out of the question. Bagehot, like Marx, viewed politics as class war, but while Marx plotted the victory of the proletariat, Bagehot sought the dominance of 'the middle classes – the ordinary majority of educated men – [who] are in the present day the despotic power in England'. The masses of Englishmen were not fit for elective government, he wrote; 'if they knew how near they were to it, they would be surprised, and almost tremble'. His theory of constitutional monarchy, so eagerly taken up by George V and his successors, was part of his scheme for keeping 'the vacant many', and their 'bovine stupidity', firmly in their place. Give them a sovereign to look up to, and the masses need not trouble their poor brains with political questions they could not possibly understand:

A republic has only difficult ideas in government; a Constitutional Monarchy has an easy idea too . . . the mass of mankind understand it . . . royalty is a government in which the attention of the nation is concentrated on one person doing interesting actions. A republic is a government in which that attention is divided between many, who are all doing uninteresting actions. Accordingly, so long as the human heart is strong and the human reason weak, royalty will be strong because it appeals to diffused feeling, and republics weak because they appeal to the understanding.

To put it more directly, the constitutional monarchy is a form of confidence trick through which those in power maintain their position by diverting the attention of the 'vacant many' away from events, actions and decisions that affect their lives and towards an institution that in reality has no effect at all upon them, other than providing a convenient outlet for their emotions, which might otherwise be directed to more dangerous purposes.

Thus, thanks to Mr Bagehot, Professor Tanner and King George V, the monarchy further endorsed the process of its own emasculation and became the political tool of the middle classes whose values, morals, concerns and aspirations have dominated the life of this country for more than a century. As well as that, the monarchy has come to symbolise all that the middle classes hold most dear, and to which the 'lower orders' are encouraged to aspire.

Yet if it has lost any real constitutional relevance (though the façade of the sovereign's 'rights and powers' has been scrupulously maintained), the British royal family has, *pari passu*, gained immensely in popular regard and has if anything grown to be perceived more and more as an important feature of the British way of life. Each monarch since 1910 has added something distinctive to the changing role of the institution, but the impetus for such changes was the example of George V, who, paradoxically, demonstrated beyond doubt that what in Bagehot's terms would be seen as weaknesses in a constitutional monarch were in popular perception his greatest assets. His simplicity, his dignity and his unswerving devotion to duty not only provided a formula for the survival of the British monarchy in a century notable for bringing about the fall of kings, but they also laid a foundation upon which his heirs could build unprecedented popularity. Whether that is what they should have been doing is another matter, on which the limitations of George V have a direct bearing.

His faith in the superiority of all things British, in the Empire and in the loyalty of subject peoples throughout the world, was touching, if naïve. In August 1897, as Duke of York, he travelled to Ireland with his wife and gained a mistaken impression of that troubled country that was to remain with him for the rest of his life. Visiting Dublin, which was to all intents and purposes an English city, and many of the great houses of the Anglo-Irish Ascendancy, the Duke was so struck by what he took to be the devotion of the Irish people to the 'mother country' that on his return home he suggested that a royal residence be established in Ireland. It never occurred to him that he had not seen the real Ireland, the Ireland that in successive elections voted overwhelmingly for Home Rule candidates; the Ireland of the Gaelic Athletic Association, which under the guise of promoting the ancient sport of hurling had found a legal way of spreading nationalist clubs throughout the country; the Ireland of the Gaelic League, founded ostensibly to promote the revival of the Irish language but in reality – as Padraic Pearse, one of the leaders of the 1916 Rising, put it – 'commencing . . . not a revolt, but a revolution . . . its appointed work was that'.[6]

Lord Salisbury, the Conservative Prime Minister whose party had used its permanent majority in the House of Lords to defeat Gladstone's Home Rule Bill and was dedicated to keeping Ireland in the Union by almost any means, cleverly exploited the Duke's enthusiasm and supported the idea of a royal home near Dublin. 'The devotion to your person which you have inspired', Salisbury wrote flatteringly to the Duke, 'will have a most valuable effect upon public feeling in Ireland, and may do much to restore the loyalty which during the last half century has been so much shaken in many districts.' However, Queen Victoria, who had wholeheartedly supported the Coercion Bill to quell Irish rioting in 1881 and had encouraged Salisbury to kill the idea of Home Rule, had no interest in attempting to charm Ireland into submission and vetoed the plan for a royal residence. In her long reign, she had seen how fragile was Irish 'loyalty'.

Her grandson retained his illusions. He fondly believed that it was the politicians who stirred up trouble among the peoples of England and Ireland, between whom there were both natural and historical affinities. His lack of education in history made him unaware that the mass of Irishmen saw themselves as a subject people governed by force, unaware of the deep and abiding hatred many Irish people felt towards the English, stretching back to Cromwell's policy of 'extirpation' and beyond and swelled immeasurably by the blatant disregard in London for conditions in Ireland during the great famine of the 1840s, when at the very minimum two-and-a-half million people died. As the historian Cecil Woodham-Smith expressed it: 'The history of what then occurred is deeply engraved on the memory of the Irish race; all hope of assimilation with England was then lost, and bitterness without parallel took possession of the Irish mind.'[7] More recently, a Limerick man summarised his feelings thus: 'The Irish people have very long memories and the English very short memories. Things might have been different if it had been the other way round.'[8]

None of this impinged upon the imperial consciousness of George V. In 1921, at the height of the Troubles, he is reported to have rebuked Lloyd George for the actions of British troops in Ireland with the words: 'I cannot have my people killed in this manner.'[9] Admirable though such sentiments were, he had still not understood that the Irish were not 'his' people, that many of them preferred to die in the furtherance of their cause than to continue to live under what they saw as subjugation. The idea that there might be virtue or justice in ending British rule simply did not occur to him. He saw the necessity of a measure of devolution, but only within the imperial framework. He was spared the sight of the ultimate severance of constitutional links between the 'Irish Free State' and what many of its citizens perceived as their former colonial master, and neither did he live to see the refusal of the Irish government to fight for the British version of liberty in 1939. Along with Bagehot's obsolete theory of constitutional monarchy, there remained in the mind of George V an idealised vision of Britain and her Empire as they had been at their zenith towards the end of the nineteenth century.

This narrow, outdated view of the world might well have been dangerous but for one thing: it was held straightforwardly, honestly and emotionally. The transparent sincerity of George V's beliefs impelled him always to act in what he considered to be the best interests of the British 'family of nations', irrespective of political pragmatism or expediency, and what those interests might be was a continual source of anxiety to him. Unity and stability were his watchwords and his commitment to the preservation of all that was great about Britain and its Empire led him to accept and even to encourage changes that would have been unthinkable in his grand-mother's or even his father's time. Ironically, it was his instinctive determination that imperial rule should continue that helped in time to bring about the loosening of its shackles.

His first world tour as heir to the throne, in 1901 just a month after the funeral of Queen Victoria, marked his first real exposure to the Empire. He had travelled the world when he was in the Royal Navy, but it appeared to have left little impression on him: he had been too immature, too involved in naval life, perhaps too preoccupied with thoughts of the home he had left behind. Since that time, his travels had been largely confined to visiting relatives in other European capitals. For a sailor, he was remarkably resistant to the idea of travelling. As Duke of York, however, when he began to appreciate the complexities of his inheritance to come, it became important that he should gain experience rather wider than that afforded by the Norfolk farm and the grouse moor. His visit to Ireland in 1897 was a start, though it was more social than formal, and its 'success' encouraged the idea that he should begin to undertake more royal duties. For the next two years, these were mostly domestic, but in the summer of 1900 the government decided that it would be in the interests of the Empire if the Duke and Duchess of York were to visit the newly created Commonwealth of Australia to open its first parliament.

That Empire had received a severe shock the previous year when the Boers of South Africa had risen up against what they saw as British attempts to intimidate them. There is a strong case for suggesting that hostilities had been deliberately provoked by the British, and certainly the outbreak of the Boer War was greeted with wild patriotic enthusiasm in London. That fervour, however, soon turned to stunned disbelief as the Boers rapidly inflicted a series of humiliating defeats on the mighty British army. What had begun as an exercise in imperial muscle-flexing was to drag on for three years as almost half a million troops drawn from all over the Empire struggled to subdue a mere twenty thousand Boer 'rebels'. The war was a watershed in British imperial policy and thinking. No longer could the Colonies and dependencies be regarded simply as a docile milch cow for the British economy and a willing buffer against expansionism on the part of rival European nations: something had to be given in return if the flow of cheap food and raw materials to Britain was to continue (the goldfields of the Rand had been at the heart of the South African war) without an enormous commitment in men and money to maintain the Empire. The Conservative government of the day decided that the 'something' should be an extension of the mystical associations of the sovereign, which had been so successful in controlling popular sentiments at home. It was easy, it was cheap and its spiritual overtones appealed to feelings higher than those of self-interest.

Arthur Balfour, the Leader of the Commons soon to succeed his uncle, Lord Salisbury, as prime minister, outlined this new policy in somewhat high-flown terms to King Edward VII shortly after his accession in 1901. The new King was reluctant to send his heir abroad for a long period at that time, but Balfour emphasised the importance of what was happening in Australia:

> The King . . . is now the greatest constitutional bond uniting together in a single Empire communities of free men separated by half the circumference of the Globe. All the patriotic sentiment which makes such an Empire possible . . . centres chiefly in him. . . . A great commonwealth is to be brought into existence, after infinite trouble and with the fairest prospects of success. Its citizens know little and care little for British Ministries and British party politics. But they know, and care for, the Empire of which they are members and for the sovereign who rules it.

In other words, let them play at politics in their own country and in their own way, but let them remain Britain's vassal through allegiance to the King-Emperor – Bagehot's confidence trick taken a stage farther.

Edward VII was not convinced, foreseeing what this new approach would mean to the monarchy, and it is interesting to note that in a way he downgraded the Australian visit by deferring his son's elevation to Prince of Wales until after it had taken place. The Duke of York, 'always ready ... to do anything that may in any way benefit my country', had no such reservations. When the trip was first suggested, he asked Lord Salisbury to obtain Queen Victoria's permission to include Canada on the return journey to avoid 'disappointment and perhaps jealousy' in the oldest Dominion.

In March 1901, the Duke and Duchess boarded the specially refitted liner SS *Ophir* at Portsmouth for what had grown into a world tour that would last eight months. The King and Queen saw them off, amid echoes of the Duke's Navy days when he had suffered so much from homesickness: 'The leave-taking was terrible,' he wrote. 'I was very much affected & could hardly speak ... & broke down quite.' He later told his parents that he and May had gone to their cabins and had a good cry.

The couple visited Gibraltar, Malta, Aden, Ceylon, Singapore, Australia, Mauritius, South Africa and Canada. A very detailed and picturesque account of their voyage was written by the Duke's assistant private secretary, Sir Donald Mackenzie Wallace, and published under the title *The Web of Empire*. The Duke's own account was more matter-of-fact: in 231 days, he noted in his diary, they travelled 45,000 miles of which 12,000 were on land; in the course of this, they laid 21 foundation-stones, received 544 addresses, presented 4,329 medals and shook hands with 24,855 people (and that was only at official receptions). 'Our object', he told Queen Alexandra in letters, 'is to please as many people as possible. ... Of course our tour is most interesting, but it is very tiring and there is no place like dear old England for me.' It must not be thought that he was enjoying himself; he was simply doing his duty.

He was learning, too, what that duty meant. He observed the Colonies' deep sentimental attachment to and reverence for Queen Victoria, the great mother-figure, and came to understand for himself the power of the mystic qualities of monarchy, though not in the manipulative sense in which politicians viewed it. At the same time, while never doubting that imperial rule was what the Colonies and dependencies wanted, and indeed was best for them, he realised that for the Empire to be maintained these far-flung peoples must subscribe to it more as an idea than as a fact: it must transcend their local politics, their devolved governments and their narrower patriotic sentiments and it must also rise above the party politics of Britain. At a speech in the City of London a month after his return home, he stressed the 'loyalty to the Crown and attachment to the Old Country' he had encountered on his tour, but he pointed out that the motherland must prove the strength of her own attachment 'to her children by sending them of her best'. As an old-fashioned imperialist, he could not imagine that the countries of the Empire might aspire to equality with Britain. They were always to be 'children'. But as a man ruled more by emotion than by reason, he saw the role of 'father' as one for himself, not for Britain and its government. It was an idea that would persist in the monarchy as the Empire retreated into the Commonwealth and the Commonwealth faded into just another moth-eaten relic of a glorious past. Indeed, the concept of the symbolic and impartial head of a family of nations, which Britain could use as an excuse to pretend that it was still a world leader, proved to be one of the chief reasons for the monarchy's survival.

The idea of ideal fatherhood fostered by the Duke of York's colonial tour in 1901 was reinforced and given expression by his visit to India, as Prince of Wales, in 1905. Convinced by the maharajahs who entertained him, by complacent British officials and by well-orchestrated festivals of welcome, that the rise of Indian nationalism was not a real threat to the Raj, he asked the president of the Congress Party, Gophal Gokale: 'Would the peoples of India be happier if you ran the country?' Yet behind the apparent arrogance of that statement was an appreciation that all was not well with the Raj. 'I cannot help thinking', he said, 'that the task of governing India will be made easier if we, on our part, infuse into it a wider element of sympathy. May we not . . . hope for a still fuller measure of trust and confidence in our earnest desire and efforts to promote the well-being and to further the best interests of every class?' He had noticed a tendency on the part of the British in India to look upon 'the Natives' as a conquered and downtrodden race – they did not even observe the courtesies usual between superiors and inferiors at home! That allowed the Congress agitators to portray the British 'to the ignorant masses as monsters and tyrants'. To counter such nationalist propaganda, the Prince suggested a limited form of provincial self-determination – a view very different from that of the Viceroy, Lord Curzon, who regarded the three hundred million people in his charge as 'less than schoolchildren, crooked-minded and corrupt'.

The Prince's instinctive desire to maintain imperial rule by being a father to all his peoples, of all races, creeds and classes, was an ideal that was historically impossible. The concept of liberty and the notion of subjugation, no matter how benevolent the intent, are irreconcilable.

The crowning paradox: Prince Albert, seen with Queen Victoria in a photograph dating from 1861, believed the sovereign had a central role in the business of government and he attempted to make the monarchy an impartial political force. After his death, the Queen tried to remain true to Albert's concept, but, persuaded by the flattery of Disraeli, she allowed herself to be turned into the sentimental symbol of imperial splendour and national self-confidence depicted in a photograph of her taken in 1882. The resulting confusion between the purpose and the image of the monarchy has been apparent ever since.

Puppet of the politicians: King Edward VII, photographed with the German Kaiser in 1906, 'not only accepted the constitutional practice that policy must be that of his Ministers, but he preferred that it be so,' according to the Foreign Secretary of the day, Sir Edward Grey. The King enjoyed visits abroad, but 'did not care for long and sustained discussion' about political matters. That suited the politicians perfectly and helped to establish the usefulness of the royal tour as a public relations vehicle.

'The very best possible training for any boy': Such was the assessment of King Edward VII of the value of a career in the Royal Navy, but in the cases of George V (pictured in his naval uniform at the age of nineteen), Edward VIII (an officer in purely honorary terms in 1918) and George VI (as a lieutenant towards the end of the First World War), it may be argued that their development and certainly their education were limited by early entry into the Navy.

The styles may change, but the purpose is the same. King George V with Queen Mary, in formal attire at the Chelsea Flower Show in 1924, and King George VI with Queen Elizabeth, suitably garbed for a visit to a nickel mine in 1939, fulfil the expectation that the royal family must be constantly on view. Since the reign of George V, the demands for royal appearances have increased enormously, yet the value of this ceaseless activity has rarely been seriously questioned.

Dressed in what he called his 'preposterous rig', Prince Edward takes his father's hand after his investiture as Prince of Wales at Caernarvon Castle in 1911. The ceremony brought to the surface the ambiguities of the Prince's attitude towards his position – ambiguities that would help to drive him from the throne twenty-five years later. The accepted reason for his abdication was his desire to marry Wallis Simpson, with whom he is pictured on their wedding day, June 3rd, 1937. Closer examination of the context, however, suggests that it was Edward VIII himself, not Mrs Simpson, who was unacceptable to the British Establishment.

'Now sits Expectation in the air. . . .' The wireless served to reinforce the impression that the monarchy was moving closer to the people, and the royal Christmas broadcast – which George V is seen inaugurating in 1935 – rapidly assumed the character of a British tradition. But control remained with the politicians: Edward VIII was denied the opportunity to speak directly to his subjects until after his abdication. For George VI, radio was a means of rallying the Empire behind Britain during the Second World War, as the uniform suggests in a photograph taken in September 1939.

George VI, pictured on the balcony of Buckingham Palace with Queen Elizabeth and the Princesses Elizabeth and Margaret after the coronation in 1937. 'A family on the throne . . . brings down the pride of sovereignty to the level of petty life,' wrote Walter Bagehot. More recently, it seems sovereignty has been reduced to the level of petty life.

Ambassador from the Court of St James: George VI with President Roosevelt during the royal tour of the United States in 1939. The King's visit helped to soften American public opinion so that the President could offer practical wartime help to Britain, an example of the use of the monarchy for diplomatic purposes in circumstances when overt political contacts would be controversial. In fact, the King was furthering American foreign policy and unwittingly contributing to the decline of Britain as a world power.

A trouble shared . . . George VI, in the role of symbolic war leader, meets victims of the London Blitz in September 1940. The determination of the King and Queen to face the same dangers as ordinary people was not only of immense value in terms of both propaganda and morale but it also introduced a new and, as it turned out, perhaps counter-productive sense of familiarity in the relationship between the monarchy and its subjects.

At the time, however, his opinions and suggestions were welcomed enthusiastically as expressions of sound judgment and good sense. Many enlightened minds, and many pragmatic ones, had been disturbed by the opprobrium heaped on the British Empire by some of Britain's European neighbours during the South African war and were coming to the conclusion that imperialism in its nineteenth-century form had outlived its benefits. But the idea of King George V as the 'imperial democrat', which I mentioned earlier, is somewhat misleading. What the King wanted was to preserve the status quo and he correctly foresaw that such an end could not be achieved by political and/or military domination: such 'democratic' reforms as he envisaged in the Colonies and dependencies were mainly for the purpose of soothing nationalistic feelings so that the sun really would never set on the Empire. When in 1930 he bemoaned the loss of Gladstone's Home Rule Bill, it was because 'the Empire now would not have had the Irish Free State giving us so much trouble'. What serious reformers – such as those who began to gain the ascendancy with the Liberals' landslide election victory of 1906 – questioned was the very existence of the Empire, and in time they would use George V's commitment to 'fatherhood' and the mystical bond of monarchy to start dismantling the very edifice that commitment was meant to protect.

It is sad, perhaps even a little tragic, that the idealism, practical common sense and selfless devotion of King George V were used by political brains incomparably more acute than his not only to undermine much of what he stood for but also to obstruct, perhaps permanently, any possibility of a monarchy with true constitutional relevance. More tragic is the fact that in his bluff, simple-minded dedication to his duty as he saw it, he unwittingly took part in a process of social engineering and political myth-making that would ultimately hasten rather than arrest an economic, moral and spiritual decline that would have been profoundly distasteful to him. That process was carried out under the banner of reform, of fairness and of justice, and many involved in it – including George V himself – believed in those ideals. But it was also a piece of sleight-of-hand. The mediocracy did precisely what Walter Bagehot had advised: it used the mystique and dignity of the monarchy to disguise what was really happening, to conceal the fact that the middle-class 'despotic power' would embrace democracy only so far as would suit its purpose, which was fundamentally to prevent the 'vacant masses' from gaining any real control over their lives.

In 1936, Sir Arthur Bryant wrote of George V: 'That slight, kingly figure and kindly bearded face came to mean to struggling men and women all over the world the assurance that in the end virtue would triumph and the hard-won decencies and dignities of our common humanity be preserved.' It was a mirage. That same year, two million of the late King's subjects in Britain were unemployed: what were the dignities and decencies accorded to them? 'Something must be done,' the new King, Edward VIII, would say. But the sovereign could do nothing except watch from the sidelines and mouth platitudes. In 1912, Lord Hugh Cecil had written: 'I can imagine that after another twenty years of politics on their present lines, the independent leadership of a "patriot king" would be highly popular.'[10] Any such opportunity had been lost even as Cecil was writing. Upon the accession of George V, the Liberal Prime Minister, Herbert Asquith, had made clear what was and would continue to be the prevailing political view – that the sovereign could act and speak only according to the advice of his ministers. From then on, the basis of the monarchy's existence was not the exercise of the few prerogatives remaining to it, but its total lack of constitutional authority. Its survival would depend solely upon its popularity.

Cecil complained that 'to do what is universally approved is to do little more than what is mechanical. It is not very difficult to ascertain with the help of able advisers what acts will fall within the category of general approbation; and that comprises all that a modern King of our country has publicly to do.' The cost to not just the monarchy but also the nation of such an 'inoperative ornament' could be high, he suggested, given 'the feeling which seems to be growing strong and widespread that party politicians and organisations are not entirely trustworthy, and yet have made themselves so strong that resistance to them is hopeless'. He was right. Mistrust of politicians and a sense of powerlessness have grown rather than diminished alongside the supposed spread of democracy, but they have been diffused and neutralised by the careful preservation of the monarchical myth. The sovereign has been presented as 'above' politics and therefore completely to be trusted, a force *for* moderation and stability and *against* the unpredictable consequences of change. That is exactly what the mediocracy wants. Of course, there have been concessions to popular demand and there have been sweeping changes. On the surface, Britain now is unrecognisable against what it was when George V came to the throne. Fundamentally, however, the polity of Britain has changed little since 1910. As recently as the 1987 general election, socialism was condemned as 'a foreign ideology'. It is a phrase George V himself might have used. After the 1906 general election, the then Prince of Wales wrote: 'I see that a great number of Labour members have been returned which is rather a dangerous sign, but I hope they are not all Socialists.'

Things might have been different. Prince Albert foresaw the possibility of a political monarchy that was not partisan. Lord Hugh Cecil imagined it, too: 'The King might really be above party, while playing an active part in political battles.' But, to quote the political scientist J. H. Grainger:

> As a focus for loyalty, the monarch who reigned was preferred to the monarch who ruled. . . . More closely confined as an office than any other of Church and state, becoming almost exclusively concerned with its own composure, the smooth mechanism of its own performance and the rigour of its duties, monarchy provided not shaping rule but a kind of cure for public life.[11]

That summarises perfectly the role George V selected for himself, 'the sustained and sustaining gentleman doing his duty,' as Sir Arthur Bryant put it.

Certainly he was a popular monarch, and that in itself was something of an achievement in an age of radicalism, conflict and pressure for the devolution of power downwards. He symbolised so well the Bagehotian concept of constitutional monarchy that it was readily accepted by the great mass of people in Britain and throughout the Empire. It was an image he nurtured through his self-imposed burden of 'fatherhood'. But his very success in the role he chose for himself inhibited any real development of the monarchy as a force for good and militated against a cleansing re-examination of basic British assumptions, both political and social, that might have eased the pain of decline from imperial splendour and even renewed the nation's strengths. Half a century after the death of George V, the old prejudices and obstacles of the class system remain depressingly obvious; the gulf between capital and labour – the 'them and us' mentality – has changed hardly at all; suspicion and mistrust of foreigners, the sense that we are somehow better than they are, still flourish, and in spite of all our pious talk of democracy, our antiquated voting system means that the political party in power still governs on the mandate of a minority. We have endorsed the style of change but failed to embrace its substance.

Of course, none of this is the fault of George V and his successors. He and they were and are well-intentioned, patriotic and concerned about fairness and justice. With one obvious exception they have performed the duties required of them with exemplary devotion and their popularity as people has increased markedly in line with their visibility to the public. But a monarchy that is inoperative in real constitutional terms can be as inimical to the good of a nation as one that is self-willed or partisan. A monarchy whose legitimacy depended on powerlessness, Lord Hugh Cecil believed, would surely die. Ours has not died, but it has become irrelevant. That, unfortunately, is the legacy of George V's limitations. When the King died in 1936, the poet Edmund Blunden wrote an elegy in which he represented George V as the personification of 'the honest man's conviction, selflessness, good will'. These are admirable qualities indeed, but they were perhaps not enough.

8

The People's King

When George V came to the throne, the British electorate numbered 7,700,000 men. By the time the King died there were more than thirty million voters, including women, in the United Kingdom. Those bald statistics alone reflect a striking change in the position of the monarchy during the intervening quarter of a century. The actual disposition of political power was broadly similar in 1936 to what it had been in 1910, but over the years its acquisition became an entirely different matter. The mandate of governments began to depend on universal suffrage, rather than the support of relatively small cliques with shared aims and interests. That gave politicians greater strength, but it also made them vulnerable: the outcome of elections became less predictable as political parties were forced to broaden their appeal, and with a growing number of electors there was nothing to prevent the rise of new and perhaps dangerous political forces; the emergence of the Labour Party had sent shivers of alarm through the Establishment and had even provoked fears of revolution. Some influence was needed to maintain stability and cohesion, allowing governments to pursue, for reasons of their own, policies that might be unpopular but would not lead to extreme reactions. The source of such influence was, of course, already in place – the constitutional monarchy.

By 1910 any actual power residing in the sovereign had, as we have seen, been removed. It had also been demonstrated that the royal prerogatives relating to consultation, encouragement and warning could be either observed or ignored according to the will of ministers. The mystique and pageantry of monarchy, however, had been carefully preserved, exercising, as Disraeli had foreseen, an almost magical grip on the emotions of an increasingly restive but still complaisant populace. What was needed was a sovereign who could somehow be identified as a representative of the common people, almost as their servant, in whose dignity they could share with pride and whose interests they could perceive as parallel to their own. George V, straightforward and unimaginative, brought up with the discipline and sense of duty demanded by the Royal Navy, was perfect for the role.

The Prime Minister, Stanley Baldwin, said after the King's death:

> Day by day he discharged those duties which thronged upon him, with his will rigorously trained to place the public interest first and last . . . the sure instinct of our people gradually discerned that whatever human frailties or limitations have attached to their King, his sense of duty to his people amounted to genius.

The leader of the Labour Party, Clement Attlee, summed up the value of such a king as a point of stability in a distracted world:

> The movements of mass hysteria which have been witnessed elsewhere have passed this country by. One reason has been the presence of a King who commanded the respect and affection of his people, who was beyond the spirit of faction, and there has been no need to elevate some individual party leader to a national hero, because the King was there to express the views of his people.

There was a good deal of truth in what the two leaders said, but also a strong measure of sanctimonious claptrap. They were the same men who, less than a year later, would combine either actively or passively to force from the throne a king who had been the most popular royal figure in history up to that time, who had commanded the respect and support of great numbers of his people, a king described by even that great leveller Lloyd George as sympathising with the lowliest of his subjects, but one who did not conform to the requirements demanded by the mediocracy. Baldwin was never to utter a greater truth than when he said that the 'power' of the monarchy 'must depend on the character and the quality of him who sits upon the throne', but to the words character and quality he should have added 'compliance'.

The rules of the royal game were outlined for George V as soon as he succeeded his father. Towards the end of the reign of Edward VII, the radical elements in the ruling Liberal Party had in their hands the means to trump the last remaining ace the monarchy possessed – its indirect power of veto through the House of Lords. Unfortunately for the politicians, the King died before the vital card could be played.

'Do not know what to think of this new catastrophe,' Lloyd George had observed. 'We reckoned without taking the Great Ruler into account.'[1]

The radical wing of the Liberal Party had long cherished an ambition to neutralise the Tory peers whose overwhelming majority in the House of Lords prevented the passage of any legislation that offended their conservative sensibilities. (More moderate Liberals had broken with the main body of the party over Gladstone's Home Rule Bill in 1893, calling themselves Liberal Unionists and voting with the Tories in both Commons and Lords.) The Radicals believed their day had come in 1906, when Sir Henry Campbell-Bannerman led them to a sweeping election victory on a programme of root-and-branch reform. Supported by Labour members and Irish Nationalists, the Liberals could count on a Commons majority of 356, yet because of the Lords' power of veto the Tories could still boast that it was they, in or out of office, who controlled 'the destinies of this great nation'. Bill after bill was gutted or killed by the Tory and Liberal Unionist peers. Matters came to a head three years later when the Chancellor, Lloyd George, introduced a budget that sought to impose a series of new taxes on the rich, especially landowners. The landed aristocrats in the House of Lords were incensed, and for the first time in two centuries the peers vetoed a money bill.

With the government unable to raise finance, there was a general election in January 1910. The Tories regained a hundred seats, but the Liberals and their allies retained a majority sizeable enough to persuade the Lords that Lloyd George's budget must be passed. The fundamental problem of the Lords' veto remained, though, and Herbert Asquith, who had succeeded Campbell-Bannerman as prime minister, found himself in a double-bind. First, it would be impossible for the Liberals to govern in the way they wished if proposed legislation was to be either subject to the will of the peers or the cause of repeated general elections. Second, Labour and the Irish Nationalists, each for their own reasons, made their continued support of the Liberal government contingent upon the removal of the Lords' power of veto. The Liberals could not continue in office without the Labour and Irish Nationalist votes, and the election result was hardly an endorsement of basic constitutional reform. And, of course, the Lords would have to be forced to acquiesce in their own diminution.

Campbell-Bannerman had introduced a Commons resolution in 1907 seeking to restrict the powers of the Lords. Asquith followed this up in February 1910 by having King Edward announce, in the Speech from the Throne at the opening of the new parliament, that the government would introduce measures to secure the authority of the House of Commons over finance and its predominance in legislation. There had already been talk before the election of forcing the Lords to accept such measures by obtaining guarantees from the King that, if the Lords rejected the government's plans, he would create sufficient new Liberal peers to ensure their passage at a second attempt. The ailing King, seriously disturbed at the prospect of being used to destroy the House of Lords, which he saw as the monarchy's last ally in a battle against a sort of democratic dictatorship, went to Biarritz at the end of February to escape the constitutional imbroglio and to await, with great trepidation, the Liberals' next moves. On April 14th, Asquith's promised measures were passed by the Commons: the Lords' veto would be abolished and, to counterbalance the greater authority thus given to the Commons, parliaments would run for only five years instead of the existing seven. Asquith immediately introduced the Parliament Bill to effect these changes, warning the Lords that if they rejected the Bill 'we shall feel it our duty . . . to tender advice to the Crown as to the steps which will have to be taken. . . .' What those steps might be he refused to specify, but he clearly had in mind the mass creation of Liberal peers, for he also gave a warning that if the government's advice was not acted upon by the King, 'we shall then either resign our offices or recommend a dissolution of Parliament'. That would mean either a minority Tory government with no mandate or an election fought on the issue of peers versus the people.

The Lords were sufficiently chastened to approve Lloyd George's budget on April 28th, the day after the King returned from Biarritz. The way was now clear for the battle over the Parliament Bill – or so it seemed until May 6th, when King Edward VII died.

It is not clear what King Edward might have done had he been confronted by a demand from Asquith to create up to five hundred new peers in order to ensure the passage of the Parliament Bill. The Liberals' assumption, backed by such precedents as there were, was that the King must abide by his prime minister's advice. Others, however, believed such a demand would have been unconstitutional and the King would have been justified in rejecting it. What is certain is that the King did not discuss the complexities of the matter with his son and that George V, lacking political experience and consumed with grief at his father's death, had no real idea of what his options were. The matter was complicated by the attitude of the Tory leader, Arthur Balfour. In April 1910, before Edward VII died, Balfour indicated that he would be prepared to form a minority government in order to protect the sovereign from embarrassment by giving him the chance to avoid both the forcible creation of peers and an unwanted general election. By the following October, however, when the issue became critical and the new King found himself being dragged up what looked like a constitutional blind alley, Balfour appears to have changed his mind.[2]

At first, Asquith trod carefully, explaining the situation to George V but forbearing to seek a guarantee from the King that he would use his power to create peers if necessary. The best course, the Prime Minister thought, would be a conference of senior members of the two main parties to prepare the way for passage of the Parliament Bill – a suggestion upon which the King seized eagerly, partly out of a natural desire to avoid confrontation but also because it gave him breathing-space in which to review his own position. Asquith was not being entirely altruistic, though he had some sympathy with the new King's predicament. The Prime Minister knew that the inconclusive result of the recent election did not give him the authority to push ahead with reform of the House of Lords and the Irish Nationalists had threatened that if he went to the country again, they would not support him without having first received assurances that an Irish Home Rule Bill would be introduced in the next parliament. Asquith needed time to marshal his forces and to prepare the voters for yet another trip to the polls. When the inter-party conference broke down, predictably enough, early in November 1910, the Prime Minister went straight to the King and asked for a dissolution.

At this point, the King's political naïvety contributed to a misunderstanding that was to rankle with him for many years afterwards. Asquith had promised George V that he would seek no guarantee regarding the creation of peers during the current parliament; but he had also said, in the House of Commons, that he would not call another election unless he could be sure that if the Liberals won their policies – chief among which, of course, was the Parliament Bill – would pass into law, i.e. would not be vetoed in the Lords. The matter was therefore clear in the Prime Minister's mind when he visited the King at Sandringham on November 11th to recommend the dissolution of parliament. The sovereign had no option other than to create new peers to bring the House of Lords into line if requested to do so by an incoming Liberal government, so it was perfectly reasonable to make that clear in advance of the election: constitutional practice would be upheld and Asquith's promise not to go to the country without the certainty of victory over the Lords would be fulfilled. Unfortunately, the Prime Minister failed to put this to the

King in the clearest possible terms, confining himself to observing that 'the matter should be put in train for final settlement', discoursing in a general way about the royal prerogative to create peers and offering the opinion that the mere threat of such action would be sufficient to quell the Lords. What the King, in his anxiety not to be associated with what he considered a shabby affair, understood from this conversation was that he had not been asked for a guarantee that he would exercise his prerogative if required – a fact which he and one of his private secretaries, Sir Arthur Bigge (who became Lord Stamfordham in 1911), noted with satisfaction and relief.

As a result, it came as a severe shock to the King when, three days later, his other private secretary, Lord Knollys, was asked directly by the Prime Minister for the royal guarantee upon which Asquith's election strategy, and his reputation, depended. Knollys presented this to George V as a change of tactics on Asquith's part and the King replied peremptorily by telegram: 'His Majesty regrets that it would be impossible for him to give contingent guarantees and he reminds Mr Asquith of his promise not to seek for any during the present Parliament.' Yet the Prime Minister's position, by his own account, had not changed. He was not seeking a guarantee for the current parliament, but for the next one, in line with his assumption that since the King was bound to accept his ministers' advice, it should be understood from the start of the election campaign that a recalcitrant House of Lords would be swamped with peers willing to vote for the Parliament Bill if the Liberals were returned to office by the people. His error was in failing to spell this out to the King at the November 11th audience.

A sovereign with a sharper brain and more political acumen would have grasped the implications and ramifications of what was happening. An elected government could not tolerate a situation in which one of the main elements of policy upon which it had been voted into power was to be frustrated by an unelected and unrepresentative upper house. If the Lords refused to recognise the will of the people, they must be made to reflect it, and this could only be done by an infusion of peers with Liberal sympathies. But George V was not a natural democrat in the modern sense and lacked the acuity to see the fundamental nature of the conflict between the two Houses of Parliament. Furthermore, he disliked and distrusted Liberals, whom he saw as hardly any different from socialist revolutionaries; indeed, not long before his accession the writer Edmund Gosse had reported him to have been 'loud and stupid' in his criticism of the Liberal government and its leadership. 'The whole atmosphere reeks with

Toryism,' Lloyd George wrote from Balmoral in September 1911. 'I can breathe it & it depresses & sickens me. . . . The King is hostile to the bone to all who are working to lift the workmen out of the mire. So is the Queen. They talk exactly as the late King & the Kaiser did. . . .' Allowing for an element of Celtic hyperbole there, it seems clear that the sympathies of George V were with the Tories in the sense, at least, that while he accepted the inevitability of social change, it was desirable that such change should not upset the status quo. He believed in an old-fashioned hierarchical system and in paternalism: he was all for improving the lot of those at the bottom of the social scale, so long as that did not adversely affect those at the top.

His chief worry in the squabble over the Parliament Bill, however, was that the impartiality of the monarchy would be compromised. One of the tenets he had absorbed from his imperfect and cursory study of Bagehot was that the sovereign must be above politics. What Asquith was demanding seemed to the King to be forcing him to take sides. What if he were to give the Prime Minister the guarantee he wanted and the Tories were to win the election – could they not then accuse him of having behaved unconstitutionally by showing partiality? And if he withheld the guarantee and the Liberals won, might he not be seen as having favoured the Tories? He was, in addition, angered by what appeared to be a personal affront, a suspicion on the part of the Liberals that if they received popular support for their attack on the Lords' veto, they might not be able to count on the King's acceptance of their advice to pack the upper chamber with Liberals, should that be required. Such a suspicion might well have lurked in the minds of several senior Cabinet members, provoked largely by the King himself, but to a man convinced that he would always know where his duty lay, the sort of pressure under which ministers were putting him was intolerable. Hence his abrupt rejection of Asquith's request.

The Cabinet, however, did not intend to take no for an answer. Their view was that the King was constitutionally obliged to take the advice of ministers and constitutionally empowered to create peers, and the guarantee they sought was intended to demonstrate to the Opposition that it had better think carefully before embarking on a course of action that might, if carried to its logical conclusion, reduce parliamentary procedure to the level of farce. Asquith had said he believed the mere threat would be sufficient to concentrate Opposition minds and the King would never actually be called upon to create five hundred new peers, but the mind of George V was far too straightforward to appreciate the principle of *reductio ad absurdum*. The Cabinet therefore fired a warning shot wrapped in what might appear to be a compromise: they insisted on a royal guarantee before the election, but suggested 'that it would be undesirable, in the interests of the State, that any communication of the intentions of the Crown should be made public, unless and until the actual occasion should arise'. That, an enthusiastic Lord Knollys told the King, was altogether different from the previous demand.

Indeed it was different, though neither Knollys nor the King really knew why. Knollys felt that secrecy would somehow make it easier for the King to remain impartial, presumably on the ground that his prerogative would not be used openly as a political weapon. The King thought it was all rather underhanded: 'I have never in my life done anything I was ashamed to confess,' he said later. 'And I have never been accustomed to conceal things.'[3] Only Sir Arthur Bigge saw the truth of the matter. It was not the King's duty, he noted acidly, to save the Prime Minister from the consequences of a rash promise, made to placate the Radicals in his party, that he would not go to the country without a guarantee from the King.

The fact is that by giving a secret guarantee rather than a public one, the King could be said to be involving himself more rather than less in party politics. Since the Opposition would not be aware of it, such a guarantee would not serve to give them fair warning of what obduracy on their part might lead to. Its only purpose must have been to reassure the Liberal left wing, the Labour Party and the Irish Nationalists that if they strove for an Asquith victory in the coming election they could be certain that their desire to curb the House of Lords would be fulfilled one way or another. Thus what was presented by the Cabinet as a concession to the sensibilities of the King was nothing of the sort. Nevertheless, the King, threatened by Asquith and his senior colleagues and encouraged by Knollys, did give a secret undertaking that he would pack the upper chamber with Liberal peers if asked to do so after a Liberal election victory. Striving earnestly to maintain the impartiality considered essential by Bagehot, he fell into the trap of acting in the interests of one of the main political parties because he feared that by doing otherwise he would be perceived as favouring its opponent.

He felt humiliated by being forced into this position, the more so when he learned three years later that Knollys, who had been private secretary to Edward VII, had failed to tell his new master of Balfour's willingness in April 1910 to try to form an alternative government. That information, he noted in January 1914 after Knollys's retirement, would undoubtedly have changed his attitude towards Asquith's demand. Now it seemed he had been not only bullied but also deceived. Yet there is convincing evidence that by the autumn of 1910 Balfour would have been reluctant to receive the King's summons. The Tory leader had come to realise that even if he could put together an administration, it would almost immediately be defeated in the Commons and, given the mood of the country, the Liberals would almost certainly win the ensuing general election. That would have provoked a constitutional crisis far graver than the one the King imagined he was already in. Knollys, with almost half a century of political experience behind him, was guilty not of deceiving George V but of greater shrewdness than his sovereign. In fact, by omission, the private secretary did the monarchy a favour.

The Liberals did win the general election, with a majority of 126, and the Parliament Bill was passed by the House of Commons on May 15th, 1911. Knowing nothing of the King's guarantee, the Tory peers vowed so to emasculate the Bill as to make it meaningless. Asquith stayed his hand until the bread and circuses surrounding George V's coronation on June 22nd had quite subsided; then in the third week of July the Prime Minister announced that the King had signified it would be his duty to accept the advice of his ministers and create as many new peers as necessary to ensure passage of the Parliament Bill through the Lords in the form in which it had been passed by the Commons. Still some Tories held out and at one stage the Prime Minister, with a list of 245 names in his pocket, gave the King two days in which to play his starring role in the final, farcical act of the drama. It was unnecessary. On August 10th, with 300 Tories abstaining, the Lords passed the Parliament Bill unamended by a majority of seventeen. Cries of betrayal went up from many titled Tories and the King received a series of accusing, anonymous letters. Elsewhere, however, the Parliament Act, even though to most of the population it was a dimly understood and arcane piece of legislation, was seen as a triumph for democracy. The power of privilege had been bent to the popular will, and George V had helped to make it possible. The perception of 'the people's king' began to take root. Far from being damaged, the status of the monarchy had, almost by accident, been greatly enhanced.

This development could not have been more timely. The early years of the twentieth century are often regarded nostalgically as the peaceful twilight of a golden age. In the words of the song, it ain't necessarily so. The vision of dear old England sinking gracefully into the imperial sunset may be true in part, but while the rich man played in his castle, the poor man was already beginning to hammer at his gate, no longer convinced that God had ordered his estate. The country enjoyed peace and growing prosperity, but as capital boomed, labour suffered. Between 1907 and 1909, unemployment doubled and wage-rates dropped. In 1914 the purchasing power of a working man's wage was less than it had been in 1896, yet in roughly the same timescale tax assessments of profits, interest and dividends increased by more than half. The bewilderment and frustration of the working classes exploded during the hot summer of 1911 in a series of strikes and riots involving almost a million people. Troops were mobilised, police forces were strengthened and the upper classes began to arm themselves with guns: the bitter scent of revolution was in the air. The English gentleman might have enjoyed his leisure and pleasure in the years leading up to the First World War, but he did so with many a glance over his shoulder.

The feared popular uprising never materialised, however, thanks partly to swift evasive action on the part of the new ruling mediocracy and partly to King George V.

The Liberals contained in their ranks genuine idealists committed to greater fairness and social justice, but at the same time, like most politicians, they directed a good deal of their energies towards maintaining themselves in power. Democracy means different things to different peoples. In modern Britain it has generally been defined as the voluntary surrender of individual power to a ruling elite selected on the basis of its appeal to the greatest number of individuals, a simple majority no matter how slender. In practice that has meant an adversarial style of politics as opposing parties vie to gain and maintain themselves in office, which in turn has led to the creation of party machines whose sole purpose is to oppose each other, without regard to what is objectively good for the country. The British principle of democracy has also produced a carrot-and-stick method of government, with promises made to win adherents and legislation used to coerce opposing groups, whose supporters, taken together, may in fact outnumber those of a party in office.

The mediocracy wrested power from the traditional, hereditary ruling class by broadening the franchise and claiming to represent the aspirations of the common man, but it did so within limits that conformed to its own design. Many common men, however, understood what was happening and, having been allowed to approach as far as the doors of Parliament, saw no reason why they should not enter and represent themselves. Bagehot's new despotic power responded by offering carrots as required to satisfy working-class appetites. The Liberals introduced new taxes on the rich, made provision for old age pensions and gave trade unions a measure of protection from legal redress against strikes and other forms of industrial protest. One of the most significant results of the 1911 upheavals was the National Insurance Act, which, limited though it was in its provisions for sickness and unemployment benefits, established the principle of the welfare state. The legal stick was also brought to bear: the five-week miners' strike of 1912 provoked the first ever government intervention in an industrial dispute, when the Liberals pushed through a Minimum Wages Act that forced the coal owners to accept a settlement. By such means the rise of the proletariat was contained and controlled and the dream of socialist revolution remained no more than that. Real power continued to rest in the hands of the mediocracy.

The attitude of George V in all this was remarkable, if paradoxical. The Liberal Foreign Secretary, Sir Edward Grey, opined in 1925 that the strength and endurance of the British monarchy was the result of its adaptability to change. Yet few men would have welcomed change less than George V. As his domestic routine was seldom varied, other than reluctantly and in exceptional circumstances, so he sought to preserve the order and tranquillity of the England he had known and loved so much as a young man. Never exposed to the darker, more selfish and less admirable aspects of what Victorians considered to be their philosophy – indeed, lacking interest and instruction in philosophy of any kind – the King saw the destruction of the old order and the questioning of old standards as causes of regret. There was hardly a development or a break with tradition that he did not challenge.

At the same time, however, there was always in his mind the Bagehotian image of the sovereign symbol of statehood, the non-ideological monarch whose main purpose was to represent and to act as the lodestar of national unity. He had no power to change, or to prevent change, dearly as he might have wished to. He once said rather sadly of his children, 'You can only watch them going their own way and can do nothing to stop them.'[4] It was a comment that might have applied equally to his metaphorical children, his subjects. In the circumstances, his duty, as he saw it, was to ensure that no matter how great the stresses placed on it, the fabric of what was essentially English society should remain intact. Putting it more succinctly, perhaps more crudely, George V believed the job of the sovereign was to forestall the possibility of change gathering the momentum of revolution. As the socialist intellectual Harold Laski expressed it, the King became an emollient.[5] This has been a key aspect of the monarchy ever since.

In the alarming and highly-charged atmosphere of 1911–12, some balm was necessary to soothe the extra-parliamentary fever of working people suddenly struck by the realisation that the conferment of votes on them did not mean they had any greater ability to improve their lot. The King was disturbed at the violence attending the industrial protests, concerned that order might not be maintained (or at least, as he learned from Winston Churchill, not without bloodshed),[6] and like many others was haunted by fear of the spread of socialism. He kept in close touch with ministers as the government – perhaps it was fortunate that there was a fairly radical Liberal administration at the time – made such concessions as were thought necessary and proper, sometimes in the teeth of fierce Tory opposition. The mediocracy was still feeling its way, still uncertain as to how it should contain the forces below upon which it now depended for its power. It was at this point that George V, to whom the prospect of class struggle continued to cause anxiety, began to do some of the government's work for it.

The credit for the idea is generally given to the then Archbishop of York, Cosmo Gordon Lang, a one-time Presbyterian from a middle-class Scottish family who, in his rise through the hierarchy of the Church of England (he was to become Archbishop of Canterbury in 1928), had gained a wide reputation for social work, particularly in the East End of London. In 1912, Lang suggested to the King that much good would come from royal visits to provincial towns and industrial centres, not a royal progress in the medieval sense, to let the people see their sovereign, but rather the reverse – to show the people that the King was seeing them. The King agreed. He had, after all, read Bagehot's concept of a royal family bringing the pride of sovereignty down to the level of petty life. So the King and Queen embarked on visits to Yorkshire factories, Staffordshire potteries, Midlands railway centres and Welsh coalmines. In 1913 they spent seven days touring the drab industrial towns of Lancashire, ending their journey in Liverpool to open a new dock. 'We have now visited practically every town of importance in Lancashire & motored 220 miles & seen several million people,' the King noted in his diary with his customary brevity.

The Archbishop of York's advice proved to be correct. As a result of these visits, the King fondly believed that he was getting to know his people, and they received the impression that they were becoming acquainted with him. It was all a myth, but it was one that stuck.

'These visits, one felt, were no mere sight-seeing,' a commentator observed. 'They were . . . expressions of homely friendliness for the simple folk. . . .'[7] More children who needed a father-figure. And the curious contradiction of the distance between the monarch and a government that was supposedly 'his' became apparent. 'If the politicians were out of touch with the things that really mattered, were not the King and Queen doing what they could to redress the balance?'[8] This was Bagehot's constitutional confidence trick in action. The masses were considered too stupid to comprehend the exigencies of the political structure of which they were theoretically a part and which their ignorance therefore threatened. Rather than being confronted with and educated in the often unpalatable realities of representative democracy – the inevitable conflict between individual and collective well-being, for instance – the people were instead offered a palliative.

'The monarchy, to put it bluntly, has been sold to the democracy as the symbol of itself,' Harold Laski wrote in 1937. No one was more eager to buy the idea than George V. In doing so he entered into a well-intentioned but ultimately profitless conspiracy with people who, like himself, sought simple answers to immensely difficult questions in an increasingly complex world. He also condemned his successors, and not only those who occupied the throne, to lives of almost ceaseless activity and ever greater visibility, the purpose of which no one now bothers to question and the effect of which is to have made the present royal family an apparently inexhaustible source of entertainment for television viewers and readers of newspapers and magazines.

One of the saddest aspects of this process has been that the royals and their advisers seem to have been unable to think of any other justification for the survival of the monarchy. In 1917, as the full extent of the disaster of the First World War was becoming apparent and bringing into disrepute the concept of 'King and Country' that had encouraged an entire generation to commit suicide, one of George V's assistant private secretaries, Major Clive Wigram, began to crystallise the idea of the royal family as a public relations organisation. Better use should be made of the press, he suggested, to publicise the work of the King and the value to the nation of the monarchy in the face of a new upsurge of republican sentiment and agitation. It was Wigram who first proposed the appointment of a full-time press secretary at Buckingham Palace and the provision of a budget for what he referred to as propaganda purposes. Royal tours such as those following the pre-war industrial unrest should receive the widest possible coverage, Wigram thought, and since it was quite likely that the country would have a Labour government before long, contact should be established with those to whom the working classes were now looking as their political voice. Receptions at the Palace should be opened to as wide a range of people as possible, on the lines of the White House functions established by American presidents.[9] A royal press secretary was appointed in 1918 and the office was maintained until 1931, when its functions were taken over by an assistant private secretary. By then, the well-established national press was more than alive to its royal responsibilities and their rewards in terms of circulation, and the spread of broadcasting had allowed the King to address himself directly to all those of his subjects who owned wireless sets. The Buckingham Palace press office was reconstituted in 1944, just as the effects of another great war were about to produce fundamental changes in public opinion.

Meanwhile, contradiction was piled upon paradox. As the monarchy was seen to 'change with the times', its chief guardian changed not at all. In his late forties, the temper of George V remained much as it had been in his youth: Asquith described him as 'hysterical' and others have spoken of his extreme sensitivity to criticism, first noted by Mr Dalton in the schoolroom.[10] Yet he was always quick to criticise others, sometimes for the most minor offences, and he found it hard to accept that he was not always right. He had a childish tendency to blame misfortunes and mistakes on other people and he expressed himself in private letters much as he had done when writing to his mother as a young man. And always the past remained alive in his mind. 'What have we come to?' he enquired sadly when faced with a suffragette at a race meeting. 'What would Grandmama have thought?' he asked one of his younger royal cousins during the First World War when she sought his permission to travel by bus; in 1924 it was, what would Grandmama have thought of a Labour government?[11] Indeed, the customs, manners and appearance of the Court remained almost exactly as they had been in Queen Victoria's time. The 'democratic' George V refused to receive an actress married to a peer and barred from the royal enclosure at Ascot a major-general's twin daughters who followed the same profession. Time-honoured modes of address were rigidly applied and failure to observe them brought instant rebuke. The King was much concerned with the niceties of proper attire. He once delivered a sharp reproof to the Lord Chancellor, Lord Birkenhead, for allowing himself to be photographed by the press in Downing Street without a top hat. Birkenhead was moved to reply waspishly that even in earlier, more formal times, lord chancellors had not been judged on the basis of what they wore on their heads.[12]

Ministers attending Court functions were required to appear in the appropriate uniform, including cocked hat and sword; ladies were expected to don the feathers and trains of a bygone era. The members of the first Labour Cabinet in 1924 found a large part of their early days in office taken up by a protracted exchange of letters discussing what might be done to accommodate at Court men to whom knee-breeches and coats of green, white and gold were either inaccessible, on account of their cost, or a joke. One suggestion was that they dress in the black garb of the officers of Parliament, while Lord Stamfordham recommended Moss Bros, which he had heard was dependable, for cut-price Court dress. Finally, the King demonstrated the spirit of democracy by allowing those who wished to settle for full evening dress.

George V liked to be surrounded by the familiar, be it people, places or objects, and his loyalties remained constant. His intimate circle of friends remained relatively small, mostly sporting or naval cronies, and his much vaunted relationships with Labour politicians such as Ramsay MacDonald and J. H. Thomas – often cited as showing the King's common touch – should not be taken too seriously. MacDonald, with his Celtic reverence for history and love of glamour, rose to the occasion when he was received at Windsor, Sandringham and Balmoral. At Court functions he afforded himself the complete regalia of the Privy Councillor. In terms of Labour Party history there is a tendency to regard him as a class traitor. As for Jimmy Thomas, his colleague Philip Snowden, MacDonald's chancellor, once remarked:

> I have calculated that he spends three whole weeks each year attending Labour conferences, and one hundred and fifty days attending lunches and dinners of various societies. I have calculated, too, that at these he consumes nine gallons of champagne and that his laundry bill for starched shirts amounts to £18 a year.

With men such as these, George V was not exactly coming down to the level of ordinary working-class life.

One of the King's most tenacious loyalties was towards the military and he regarded his role as its titular head with the utmost seriousness. During the First World War, he was loud in his defence of army commanders in the face of what he considered to be unwarranted and dangerous interference by Lloyd George's War Cabinet, even though British strategy on the Western Front had been disastrous. The commander-in-chief, Sir Douglas Haig, was a particular friend, being the first non-royal ever to be married in the private chapel of

Buckingham Palace, and he kept in close contact with the King on military matters – 'no doubt from patriotic motives,' as A. J. P. Taylor commented tartly. In 1917, as Allied losses mounted and the impression grew that, as a German put it, the British troops were 'lions led by donkeys', Lloyd George showed his displeasure at Haig's failures by agreeing to a French supreme commander. The King, who believed fighting wars was the business of soldiers rather than politicians, leapt to Haig's defence, assuring him that he would do his best 'to protect your interests': for a sovereign so insistent on royal impartiality and constitutional practice it was a rash promise, even though Lloyd George had not consulted him beforehand. In the event there was neither anything the King could do for Haig nor any success for the French initiative. The stalemate on the Western Front continued and Haig's conviction that his policy was correct resulted in the tragedy of Passchendaele.

Lloyd George, desperate for a breakthrough in order to quell mounting disaffection at home, next turned on the Chief of the Imperial General Staff, Sir William Robertson. The Prime Minister wanted to replace Robertson with a man more willing and able to work with the French in formulating a co-ordinated strategy among the Allies, who had now been joined by the Americans. Robertson refused to budge and once again the King's judgment was impaired by loyalty to a man he admired. He informed Lloyd George that Robertson's removal would be the cause of resentment in the army and the country and of rejoicing by the enemy. Lloyd George pointed out that the army hardly knew Robertson, who had not fought at the front and rarely even visited it; furthermore, the CIGS had displayed remarkable lack of skill as a strategist and had been wrong more often than he was right. 'If he doesn't look out,' the King noted darkly, 'his government will fall.' It was a mark of his misunderstanding of the political realities, of the mood of the nation and perhaps even of the requirements of leadership. At the beginning of 1918, Lloyd George, whatever his faults, was the only man capable of inspiring and sustaining Britain in the renewed efforts that would eventually win the war: that was acknowledged even by the Tory leader, Andrew Bonar Law, who alone among senior politicians at the time might have been able to form an alternative administration. After a threat of resignation from the Prime Minister, Robertson went, followed soon by the Chief of the Air Staff, General Sir Hugh Trenchard, again under protest from the King, whom Lloyd George felt obliged to warn that he was encouraging mutiny by championing military officers in direct contravention of the wishes of the civilian government.

It was so often the way. George V interfered ceaselessly and apparently tirelessly in the business of government – as he was constitutionally entitled to do – but the monarch whom Clement Attlee would later praise somewhat too fulsomely for his 'sympathy with new ideas' was more likely to be trying to warn and resist than to encourage and initiate. He was not in any sense a creative man or an imaginative one, therefore he lacked insight into the nature of change and was afraid of it. Change was inevitable, that he did understand, but to the King it brought uncertainty and instability: there was no knowing where it might lead. He sought refuge in compromise and moderation, and there lay both his saving grace and much of his popular appeal. One of the problems with representative democracy as a system is that it can easily be appropriated by zealots or fanatics to impose their views on others who do not share them. There has long been awareness of this in England, so that extremism of any kind is generally mistrusted. That suspicion has been both fostered and exploited by the mediocracy in order to maintain its supremacy in national life. The educated middle class claims for itself the guardianship of reason and 'fair play', of doing what is right and of knowing what is best. In George V, the mediocracy had its ideal symbol during the turbulent years following the First World War, as extremism flourished in an atmosphere of mingled hope and despair.

The King's intervention on the side of compromise and conciliation in the Irish crisis of 1921 was undoubtedly helpful to the British government at the time, since it both calmed Protestant fears in the Six Counties and helped to create conditions that led to a truce between Britain and the unilaterally declared Republic headed by Eamon de Valera. Prompted by his friend General Smuts, prime minister of the Union of South Africa, the King suggested that he should make a personal appeal to all Irishmen when he went to Belfast to open one of the two devolved parliaments (the other was, of course, in Dublin) created by Lloyd George. The speech was written by Sir Edward Grigg, a former *Times* journalist and then a private secretary to Lloyd George, but the fact that its sentiments appeared to come directly from the King was crucial:

> I speak from a full heart when I pray that my coming to Ireland today may prove to be the first step towards the end of strife amongst her people, whatever their race or creed. In that hope I appeal to all Irishmen to pause, to stretch out the hand of forebearance and conciliation, to forgive and forget, and to join in making for the land they love a new era of peace, contentment and goodwill.

In the light of history it was, of course, a royal palliative that failed utterly, and the effects of that failure remain depressingly obvious today, when it is the North of Ireland rather than the South that is under what amounts to British military occupation and the parliament that George V opened with such hope is suspended, perhaps permanently. In 1921, though, the King's speech helped to establish a line of escape from an increasingly untenable position on both sides of the Irish Sea. It also helped to establish the King in the perception of the majority of the British people as a fount of moderation and a guardian of democracy. He had acted out of the conviction that he was the father of all his people, and large numbers of those people were prepared to accept him as such. The fact that neither the King nor those of his subjects who cheered him so vociferously really knew anything about each other, that it was no more than an illusion they were creating, seems not to have occurred to anybody.

To be sure, the King's peregrinations inspired by the Archbishop of York probably meant that he had seen a good deal more of ordinary British life than many of the Liberal and Tory politicians of the day, and the general warmth of the welcome he and the Queen had received in various parts of the country had naturally induced in him a certain sympathy for the 'simple folk'. But seeing and experiencing do not always lead to understanding, especially in a mind unaccustomed to analysis and reflection. George V was no Bourbon, learning nothing and forgetting nothing. 'I am not a clever man,' he once said, 'but if I had not picked up something from all the brains I've met, I would be an idiot.'[13] Yet what he learned was filtered through the prism of the past, *his* past. Life had been better then, more straightforward, less fearful: he could not see why anyone would want to abandon the old certainties in favour of dangerous new ideas.

In Sir Arthur Bryant's 1936 hagiography there is a particularly significant passage referring to the decade following the First World War:

> In those hectic years, when all standards seemed to be in the melting pot and many ugly heresies of thought and conduct flourished for a season, the King had continued to show by his high and sustained example what manner of man an Englishman could be. He and the Queen represented the secret convictions of every decent British man and woman at a time when the intellectual leaders of the nation were preaching the gospel of disintegration and many of its social leaders were making bad manners and loose living a social fashion.

To challenge previously accepted dogma was heretical, indecent and un-English. The word 'un-English' was one that King George V found himself using more and more frequently as the years of his reign passed. But Bryant was also voicing the opinion of the 'respectable' middle classes, who had used their social and economic inferiors to obtain power but now wondered anxiously whether, with the example of the Russian Revolution before them, the masses could still be controlled. George V, broadly middle class in perception himself, accepted the mediocracy as the established order. He believed, with simple sincerity, that the bourgeois state was the best, indeed the only one, acceptable to English ideals and acted always with the aim of supporting and maintaining that state.

Bryant, a model of the mediocracy, wrote:

> More, I believe, than by any other influence, the change in public opinion during the last decade of his reign towards decency of conduct, self-control and national pride was brought about by the personal example of the King and Queen. At one time they seemed almost alone. Gradually the country came round to them. It was the throne which restored to the people of Great Britain the leadership and confidence of which they were in need.

With hindsight one may view it in another way. There is a strong case for suggesting that Britain between the wars lacked both leadership and confidence: why else would it have fawned on the deluded Mussolini and cringed before the demented Hitler? It may be argued that the single most important reason why the uninspired and uninspiring leaders of 1925 to 1939 were allowed to continue with their ineffectual flounderings was that the attention of the people they presumed to lead had been diverted towards the new romance of 'democratic' monarchy. The people had been encouraged to believe that their simple, honest, dutiful, God-fearing King was the embodiment of their hopes and fears, their ambitions and dreams, their pride and patriotism; that he shared their successes and their suffering; that he repaid their loyalty with service; that if they challenged the established order, they challenged him and therefore everything that was great about Britain.

Why did they accept it? Walter Bagehot knew the answer to that half a century before. Partly it was because George V, in Bryant's encomium:

possessed a remarkable simplicity and balance of character. There was a certain broad humanity about him . . . he was just precisely what the ordinary, decent man in his best moments would have liked himself to be . . . he took his stand from the simple lesson he had learned as a boy – the unflinching and literal fulfilment in all places and all circumstances of what he knew to be his duty.

Who, in all conscience, could stand against a system symbolised by a man such as that? No matter what its deficiencies, there must be something basically good and sound about it. For the rest, it was a matter of the alternative. The people of Britain had seen the chaos attendant upon the collapse of the other great imperial houses of Europe and they were not prepared to take the risk, even in the hope of improving their common lot. Blinded by the mystique of constitutional monarchy, they did not see the difference between the Austrians, the Germans, the Russians and themselves. It did not occur to them that, having sacrificed a generation in the name of liberty, greater freedom was being denied to them in the name of stability. As Bagehot had predicted, the masses preferred simple concepts to difficult ones.

That George V did his best for his people and his country is beyond doubt. Yet in absolute terms he was doing nothing. In 1924 Lord Grey of Fallodon wrote that in earlier centuries it must have seemed improbable that the monarchy could have developed to the position it now enjoyed without either being a check on democracy or being reduced to futility.[14] That the constitutional monarchy exemplified by George V has in some ways degenerated into both those conditions should be obvious as we near the end of the twentieth century.

PART 2

Monarchy for the Mass Market

9

'Royalty of Virtue'

The governing factor in the life and reign of King George V was a sense of duty. There is no evidence that he actually enjoyed being a monarch: it was a position to which he had been called, a task he had to fulfil, and since he regarded obedience as one of the highest virtues, he naturally felt it was incumbent upon him to meet his obligations without question or complaint. He was always nervous when appearing in public, and particularly when he had to make a speech, yet he became the most publicly visible and communicative sovereign Britain had ever seen. He disliked ceremonial, but he helped to establish the modern spectacle of monarchy. Left to his own inclinations, he would have remained close to hearth and home, an obscure country squire whose course followed the seasons, overseeing his farmlands and his horses, shooting birds and small animals, using his naval training to sail for pleasure and, for intellectual stimulation, sticking stamps into his albums. Yet he worked meticulously through the red despatch boxes arriving daily from Westminster and corresponded feverishly on the minutest detail of government business. On his industry, dedication and selflessness in the service of his country, no one could fault him.

There is, however, one aspect of the King's dutifulness that has largely been ignored, the one that perhaps guided him more than any other and had the most profound implications for his successors. Superior even to his duty to his nation and its people was the duty owed to the principle of hereditary monarchy, to its survival. These were perilous times for monarchies. Within months of the accession of George V, King Manuel of Portugal was overthrown by republicans and obliged to flee to Gibraltar, whence he was brought to England at the prompting of the King (despite the misgivings of the Foreign Office) in the British royal yacht, *Victoria and Albert*. Within the first decade of his reign, George V witnessed the downfall of the Romanovs, the Habsburgs and the Hohenzollerns. He was no doubt aware of Queen Victoria's attitude of *après nous le déluge* and of his father's depression, towards the end of his reign, at the growth of the 'social-istic' tendencies he saw about him. In view of all this, George V's approach to kingship was conditioned in no small way by his determination to protect and secure the position of the monarchy for the future.

In the early years of the twentieth century, the rise of the labour movement brought with it an upsurge of republican sentiment such as had once been perceived to threaten the reign of Queen Victoria. Socialism, with its neo-religious principles of morality, equality and justice, inevitably challenged the uses and abuses of privilege. Since the monarchy was at the pinnacle of privilege, many socialists believed, with good reason, that its abolition would automatically bring down the entire structure. Queen Victoria, guided as always by the views of Prince Albert, had sought to deflect the threat by dissociating the monarchy from the excesses of the aristocracy and aligning it with the industrious, well-intentioned and respectable middle class. King Edward VII, believing firmly in privilege, had followed his own self-indulgent course relying on the Disraelian concept of majesty and his personal magnetism to show that there was no harm in it. The response of George V was, as became his habit, to meet the challenge halfway, albeit reluctantly. One of his attempts to defuse the consti-tutional crisis over the Lords' veto involved suggesting the creation of life peers, ennobled on the basis of merit rather than birth and denied the right to bequeath their titles. At the time nobody was much interested: establishing the supremacy of the Commons was the important thing, while hereditable honours, in the contemporary social climate, were considered indispensable instruments of patronage, so long as the political power of their recipients was restricted. Fifty years later, the 'dilution' of the House of Lords through the introduction of life peers would help to justify its continued existence.

The containment of the House of Lords was hailed as a victory for democracy and, as I have shown, one in which the King was seen to be on the side of the people. That, however, counted for little in the jingoistic hysteria of the First World War. The hatred of things German whipped up in order to motivate the members and the families of what has been described as the last great peasant army ever raised had rebounded to the extent of provoking deep and sometimes violently expressed hostility towards people in Britain thought to have German connections or sympathies. For example, the Lord

Chancellor, Lord Haldane, who as war minister had done more than anyone to ensure that the country actually had the ability to take up arms against the Kaiser, was forced to leave his post for no better reason than that he had once called Germany his spiritual home, having spent some of his student days at Heidelberg University. As early as the autumn of 1914, the First Sea Lord, Prince Louis of Battenberg, had had to be removed because of a vicious campaign against him on account of 'my birth and parentage'. Prince Louis was a cousin of George V by marriage. It was but a step for the Hun-hunters to attack the King himself.

The early salvos were cautious. H. G. Wells wondered in print about the effect on the war-effort of 'an alien and uninspiring Court', prompting George V to retort that he might be uninspiring but he was damned if he was an alien. Yet the British royal line at that time was Hanoverian and, thanks to Prince Albert, its dynastic name was Saxe-Coburg and Gotha; the King was a first cousin of the Kaiser; Queen Mary was a princess of the House of Teck; among their relatives were representatives of German princedoms and dukedoms, British citizens to be sure, but named for Schleswig-Holstein, Gleichen, Hohenlohe-Langenburg and so on. The Hun-haters began a campaign of vilification, which gathered momentum as the loss of British lives mounted and the bloody stalemate on the Western Front continued. By the spring of 1917, Lloyd George was receiving a stream of anonymous letters asking him how he thought Britain could ever win the war when it had a royal family most of whose lineage, and perhaps some of whose sympathies, belonged to the enemy.

George V was shocked and outraged. His Prime Minister was alarmed. The first phase of the Russian Revolution had forced Tsar Nicholas II to abdicate on March 15th, encouraging radical socialists in Britain to plan the formation of workers' and soldiers' councils and to call a revolutionary convention in Leeds. Lloyd George concluded that for the sake of national unity the German names and titles would have to go. It was probably an unnecessary gesture. The King's exemplary conduct and devotion to public duty had inspired nothing but confidence in most people, both before and during the war. The fanatical anti-German campaigners were a tiny minority and that they received any support at all was the result more of bitterness occasioned by the failure and huge loss of life attending British military operations than of any animosity towards the royal family. After all, everyone knew that the King had visited the front, that his heir, Prince Edward, had personally experienced the horror and misery of the trenches, and that his second son, Prince Albert, had taken part in the great naval battle of Jutland in 1916. Royal patriotism was hardly to be questioned. As for the 'revolution', that was no more than a dream in the heads of a few idealists: there was little comparison between the bourgeois state of Britain and the autocracy of Tsarist Russia. But the King's confidence failed him and he agreed to Lloyd George's public relations exercise.

The royal family could not slough off its German ancestry, but on July 18th, 1917, it made its nomenclature quintessentially English: the House of Windsor. The peripheral members became Carisbrooke and Cambridge (though that, in fact, was merely a conversion into a marquessate of a Hanoverian dukedom), Milford Haven, Mountbatten and so on. In a nation that has taken such pride in its history, the realities of that history were covered up to satisfy xenophobia. The tactic silenced the Hun-haters, though only for a short time, but did nothing more than disguise the cracks in national unity that the war had exposed. In 1918–19, for instance, thirty-two million working days were lost because of industrial protest – even the police went on strike, demanding recognition of their union. Still, the King had removed the monarchy from the cockpit of division and discontent, and that pleased him.

In 1917, the King's determination to protect the monarchy at all costs thrust him into a moral dilemma from which he did not emerge with much credit. After the so-called February Revolution in Russia, Tsar Nicholas and his family were placed under arrest, partly for their own safety, by the Provisional Government headed by Prince George Lvov and Alexander Kerensky.[1] 'Nicky' was both a first cousin and a close friend of George V, and his predicament naturally agitated the King, who on March 19th sent the Tsar a telegram (though it never reached its intended recipient): 'Events of last week have deeply distressed me. My thoughts are constantly with you and I shall always remain your true and devoted friend, as you know I have been in the past.' He had helped to 'rescue' King Manuel of Portugal; it might have been thought that he would do at least as much for his unfortunate cousin. The opportunity was provided by the Provisional Government itself when it requested that the imperial family should be granted asylum in England. Lloyd George, Bonar Law and Lord Stamfordham agreed that the Russian request should be met and that asylum should be offered at any rate for the duration of the war.

A week later, however, George V had had second thoughts. He told the Foreign Secretary, Arthur Balfour, that while he had a strong personal friendship for the Tsar and would do anything to help him, that did not, in effect, include bringing him to England. Balfour said that since the invitation had been relayed to the Russian government, it could not at that stage be withdrawn. By April 6th, the King was becoming panicky. Stamfordham wrote to the Foreign Secretary:

His Majesty receives letters from people in all classes of life, known or unknown to him, saying how much the matter is being discussed, not only in clubs, but by working men, and that Labour Members in the House of Commons are expressing adverse opinions to the proposal.

What was particularly upsetting His Majesty was that *he* was popularly credited with having instigated the offer of asylum to the Tsar, and he feared that such talk would associate him with Russian autocracy in the minds of British republicans who had been heartened by the example of the February Revolution. A second note sent by Stamfordham to Balfour on April 16th evinced something approaching hysteria:

He must beg you to represent to the Prime Minister that from all he hears and reads in the press, the residence in this country of the ex-Emperor and Empress would be strongly resented by the public, and would undoubtedly compromise the position of the King and Queen.

Lloyd George, seeing wider political difficulties involving the Germans, the gathering forces of Bolshevism in Russia and the conduct of the war, allowed the King to have his way and fell back upon the time-honoured British tactic of stonewalling. On July 16th, 1918, the Tsar, his wife and their five children were murdered by Bolsheviks in a cellar in the Urals town of Ekaterinburg. 'It was a foul murder,' George V wrote. 'I was devoted to Nicky . . .' Not devoted enough, it seems, to place humanitarian principles above the desire to protect his own position. That there was serious disaffection in Britain in 1917 is beyond doubt, but it must also be said that the likelihood of a home-grown version of the Russian Revolution was minimal: the King would certainly have been criticised for offering asylum to the Tsar, but he would not have been overthrown. It is perhaps significant that his part in the effective withdrawal of the British offer was not broadcast. Having achieved his aim, the King simply washed his hands of the affair. In later years, it was Lloyd George who took the blame for abandoning the Tsar and his family to their fate, a distortion of the truth assiduously promulgated by the Tsarina's nephew, Lord Mountbatten.

This curious detachment of George V, the almost compulsive need to interfere in public affairs combined with an equally obsessive desire to do nothing that might attract criticism, was evident, too, during the long-running Irish Home Rule crisis. Herbert Asquith had variously described the King as 'hysterical' and '*émotionné*'; in 1920 Lloyd George branded him 'an old coward' who was 'frightened to death' of the worsening situation in Ireland 'and anxious to make it clear that he has nothing to do with it'.[2]

The King had been haunted by the nightmare raised in 1912 by the Tory leader, Bonar Law, who had pointed out that the Home Rule Bill introduced by the Liberals placed the sovereign in an invidious position. The Liberals would get the Bill through the Commons and because of the Parliament Act it could not be rejected by the anti-Home Rule Tories in the House of Lords, but it would automatically reach its final stage – the royal assent – in two years. If the assent was forthcoming, the King would be condemned by half the country; if it was not, he would be damned by the other half; in either case, he would be unpopular in Ireland, since he would be forced to choose between the loyalists of the Six Counties and the nationalists of the South.

His first attempt to escape from the impasse was the Buckingham Palace Conference of 1914. It was irrelevant and a failure, but at least it served to place the King as a force for moderation and restraint. Then the war intervened, and the carnage in continental Europe reduced almost to a sideshow the brutal repression of the 1916 Easter Rising in Dublin. With the European peace came renewed Irish conflict: Sinn Fein declared a republic in Dublin, with de Valera as president, and began a terrorist campaign to get the British out. Britain responded by sending in the notorious 'Black and Tans', so called because of their khaki uniforms with black hats and armbands. Finally, in 1921, there came the King's intervention in the form of his appeal to all Irishmen when he opened the Belfast parliament. It was, according to A. J. P. Taylor, 'perhaps the greatest service performed by a British monarch in modern times'.[3] Yet what did it actually achieve? 'A terrible chapter in British history was closed,' Taylor wrote. But the history of Ireland would continue to be written in blood, and still is today, and even for Britain the chapter was far from closed. All the King had done was extricate himself. He had been seen to do his duty in the interests of all his people. What happened after that, no matter how much he might deplore and regret it, was not his responsibility.

Lloyd George was wrong to call the King a coward. A lack of courage was not one of his faults. Kingship, even in what we understand as constitutional monarchy, is a daunting enough task for any man and George V came to it in middle age, after a life that, as I have shown, had in no sense prepared him for what he was to face. A certain bewildered detachment and a failure to leave any deep or lasting impression on his times and on history were perhaps only to be expected. But there was in his nervous, excitable, essentially diffident nature an element of fear that manifested itself in a rather negative urge towards self-protection. Both Asquith and Lloyd George felt they had cause to complain that when they consulted George V his first thought was often for his own position, the effect that a particular course of action might have upon his reputation and the standing of the monarchy in general.[4] If he was afraid of anything, it seems to have been the great mass of the people over whom he reigned. 'I didn't realise they felt like this,' he commented on the outpouring of popular sentiment at the celebration of his silver jubilee in 1935. 'I am beginning to think they must really like me for myself.' He was mistaken. They could not like him for himself because they did not know him. What people had fallen for was not a monarch, but the image of monarchy which he had come to represent.

In 1889, an American bishop named Henry C. Potter had warned his countrymen that:

> If there be no nobility of descent in a nation, all the more indispensable it is that there should be nobility of ascent – a character in them that bear rule, so fine and high and pure, that as men come within the circle of its influence, they involuntarily pay homage to that which is the pre-eminent distinction, the Royalty of Virtue.

In the Britain of George V, nobility of descent no longer ensured a lease on power. The mediocracy had successfully challenged it from the mid-nineteenth century onwards and by 1911 its victory was complete. By that time also, however, the aspirations of the working classes, awoken and pandered to by the new despotic power as a means of securing its political base, were rising to challenge the mediocracy itself. Unable to fall back on any nobility of descent, which it had itself discredited, and equally lacking any claim to nobility of ascent because of the nature of party politics, the educated middle class that provided national leadership found a distinction to which almost everyone was prepared to pay homage – a very literal version of Potter's royalty of virtue.

George V's strengths, weaknesses and limitations made him the perfect candidate to become what the Australian statesman Sir Robert Menzies called 'the first great constitutional monarch'. Unlike his father, George V was no philanderer or sybarite and could not be associated with aristocratic excess, so that he was seen as being on the side of common morality. Unlike the Prince Consort, he lacked the political acumen to initiate, to obstruct or seriously to influence national policy, so that he was no threat to the English sense of democracy. Unlike Queen Victoria, he was not steeped in the micropolitics of Court life (though he continued to observe the niceties of Victorian etiquette, manners and appearance), so that he could be identified almost personally with the populace at large. On the other hand, he shared with the mediocrats – and, it must be admitted, considerable numbers of others who aspired to middle-class values – an insular suspicion of and scorn for foreigners, a commitment to conventional respectability and the value of hard work, a belief in empire as a civilising influence, a desire for peace and order combined with a readiness to go to war if circumstances made that appear necessary, a mistrust of intellectuals and an unreasoning dread of socialism. If Edward VII had all the faults of which the Englishman was accused, George V was a model of most of the virtues of which the Englishman was proud. His was the kind of nobility to which all, if they felt so inclined, could lay claim and which affected everyone who came into contact with it.

Such were the emotional ties between the great majority of the British people and the constitutional monarchy that George V, simply on account of his character, came to represent. But there were more tangible links, too. Chief among these was the King's earnest and obvious desire to serve not only the nation and the government but also the people themselves. Of course there had been for generations an assumption that sovereigns (with one or two notable exceptions) could be expected to act in the national interest. What distinguished George V from his predecessors was the practical nature of his service, combined with the fact that he clearly saw the national interest not as some political abstraction but in terms of the unity and well-being of the people.

The potential for this practical aspect of the monarchy was demonstrated as early as 1901, when the then Duke of York returned from his first colonial tour. In a speech at the Guildhall in London, he told the assembled businessmen and City dignitaries: 'I venture to allude to the impression which seemed generally to prevail among our brethren across the seas, that the Old Country must wake up if she intends to maintain her old position of pre-eminence in her Colonial trade against foreign competitors.' Next day the press was full of headlines saying 'Wake up, England!' and leading articles that the Duke thought 'very civil'. King Edward had huffed and puffed at the suggestion that his son's tour should descend to the level of trade and commerce, but his disdain was certainly not shared by a significant proportion of his subjects. To adapt the famous dictum of Calvin Coolidge, the business of the middle classes is business, and the mediocracy was alive to the marketing possibilities offered by a well-timed royal visit. The descendants of George V would find themselves becoming the most widely travelled royal family in the world, much of their journeying not unconnected with trade fairs, 'British Weeks' and the desire to increase exports.

The King's willingness to serve, to be useful and to play father to his people took the monarchy in new directions and established new 'traditions'. One of the most enduring was the royal Christmas broadcast. The idea came originally from John (later Lord) Reith, the first general manager of the British Broadcasting Corporation, in 1923, but the King, with his hatred of public speaking, would have none of it. The following April, however, millions of his subjects heard his voice for the first time when the BBC broadcast the King's speech opening a British Empire Exhibition at Wembley. During the next few years, the expanding medium of radio carried some of the King's speeches on state occasions into the homes of his people, but it was not until 1932 that he was prevailed upon to deliver the inaugural Christmas Day message. Full of misgivings, he faced a microphone in a small room at Sandringham, the table at which he sat covered by a heavy cloth to absorb the rustle of his text as his hands shook with nervousness. The words, written by Rudyard Kipling, set the tone of bland banality that would come to be expected of royal utterances in an age of mass communications:

Through one of the marvels of modern science, I am enabled, this Christmas Day, to speak to all my peoples throughout the Empire. I take it as a good omen that wireless should have reached its present perfection at a time when the Empire has been linked in closer union, for it offers us immense possibilities to make that union closer still. I speak now from my home and from my heart to you all; to men and women so cut off by the snows, the deserts or the seas that only voices out of the air can reach them . . . .

It was an enormous success and once again the King who hated change became an innovator in spite of himself. He protested vehemently at the thought of annual performances but was persuaded that it was what the public wanted, and this constitutional monarch believed that what the public expected of its sovereign, it must have. That, in the eyes of the ruling mediocracy and, indeed, the population at large, was perhaps the greatest virtue of George V. 'The festivities will entail a lot of extra work, and I shall be pleased when they are all over,' the King wrote of the celebrations marking his twenty-five years on the throne. He was approaching his seventieth birthday and since 1929 he had been in uncertain health following a near-fatal illness, but the government wanted a jubilee jamboree to restore national morale after years of recession and misery (also to serve as a display of unity in the face of the growing menace of the European dictators) and the ageing King, as always, did his duty. Within six months he was dead.

On the evening of Monday, January 20th, 1936, came a medical bulletin from Sandringham, where the royal family had, as usual, been spending the Christmas holiday. 'The King's life', said the bulletin, 'is moving peacefully towards its close.' The process, it has recently become known, was helped by doses of morphine administered by the King's doctor, Lord Dawson of Penn.[5] That was to provide a controversy for the future, but for the monarchy the future was now – and it promised to be very different. The new King, Edward VIII, had both definite views and distinct doubts about the role of the sovereign. As Sir Ivor Jennings expressed it:

> During the present century, we have placed almost an intolerable burden on the royal family. They must not only head subscription lists and appear on state occasions; they must, also, inspect this and that, open this and that, lay this stone and that, and undertake a thousand other dull tasks in a blaze of publicity. We can hardly blame Edward VIII if he preferred to make toffee in the kitchen. George V had made himself a slave to public demand.

In January 1936, however, public demand was more than satisfied by the prospect of the new reign. Popular as George V had been as an icon, it was as nothing to the almost magical effect produced by his eldest son. The 1920s and, perhaps even more so, the grim Depression years of the 1930s saw a great flowering of popular heroes as ordinary folk sought escape from confusion and misery through glamour and romance. The development of radio and the rapid growth of the cinema helped to create a fantasy world that blunted the bitter realities of everyday existence as people enjoyed vicariously the allure of crooners, film stars and other idols. Edward VIII, as Prince of Wales, had all the attributes necessary for stardom: wealth, youth, good looks, charm, style, energy and a certain indefinable flair. The fact that he was also a royal with an actor's gift for working a crowd made his elevation to heroic status inevitable.

But his popularity, which exceeded that of any royal figure before him, was based on firmer foundations, too. He had travelled the world as a sort of royal roving ambassador, gaining in repute and storing up affection wherever he went. *The Times*, in a leading article at his accession, said he had 'won the hearts of unnumbered men, women and children' throughout the Empire with

> his attractive habit of identifying himself with the different nationalities ... his thoughtful tact, his kindness and sympathy, his affection for children, his delightful sense of humour ... his ready memory for faces, his freedom, for all his dignity, from personal or official side, his powers of conversation, and his remarkable talents of voice, memory and quick resourcefulness as a public speaker in other languages besides English.

Nor was that all. He had passed with distinction the test of George V's concept of the sovereign as public servant. The editorial in *The Times* continued:

> Day in and day out he has never spared himself. He has traversed and studied the country from end to end, has made friends with all sorts and conditions of its workers, has gained an inside knowledge of its industries and has taken his place under the King, his father, at the head of every national movement for the relief of sickness and suffering and want ... As a King, the people will be able to look up to him as one who has a statesmanlike knowledge and sympathetic understanding of the people of all creeds and races over whom he has been called to reign.

His address to the first Privy Council of his reign seemed to confirm all this. 'When my father stood here twenty-six years ago,' he told the Councillors gathered at St James's Palace, 'he declared that one of the objects of his life would be to uphold constitutional government. In this I am determined to follow in my father's footsteps and to work as he did throughout his life for the happiness and welfare of my subjects.'

And there was more. This was a King prepared to take the monarchy to the people not in the rather detached manner of George V, but in a personal, direct and 'democratic' way. When he visited Clydeside, ravaged by the recession and a hotbed of socialism, 'King Edward passed into the slums from a world of pride and power to the world of human misery of which no man is more ashamed than he,' according to a contemporary account.[6] He visited tenement families living six and seven to a room and met a five-year-old boy who asked if he was the new King. 'Yes, sonny,' Edward said, shaking him by the hand, 'I am your new King.' Crowds greeted him with shouts of 'Good old Teddy' and 'God bless Your Majesty', and at the official lunch with the Lord Provost of Glasgow the King told his host that people deserved better homes than the appalling places he had seen. In Edward VIII, the royalty of virtue was surely to be made flesh.

There was one noticeable gap in the new King's shining armour: at the age of forty-one he remained unmarried, unlike all his younger brothers. This had not seemed to matter while he had been Prince of Wales, indulging in a lively and not altogether reputable social life reminiscent of an earlier heir to the throne, but Britain was not used to a king without a consort. In the enthusiasm surrounding the opening of the new reign, however, the lack of a queen was generally overlooked, particularly since public interest in the more familial aspects of the monarchy had for some time been fixed upon two particularly fine examples of royal virtue, the Duke and Duchess of York.

The marriage of George V's second son, Prince Albert, and Lady Elizabeth Bowes-Lyon on April 26th, 1923, had been the greatest royal spectacle of the reign. For the first time in six hundred years the sovereign's son was married not in one of the private royal chapels, but at Westminster Abbey. Three thousand guests attended the ceremony and more than a million people thronged the streets to watch the processions. That night there was dancing in four ballrooms at the Savoy Hotel, while Harrods, Selfridge's and other big London stores decked themselves with flowers and searchlights and brought in military bands to stage their own celebrations. 'A princely marriage', the percipient Walter Bagehot had written, 'is the brilliant edition of a universal fact, and as such it rivets mankind.'

Not only was this the first princely wedding since George V's own thirty years earlier, but it was also the first time for two hundred years that an English prince had been permitted to take a non-royal wife. (Coincidentally, the previous occasion had also involved a Duke of York, later King James II, who married Lady Anne Hyde.) The new Duchess, who came from an old Scottish family, was greeted by her brother-in-law, the Prince of Wales, as a breath of fresh air in palace corridors and by *The Times* as 'all the more welcome an addition to the royal family because the public knows nothing about her'. That last point was quickly to be rectified. As soon as her engagement – or betrothal, to use the royal word – to the Duke of York was announced, the newspapers began to publish every detail they could discover about her. 'Small, dark and piquante,' she was revealed to be an excellent dancer, a good tennis player and a nicely old-fashioned young woman of high principles, intelligence and energy. Furthermore, having been brought up as a commoner (the accurate but nevertheless rather misleading term to describe the daughter of an earl descended from a king of Scotland), Elizabeth Bowes-Lyon was considered more likely than any royal to be able to identify with ordinary people. So it was to prove. The *Morning Post* observed:

At once the Duchess of York bore her rank as if it had been hers by right of birth. She took her place simply and naturally in the ever-expanding public life of her husband. He was especially interested in the social welfare of boys and men; she did similar work among women and girls. While he went over factories and workshops and shipyards, she was unwearied in visiting maternity centres, girls' clubs and housing colonies. They were together all over the United Kingdom and Ulster, crowding their days with beneficent duties, obviously happy in their strenuous work and in each other, and whether she was happier gracing state ceremonies in London, Edinburgh and Belfast, or equipped with a handkerchief drawn over her hair, to go down a Durham coalmine, there was no means of determining. That special faculty for absorption in the occasion never deserted her.

The Duke, too, had made something of a reputation for himself as a champion of the working classes, even if, as was customary with these early royal excursions into the lower regions of society, his activities were distinguished more by their press coverage than by their results. While the Prince of Wales, at the suggestion of Lloyd George's post-war government, flashed his winning smile round the world in a series of rally-the-Empire tours, his younger brother, also as a result of political prompting, was given the less exciting task of providing royal patronage for programmes of industrial welfare designed to mitigate increasing industrial unrest at home. He became president of the Industrial Welfare Society, an organisation involving employers and leaders of the labour movement in attempts to improve working conditions and to provide factory employees with amenities such as canteens, health clinics and leisure facilities. His willingness to visit any kind of industrial centre, his insistence on a complete absence of formality or special arrangements and his unassuming, sometimes self-deprecating, manner won him many supporters and the newspaper nickname of 'the Industrial Prince'.

This was no fleeting interest on the Duke's part. He remained president of the Industrial Welfare Society for sixteen years, and in 1921 himself proposed a venture that set out to promote the idea of social cohesion – the Duke of York's Camp. On Saturday, July 30th, 1921, four hundred boys gathered for the first camp at a redundant coastal airfield near Hythe in Kent. There was nothing new in the idea of offering boys from the city slums healthy holidays; what was different about this camp was that half the boys came from public schools. The Duke had invited each of a hundred industrial concerns to send two of their workers aged between seventeen and nineteen and an equal number of fee-paying schools to send two boys each. The campers would spend a week together on terms of absolute equality, indistinguishable from one another at least in dress, since they would all wear the same uniform of shirts and shorts provided by the camp. They were divided into groups of twenty, a mixture of backgrounds carefully ensured, and then encouraged to compete against each other in a series of special camp games, the conventional football and cricket having been barred on the ground that the public-school boys would be likely to possess skills greater than those of their less privileged comrades.

That first gathering was the cause of much anxiety and mistrust, not only to the pioneering participants but also to the public, the press and the Duke himself. When the patron went to inspect his handiwork, however, he was delighted with the enthusiasm he found among the boys and their supervisors, so for the next nineteen years the Duke of York's Camp was an annual event, with one exception. In 1930 the camp was cancelled because the site, at New Romney, had become in itself a tourist attraction, gaping onlookers drawn in their hundreds not by the unusual sight of working lads and Wykehamists living and playing together, but by the prospect of catching a glimpse of the Duke during his day at the camp. The following year, the camp was re-established on a new site at Southwold in Suffolk, and there it remained until the outbreak of the Second World War.

For the seven thousand boys who passed through those annual camps, the highlight of the week was always the Duke's visit. He tried to make it as unceremonious as possible, even proposing on one occasion – according to Robert Hyde, of the Industrial Welfare Society – 'that he should arrive at midnight, dress in camp kit in the morning, and wander about unrecognised and free; but he was told that the love of the public for a story of this kind would bring around him all the forces of modern publicity'. Those forces surrounded him anyway, whatever he did. Here is a special correspondent of *The Times* describing the royal day at the penultimate camp in 1938, by which time the Duke of York had reluctantly become King George VI:

> To the intense delight of his young guests, the King today broke his holiday cruise to Scotland in the Royal Yacht *Victoria and Albert* and came ashore here [at Southwold] to spend a day in the camp for 400 public school boys and young workers which he founded ... He was brought ashore in a veteran rowing boat manned by two 'old salts' ...
>
> It was the most unusual, exciting, and democratic arrival among his people that any monarch of this country can ever have made ... the 'front' and the cliffs lined with excited holidaymakers, and waiting on the beach, many of them splashing about in the sea, the 400 boys who are in camp ... The first part of the trip from the *Victoria and Albert* was made in the Royal Barge, but 100 yards from the shore the King entered the small boat. A terrific cheer went up from those waiting on the beach; the King waved his hand in greeting and smiled happily. He looked suntanned and, like everyone else in the camp, he wore shorts and an open-necked shirt, with white canvas shoes ...
>
> As quickly as they could the boys seized the nose of the boat and gave it a mighty tug ashore, and amid ringing cheers, the King jumped down on to the shingle. Then, leading his young guests through two lines of cheering holidaymakers, the King walked across the common to the camp ...
>
> After luncheon, the camp photograph was taken, and then the King joined his young guests in a merry 'sing-song' which included all the old camp favourites, among them the action song 'Under a spreading chestnut tree' ...

The day always ended with the gentle humiliation of some of the distinguished guests – politicians, industrialists, trade union leaders, public-school headmasters – accompanying the Duke of York. Their names were placed in a hat and those drawn by the Duke were required to make a speech lasting not more than three minutes, heckled or cheered on by the boys, and cut off at the end of their allotted time by an unexpected explosion as one of the boys fired a blank from a pistol.

Such informality was characteristic of both the Duke and the Duchess of York. The Duke himself admitted that his factory visits did not always proceed with the dignity associated with royalty:

> Once, to my surprise and dismay, I was dropped in a lift. Another time, a foolproof stamping machine threw out forty unstamped letters for my benefit. The threads of looms seem to break whenever I approach those machines. And yet, I find that industrialists are ready to welcome me in their midst.

As for the Duchess, her natural warmth and responsiveness charmed the ordinary people with whom she spent so much time. During a visit to Sheffield in 1934, she was taken to see Deep Pit allotments, formerly derelict land converted by more than a thousand working men into a gigantic vegetable patch. She was to have been accompanied by her husband, whom the gardeners had expected to dig up some 'Duke of York' potatoes, but the Duke had a poisoned hand and could not attend. Sensing the men's disappointment, the Duchess – white kid gloves and high-heeled shoes notwithstanding – seized a garden fork and did the digging herself, to rapturous applause.

The Yorks, both together and separately, displayed a new and exciting royal style, reinforcing in a particularly positive way the impression created by George V and developed by the Prince of Wales that the monarchy belonged to the people. More than that, the Duke and Duchess were perceived almost as being *of* the people, partly because Elizabeth had not been born royal but also because when they moved into their first real home in 1927 it was not a castle or a palace or even a country mansion, but a house in the busy thoroughfare of Piccadilly, near Hyde Park Corner. Number 145 Piccadilly could hardly be described as a modest residence – it had twenty-six bedrooms, though most of them were occupied by staff – but the fact that it was in the middle of London, indeed just a few yards from an undeniably democratic bus stop, added significantly to the popular appeal of the Yorks.

What appealed even more, however, was the establishment of the Yorks as the first royal family of the new generation, with the birth on Wednesday, April 21st, 1926 (just nine days before the start of the General Strike), of Princess Elizabeth. 'A family on the throne is an interesting idea,' Bagehot had written, and public interest in this latest addition was intense, even though she was only third in line to the throne and it was generally assumed both that her Uncle Edward would marry and produce an heir and that her own parents would have more children, possibly including a boy, so that Princess Elizabeth would be nudged farther down the line of succession. Photographs of the Princess were soon to be found on mantelpieces in homes throughout Britain and the Empire and at the age of three she had already become a 'cover girl' for *Time* magazine, which selected her as a leader of fashion, as if she herself had taken the decision to abandon the traditional nursery colours of pink and blue: 'Now every mother almost wants to buy a little yellow frock like Princess Elizabeth's.' Even before that, the Duke of York was surprised to discover how popular his first-born had become. During a tour of Australia in 1927, when Princess Elizabeth – still under a year old – had been left at home, he wrote to Queen Mary: 'It is extraordinary how her arrival is so popular out here. Wherever we go cheers are given for her as well & the children write to us about her.' Part of Antarctica was named in her honour, Princess Elizabeth Land, a song was composed for her, and her face adorned a postage stamp in Newfoundland.

As early as 1930 a market for biography had developed and John Murray published *The Story of Princess Elizabeth* by Anne Ring:

> When Princess Elizabeth's nurse . . . says in her quiet tones 'I think it is bed time now, Elizabeth,' there are no poutings or protests, just a few last laughs at Mummy's delicious bed time jokes, and then Princess Elizabeth's hand slips into her nurse's hand, and the two go off gaily together . . . to the accommodating lift, which in two seconds has whisked them up to the familiar dear domain which is theirs to hold and share.

That same year, on August 21st, the Yorks made history when their second child was born at the home of the Duchess's parents, Glamis Castle in Forfarshire: it was the first royal birth in Scotland since 1602. The Duke and Duchess had been hoping for a boy, but it was a girl they got and they named her Margaret, no doubt remembering the Maid of Norway who was Queen of Scotland in the thirteenth century.

The little Princesses filled the roles of juvenile leads for the royal family and the shining example of domesticity provided by them and their parents was celebrated widely in the press and, increasingly, in books. When the Duchess of York opened a new headquarters for the British College of Obstetricians and Gynaecologists in London, the college's president spoke for many people in telling her:

> We believe that the sanctity of the family means a great deal to the spiritual and physical welfare of our race. Your Royal Highness has given to us all a vision of the happiness of married life, and in a very beautiful way, through the little Princesses, the people have been permitted to share your joys and show their devotion to the Crown.

Thanks to the dutifulness of the King, the dashing charm of the Prince of Wales and the domestic harmony of the Duke and Duchess of York, the popularity of the royal family had reached new heights. But the towering edifice of monarchy over which George V presided was slowly being chipped away from within. 'He that hath wife and children', wrote Francis Bacon, 'hath given hostages to fortune; for they are impediments to great enterprises, either of virtue or mischief.' The great enterprise of the twentieth-century monarchy had been created round an ideal and an example of virtue; it was soon to be shaken to its foundations by mischief on the part of one of the King's hostages to fortune.

On January 22nd, 1936, two days after the death of George V, his eldest son was proclaimed King from a balcony at St James's Palace. Edward VIII was seen to be watching the ceremony from a palace window, accompanied by a woman described in the newspapers as 'the King's unknown companion'. Unknown she might have been to the new monarch's subjects, but among his friends she was only too familiar. Her name was Mrs Wallis Warfield Simpson.

10

Damnosa Hereditas

A royal family, according to Bagehot, 'introduces irrelevant facts into the business of government, but they are facts which speak to "men's bosoms", and employ their thoughts'. Wallis Simpson was just such an irrelevant fact. The story of Edward VIII and Mrs Simpson has become one of the great romances of the twentieth century. It contains the most compelling elements of both Shakespearean tragedy and the popular novelette: the lowly born woman for whom love conquered all; the king who renounced his throne and, in effect, his country to marry the woman he loved; the 'feud' between the new queen and the duchess who was wrongfully denied the honour that should have been conferred upon her by her husband's exalted rank; the sad, empty and unfulfilled life of a royal exile; the betrayals, the shame, the courage of the new king who took his brother's place, the final reconciliation in death. It is all such stuff as legends are made on.

But like any legend, this one pays less regard to truth than to drama. The determination of King Edward VIII to marry Mrs Simpson, twice divorced and an American, was certainly the trigger for the Abdication crisis, but all the available evidence suggests that the causes of the most severe shock to the English throne since the Glorious Revolution of 1688 were more complex than Mrs Simpson's shortcomings as a prospective consort and were to be seen long before her advent in Edward's somewhat idiosyncratic love life.

As early as 1911, with his investiture as Prince of Wales just a month after the coronation of his parents, David, as he was invariably known in the royal family, manifested deep misgivings about the position into which the accident of his birth had cast him. His anxieties began with what he called the 'preposterous rig' he was required to wear for the ceremony at Caernarvon Castle: a mantle and surcoat of purple velvet with ermine edging and white satin breeches. He had previously winced at the medieval garb he had been obliged to don for his investiture as a Knight of the Garter, but he had suffered in silence because he was aware of the historical associations of the uniform. The Caernarvon costume was an entirely different matter, specially designed to make, as it were, a spectacle of its wearer in front of ten thousand people. Queen Mary headed off an outright rebellion on the part of the seventeen-year-old Prince, but she could do nothing about the effect that the ceremony itself had on him. He suddenly realised, by his own account, that 'while I was prepared to fulfil my role in all this pomp and ritual, I recoiled from anything that tended to set me up as a person requiring homage'.[1]

At first sight, this might seem to be a refreshing and even praiseworthy attitude for a young prince in the so-called age of the common man. The concept of homage is an ancient one, bound up with mysticism, fealty and autocracy, and it may be properly argued that it has no place in a democratic society which, no matter how imperfectly, has the right to choose its own rulers rather than having them imposed upon it by divine intervention. In our society, however, while it has been thought necessary to retain the idea of allegiance to a sovereign, the expression of homage that idea entails has been, over the centuries, directed towards not the person but the institution, not the monarch but the monarchy. This the new Prince of Wales failed to understand. The loyalty displayed on that July day in 1911 was not for him personally, but for what he symbolised.

There may have been another failure, too. Again in his own words, the Prince was 'half-fainting of heat and nervousness'. He saw the investiture as an ordeal and, when it was all over, he knew he had experienced something that would come to be an ever greater part of his life. He must have known by then what his father suffered in the annual royal round of ceremonial and pageantry – George V, who never overcame his dislike of such things, was not one for keeping his complaints to himself – and the prospect must have terrified him. It was not that David lacked courage. During the First World War he badgered and browbeat, promised and pleaded in his attempt to be allowed to go to the Western Front, dismissing the risks with an airy 'What does it matter if I am killed? I have four brothers.' He got his way and, though barred from actual fighting, saw for himself and shared some of the horror and misery of the trenches. His abdication, though many would dismiss it as act of cowardice, was in fact the opposite. It would have been easier, and less brave, for him to have bowed to the demands of government and church (though whether the mediocracy would really have allowed him that escape route is open to question). Yet there seems to have been in David, despite his outward air of confidence, a certain weakness of character and of nerve. The kind of courage required in extreme circumstances is not the same as that needed to face the tests of everyday life, particularly when that life is royal.

During the Empire tours dreamed up for the Prince of Wales by Lloyd George in the early 1920s, Lord Mountbatten, who accompanied his cousin some of the time, noted that David was often depressed 'and said he'd like to change places with me'. In public, the Prince was ebullient and charming, doing whatever was asked of him, going out of his way to meet the people of the places he visited, performing official ceremonies, flashing his famous smile at receptions, and generally behaving exactly as was expected of a 'modern' young royal. But during the long sea voyages between countries he could sink into periods of gloom during which 'he'd shut himself up in his cabin for days, alone, face drawn, eyes brooding,' according to Lord Mountbatten. 'His staff couldn't go near him. I was the only one who dared intrude, to try to rouse him from his melancholy. He was basically a lonely person, lonely and sad.'[2]

The Prince's friend, confidante and mistress for sixteen years (apart from his occasional infidelities), Mrs Winifred Dudley Ward,[3] thought she knew the cause of that loneliness and sadness. Freda, as she was generally known, recalled hearing her lover express his longing to have a life of his own, to be an ordinary person, to have 'no more of this princing!' The Prince, she said, dismissed the role of the sovereign as that of a puppet and mere figurehead. 'Do nothing to upset the Prime Minister or the Court or the Archbishop of Canterbury! Show yourself to the people! Mind your manners! Go to church!' What modern man, he asked, wanted that sort of life?[4]

In 1925 the Society diarist Henry 'Chips' Channon, who was close to David and his circle, jotted down what proved to be a piece of unconscious prophecy. 'The Prince of Wales one feels', he wrote, 'would not raise his finger to save his future sceptre. In fact many of his intimate friends think he would be only too happy to renounce it.' That was six years before the Prince's first real meeting with Mrs Simpson and nearly a decade before he became infatuated with her.

If the Prince himself had doubts about his future, there were others who were equally concerned. While David was establishing himself, with a little help from Lloyd George, in popular esteem both at home and throughout the Empire, an old courtier felt it necessary to lecture him on his easy-going style. Sir Frederick Ponsonby, Keeper of the Privy Purse, pointed out that the Prince was breaking out of the

Bagehotian rules for sovereigns: 'Above all things your royalty is to be reverenced, and if you begin to poke about it you cannot reverence it . . . Its mystery is its life. We must not let in daylight upon magic.' The Prince of Wales, Ponsonby told him, had made himself too accessible, had come too close to the people and in so doing was risking the preservation of the monarchy's mystic influence. When the Prince protested that the world had moved on, Ponsonby pompously replied that *he* knew better, having served Queen Victoria, King Edward VII and George V, all of whom had understood that the monarchy must keep its distance.[5]

Such forebodings were shared by George V who, having been brought uncomfortably close to the accession of his eldest son through his own brush with death in the severe illness of 1928, is said to have suggested to some members of his family, while he was convalescing, that David would never sit upon the throne. By 1935 that thought had become a fervent hope. 'I pray to God that my eldest son will never marry and have children, and that nothing will come between Bertie and Lillibet [the family pet-name for Princess Elizabeth] and the throne.'[6] And to Stanley Baldwin, the Prime Minister, the old King made his famous and only too accurate prediction about his successor: 'After I am dead, the boy will ruin himself in twelve months.'[7] Baldwin knew what he meant. In 1936 he told a parliamentary colleague, 'I had rather hoped to escape the responsibility of having to take charge of the Prince as King,'[8] while at the Privy Council marking the accession of Edward VIII, the Prime Minister expressed doubt to the Labour leader, Clement Attlee, that the new King would stay the course.

Something had clearly gone wrong, something far more serious than an apparently misdirected passion. The public was expecting a dazzling new reign by a man who had become even more closely, more personally identified with ordinary people and their concerns than George V had been; a man who had grown up with the reality of representative democracy and the responsibility that appeared to place upon the sovereign; a man who, unlike his father, had known from his earliest years that he would be a king; a man of the modern age, free of the nostalgia for Victorian England that still affected the Court. When he made his first wireless broadcast as King in March 1936, it was to a record number of two million listeners. Yet politicians, courtiers and close friends of the King and his circle were far from sanguine. Even Edward himself felt a sense of foreboding when he became the occupant of Buckingham Palace. 'One never tinkers much with palaces,' he wrote in his memoirs. 'Like museums, they seem to resist change. Besides, a curious presentiment induced me to leave the rooms as they were. Somehow I had a feeling that I might not be there very long.'

It might be thought, and it has been suggested, that the new King's feelings of impermanence arose from the fact that by the time of his accession he had definitely made up his mind that he would marry Mrs Simpson.[9] There are difficulties with this theory, however. First, marriage remained as yet only in the mind of the King. Mrs Simpson, though by her own account she and her husband were going their separate ways, had not sought a divorce. She thought that her relationship with David might come to an end following his accession and even, in a letter to a relative, expressed the wish that he would follow the conventional path and marry some princess or other high-born woman, if only for the sake of appearances.[10] She might have hoped that such a marriage would divert public attention and allow their clandestine affair to continue, in the manner of Edward VII and his various paramours, but it seems obvious that she did not at that stage anticipate becoming his bride herself. The second point is that the King did not equate marriage to Mrs Simpson with abdication: it was not until November 1936 that he made his rash threat 'to go' if the government opposed the marriage, thereby handing his crown on a plate to those who wished to see the back of him. Finally, there are the much earlier indications of malaise in the heir to the throne. When George V voiced the hope that the crown would bypass David and when he made his fateful prediction to Baldwin, he knew of his son's relationship with Mrs Simpson, but never for a moment did it occur to the King or the Prime Minister that marriage was a possibility. Wallis Simpson may be identified as the immediate cause of the constitutional crisis of 1936, but the objective view of history must be that the underlying blame falls squarely on the monarchy itself.

George V became a popular monarch in spite of – indeed, almost because of – his stunted, dependent personality. He lacked the vision and perception to be anything more than a servant of the state, however it chose to use him, and the slavish obedience to duty he had learned in the Navy, combined with his personal qualities of faith, honesty and sincerity, saw him through. Had he really been the wise king some have portrayed, he would surely have been concerned to offer better preparation to his heirs, particularly to the one who would succeed him as king. He did not. Instead, he set his two eldest sons on precisely the same course he had followed himself, with the famous and fatal words, 'The Navy will teach David all he needs to know.' It might have been Edward VII speaking. To be fair, the very length of

Queen Victoria's reign had an effect on the then Duke of York's attitude. The fact that he had become heir presumptive on the death of his brother had made little difference to his life other than freeing him from his naval commitments, and it was to be a further nine years before he was required to take a slightly greater share of royal responsibility as Prince of Wales. The tranquillity and leisure of those years must have given him the impression that there was nothing very much to being heir to the throne, certainly nothing calling for special training or ability. It was only when he became king and confronted both the enormity of the job and the disadvantage at which he found himself that he tried to make up for the deficiencies in his sons' education. By then, however, the damage had been done. George V was not a man blessed with a great deal of foresight.

As I have indicated, the childhood of David and Bertie does not appear to have been the unremittingly wretched affair that some writers have imagined. It had its difficulties and anxieties, of course, but which childhood has not? Few parents are blameless in the matter of their children's shortcomings, yet it should be remembered that the successful negotiation of that period of dependence and powerlessness is conditioned to a significant extent by the personality of the child. The debate over acquired and inherited traits is a complex one, and the effects of parental behaviour can be devastating; nevertheless, some people emerge strengthened by the horrors of their childhoods while others are debilitated by comfort and affection. In the case of David and Bertie, the raw material was not encouraging. Neither was gifted intellectually and both were highly excitable and nervous. The excesses of a sadistic and mentally unbalanced nurse did not help.

This woman became so obsessively attached to David that she would pinch him or twist his arm to make him cry before he saw his mother, whose reaction to the child's distress would be to hand him back to the nurse immediately. When Bertie was born, the nurse resented him because he distracted her attention from David, so she neglected and starved the younger child as a 'punishment'. In those days it was accepted in many upper-class families that the parental writ stopped at the nursery door, and it was three years before the nurse's dangerous habits were discovered, even though many in the household knew or suspected what was going on. She was dismissed immediately and replaced by the competent and caring Charlotte Bill, whom the children called 'Lalla' and to whose influence the slight trace of Cockney vowels in the speech pattern of Edward VIII may be traced.

What lasting ill effects, if any, the two eldest Princes might have suffered as a result of their early experiences in the nursery it is impossible to say. Bertie's lifelong digestive problems have been blamed on the neglect of his first nurse, but they are more likely to have been associated with his nervous temperament. As for David, the forays into popular psychology which have linked his later relationships with women to lack of maternal affection and the manic ministrations of the nurse are both simplistic and suspect. The assumption has been that since his love affairs tended to be with married women, he was seeking a Freudian mother-figure. There are other explanations. His close friend Lady Alexandra Metcalfe, daughter of Lord Curzon, thought it was 'their sophisticated ways' that attracted him to married women, which seems to suggest that what he sought was the sense of maturity he lacked himself.

Others believe that what David needed was reassurance of his manhood, which was more likely to be provided by a sexually experienced woman than a young Society virgin. That, rather than some Oedipus complex, may explain why in his twenties he had a long relationship with a married woman twelve years his senior.[11] There has been speculation that the Prince was never a particularly accomplished lover – indeed, some have even hinted that he had latent homosexual tendencies, though the evidence for that is circumstantial and extremely slight – and that he required strong women who would take a dominant role.[12] Mrs Simpson herself later commented that David was 'full of deeply ingrained inhibitions of the most incredible kind' and that he could not have been 'a wild libertine'. As a woman with experience of two marriages, she added, she knew instinctively 'that he had never really fulfilled himself in a mature, adult relationship with a member of the opposite sex'.[13] Obviously she did not see herself as a mother-substitute. It should be remembered, too, that not all his affairs were with older women. His first great love, Freda Dudley Ward, was his junior by a year and Mrs Simpson was almost exactly two years younger than her royal suitor. Nor should the idea of the dominant woman be pushed too far: there is plenty of evidence of the Prince's stubbornness and determination to have his own way, and, if Mrs Simpson is to be believed, it was he who forced the pace of their romance.

At any rate, in childhood David at home was very much the star of the royal family that he would later become in public. Lady Airlie described him as the least inhibited of the royal children and there are many stories of his self-confidence and precocity. This had a negative effect on Bertie, who worshipped his brother and always felt second-best. Such feelings of insecurity as that engendered were heightened by the presence of his younger sister, Princess Mary. Like many men who are acutely conscious of their maleness, George V gave expression to the softer, more feminine side of his nature through a fondness for little girls, and there is no doubt that Mary was his favourite child. (The trait was to surface anew in his affection for his grandchildren, Elizabeth and Margaret.) Bertie thus occupied an unenviable position between his outgoing elder brother and his indulged sister, both of whom received, for different reasons, more attention than he did. This in itself is sufficient to produce an unusual degree of diffidence in a child, but Bertie suffered other handicaps, too. He was left-handed, he stammered and he had knock-knees.

The official biographer of King George VI, Sir John Wheeler-Bennett, pointed to a connection between the stammering and the left-handedness, claiming that being forced to write with his right hand – as was thought essential for left-handed people until comparatively recently – might have produced in Bertie a psychological condition known as the misplaced sinister, which could have affected his speech. Lady Airlie, however, remembered the little Prince stammering even before the right-hand regime was introduced and attributed the impediment to extreme nervousness. When Bertie felt at ease, she wrote, he spoke without a stammer and displayed more intelligence and character than he was credited with. This may be borne out by the recollection of Sir Louis Greig, a longtime friend and confidant of George VI, who maintained that the stammer only manifested itself when the young Prince had to speak in public. What is certain is that he received no consideration or sympathy from his siblings, who, encouraged by their father, tended to tease Bertie and mock his speech difficulties.

Bertie's knock-knees were inherited from his father (David had been mercifully spared them in his genetic inheritance) and prompted in George V the first departure from the maxim that his sons should be brought up just as he had been. The then Prince of Wales ordered that his eight-year-old son should wear splints to correct the deformity of his knees, so that he should be spared the embarrassment his father felt at his own imperfection. Much has been made of this 'torture' and the story has often been told of how the footman in whose care the two eldest boys were placed in 1902, Frederick Finch, was moved by Bertie's tears to release him from his shackles one bedtime – only to be shouted at by the irate father who pulled up his trousers and said it would be Finch's fault if Bertie grew up with knees like his own. The fact is that for the most part the young Prince Albert endured the discomfort and inconvenience of his splints with courage and little complaint, and he certainly grew to manhood with straight knees. Whether he was grateful to his father for this is not recorded.

What, in the event, he cannot have been grateful for were the limitations of his education. The early schooling of David and Bertie was undertaken by Mme Hélène Bricka, who had been governess to Princess May, but whatever beneficial effects she may have had were, in the eyes of their parents at least, seriously undermined in 1901, when the Duke and Duchess of York undertook their Australian tour and the children were left in the care of their royal grandparents for eight months. Edward VII had not abandoned his belief that childhood was a time to be enjoyed, and he and Queen Alexandra colluded blatantly in every attempt their adored grandchildren made to escape the discipline of learning. Nor was there much in the way of restraint on their behaviour, whether among the family or before guests. The boys made the most of their freedom and virtually ran riot, much to the chagrin of their parents when they returned. The Duchess of York saw fit to complain to the Queen, while the Duke's response was to impose a stricter, male-dominated regime.

It was not a success. Just as George V suffered (though he would have been the last to notice it) from his father's response to his own childhood, so David and Bertie were severely limited by their father's reaction to his upbringing, though in a quite different way. Edward VII had been resolved to raise his children in a manner directly opposed to the precepts of Prince Albert; George V, on the other hand, tried to recreate exactly the conditions of his own early education. Both were wrong. Neither understood that their sons were not the same as they had been, neither stopped to consider whether changing times might require changed techniques, or that there might have been something lacking in the formation of their own minds. Edward VII could find nothing right in his father's ideas of child-rearing and George V could find nothing wrong in the methods decreed by his father. Both believed absolutely in the correctness of their courses. No one should be surprised at this. Throughout their lives, Edward VII and George V showed little evidence of self-examination or even of self-awareness. Why should they? They were kings, and under the cobbled-up constitution of modern Britain, the monarch is subject to criticism but beyond reproach. Who was to tell them they were wrong? Under a system in which all the king or queen has to do is reign, whatever that means, only the magnifying lens of history can discern the weaknesses.

Prince Eddy and Prince George had their Mr Dalton. Prince Edward and Prince Albert in their turn had Mr Hansell. If anything, the latter had less to recommend him than the former, whose efforts had not been attended by any great success. Henry Peter Hansell, aged thirty-nine at the time of his appointment as tutor to David and Bertie in 1902, was a pedagogue of average competence but little character or imagination. He was chosen because he came from Norfolk, because he shared the Prince of Wales's passion for yachting and because he had prepared Prince Arthur of Connaught for Eton. David and Bertie, however, were not destined for public school. The intention was that they should join the Royal Navy, just as their father had done. For the sum of their general education, therefore, they were dependent on Mr Hansell, and he was utterly unequal to the task of inspiring an urge to learn in two boys who were already labouring under serious personal and intellectual disadvantages.

The atmosphere created by Hansell was uncongenial for a start. To his credit, he was aware of both the difficulties of his commission and his own limitations in attempting to fulfil it. Having been a master in conventional schools, he had an instinctive grasp of the positive aspects of 'peer pressure' (though, of course, such jargon would have been unintelligible to an Edwardian) and understood that its absence would place obstacles in the path of the Princes' development. Unfortunately, the only method he could devise to mitigate the problem of isolation was to try to copy school surroundings as faithfully as possible. Sir John Wheeler-Bennett wrote:

> He fitted up a classroom with two standard desks, a blackboard, bookshelves, etc., in a corner room of the first floor [at York Cottage]; here from 7.30 till 8.15 the boys would do their preparation before breakfast; and from 9 till 1 and between tea and supper they did their lessons.

Not only that, but the humourless Hansell, lacking any sense of the ridiculous, appointed David 'head boy' in a class of two and when he left to become a naval cadet promoted Bertie to the post, the remainder of the class consisting of Prince Henry. 'I should say', Hansell wrote in all seriousness to the Prince of Wales towards the end of 1907, 'that Prince Albert has failed to appreciate his position as "captain".' The comment tends to indicate that Prince Albert's judgment was better than his teacher's. But it would be unfair to blame Hansell alone for the deficiencies in the basic education of the Princes. He repeatedly urged their father to send them to a suitable preparatory school, but the Prince of Wales obstinately refused.

Hansell's report-books, in which he charted princely progress (or more often lack of it) for his employer, make fairly dismal reading and reflect the teacher's dismay at the consistent absence of reward for his work. The boys appear to have been lazy, inattentive, disobedient and quarrelsome. As a result of Hansell's reports, the Prince of Wales often issued the 'dread summons to the library' recalled by his eldest son, but he seems never to have wondered whether they might do better in other circumstances, despite the advice of the man he had charged with the responsibility for educating them. The thought may be unkind, but it is hard to escape entirely the impression that in his peculiar, pig-headed way the Prince of Wales did not want his sons to be well-educated. Philistinism flourished in Edwardian England, together with the curious belief that it would not do for a gentleman to be too good at anything (save perhaps blood sports) and certainly not to be seen striving to achieve excellence.

According to Hansell, Bertie began to resent the dominance of his elder brother and the pair quarrelled even more, but his academic performance did not improve after David's departure in the spring of 1907. Hansell, who had become 'headmaster' of his miniature school with the appointment of tutors in French, German, mathematics and other subjects, described his new head boy as 'at present a "scatter-brain" '. Bertie's stammer made English difficult enough for him, let alone French and German, but his greatest burden of those days in the York Cottage classroom was mathematics. The basic principles were 'beyond him' and his failure to grasp them induced both embarrassment and a deep loathing of the subject, which often combined to produce tears of despair or outbursts of impotent fury. 'You must really give up losing your temper when you make a mistake in a sum,' his father told him, no doubt trying to be kind. 'We all make mistakes sometimes, remember now you are nearly 12 years old & ought no longer to behave like a little child of 6.'[14] To Hansell, who doubted whether Bertie would be able to pass the maths section of the naval college entrance examination, the Prince of Wales wrote: 'You must be very strict & make him stick to it & do many papers.'

There followed a year of renewed efforts and serious cramming in maths, then in November and December 1908 Bertie manfully undertook the entrance examinations for the junior Royal Naval College at Osborne, part of the 'snug and nice' home his great-grandmother had found on the Isle of Wight. 'I can state as a fact that he has now reached a good standard all round,' Hansell assured the Prince of Wales, and the naval examiners appear to have agreed, though the Prince was found wanting in geometry. The oral examination must have been an ordeal because of his stammer, but he managed to impress the selection board, which observed that even if he had been a costermonger's son it would have passed him without hesitation. It in no way reflects on the Prince to wonder whether that statement should be taken absolutely at face value. Hansell had uttered a note of warning:

> Like his brother he cannot get on without 'a bit of a shove' and ... I do hope that he will not be left too much to himself ... a too literal interpretation of the direction that they are to be treated exactly the same as other boys, who have had three or four years at a private school, must lead to disaster ...

There was no disaster, but neither was naval training an unqualified success for David and Bertie. Their father had benefited from both the company and the additional instruction of John Dalton, but he did not afford a similar privilege to his sons, who in spite of their childhood isolation became the first royal children sent to face the rigours of the outside world entirely by themselves. It must have been a severe shock. The conditions were rigorous and the regime was founded on the harshness that for centuries was thought necessary to train sailors, which naturally brutalised the cadets themselves and led to widespread bullying. That apart, the two Princes were hurled without preparation from the protective custody of palaces and the ordered privacy of Sandringham into an existence *en masse*, where everything they did was in the company of a score or more of other boys. If that was 'a bit of a shove', they certainly got it, and it is interesting to note that in some ways Bertie responded rather better than David did. Both bore the rigours of their new life uncomplainingly, but while David remained somewhat apart from his fellows, Bertie endeared himself to many and, his natural shyness notwithstanding, made a number of firm friends.

In terms of education, on the other hand, David was slightly ahead of his younger brother, though neither can be said to have distinguished himself and appearances in their father's library were a regular feature of their periods of leave. On one occasion, David burst into tears in the expectation of yet another rebuke based on his end-of-term report, much to the surprise of a father who had merely wanted to inform him that the feared document actually recorded a slight improvement in the boy's performance. For the most part, however, the assessments of the Princes' work were not encouraging. Much of their time was occupied in learning the practical aspects of seamanship, so that the academic content of their training was not great, but even then David and Bertie remained firmly in the lowest reaches of their respective classes. David once exulted in the fact that he had reached a position as high as thirty-second in his class; Bertie did less well. His father wrote:

> My dear boy this will not do, if you go on like this you will be at the bottom of your Term, you are now 71st & you won't pass your examination and very probably will be *warned* [i.e. that he would not be allowed to return to the college] this term if you don't take care ... It will be a great bore, but if I find that you have not worked well at the end of this term, I shall have to get a master for you to work with all the holidays & you will have no fun at all.

David passed on to the senior naval college at Dartmouth in the spring of 1909, but at the end of the following year there were doubts that Bertie would be able to follow him. His work had shown bouts of improvement, but these were not sustained and his tutors expressed concern (though not to his father) that he might do so badly in his final examinations that Dartmouth would not accept him.[15] He certainly did badly, being rated sixty-eighth out of the sixty-eight in his class. 'I am afraid there is no disguising to you the fact that P.A. has gone a mucker,' one of the senior staff at Osborne wrote to Hansell. 'He has been quite off his head, with the excitement of getting home, for the last few days, and unfortunately as these were the days of the examinations he has quite come to grief...' Yet perhaps he escaped some parental wrath that Christmas at Sandringham, for the year 1910 had seen his father succeed to the throne on the death of Edward VII – to be plunged immediately into the crisis over the Parliament Bill.

As it happened, Bertie was allowed to go to Dartmouth (hardly surprising, really, considering that he was now second in line to the throne), but he was not to have the company of his brother for long. David was invested as Prince of Wales in the summer of 1911 and subsequently removed from Dartmouth. George V, confronted at last with the inadequacies of his own education in equipping him for kingship, decided that naval training was too narrowly based for the heir to the throne and, having listened for once to Hansell's advice, informed his son that he would be going to Oxford university. David felt cheated. He had spent four years learning to be a sailor and was now to be denied the reward of the final training cruise in a battleship. He protested that Oxford would be a further waste of time, arguing that he had 'neither the mind nor the will for books' and pleading to be sent on a world tour instead as a form of on-the-job training. The King would not hear of it, though he did compromise to the extent of allowing the new Prince of Wales to make a three-month voyage as a midshipman aboard the battleship *Hindustan*.

David's doubts about his new status have already been considered. They were heightened by this abrupt change of plan for his future. As he was to say later himself, the emphasis of his upbringing thus far had been 'strict and unaffected' and if it had done anything for him 'it was to make me desperately anxious to be treated exactly like any other boy of my age'. That had been precisely what his father had said he wanted. Yet now the King was 'beginning to remind me of the obligations of my position' and summarily requiring him to behave and feel not like any ordinary boy but like a prince. The confusion he experienced as a result was to remain with him for the rest of his life. He was unable fully to adjust to his position as Prince of Wales, later as King and, after his abdication, as the exiled Duke of Windsor.

Bertie had no such difficulties for the time being. He continued his naval career at Dartmouth, where conditions were considerably more congenial than they had been at Osborne and where he acquitted himself if not exactly creditably then at least satisfactorily – 'I think he will do,' was the ultimate verdict of his commanding officer. Still diffident and immature, he none the less seemed increasingly relaxed, joined in the fun that was permitted at the senior college and passed his leisure time pleasantly, riding horses, cross-country running and playing tennis, at which he became more than proficient. Having passed out a few places above the bottom of his year, he joined the cruiser *Cumberland* in January 1913 for a six-month cruise to the Canary Islands, the West Indies and Canada, which completed his basic training and revealed an unfortunate predisposition towards seasickness. 'I am pleased with my boy,' George V told an officer when Bertie left the *Cumberland*.[16] The Prince was following in his father's footsteps, though how closely it would be twenty-three years before he would, to his infinite dismay, discover.

Such, then, was the education of the new generation of the royal family. In the case of Prince Albert, it differed hardly at all from that of his father and its effect was much the same. Any outstanding traits of mind or personality he might have possessed had been crushed, leaving a bland, underdeveloped character to be moulded chiefly by circumstance. His main attributes were determination, courage and obedience to the call of duty, combined with unassuming modesty, generosity of spirit and – much more than his father – a keen sense of common humanity. As for his handicaps, they were his diffidence and nervousness, a limited intellect and an immature instability of temper. For the Prince of Wales it was different. The inadequacies of the royal system of education served mainly to underpin the more negative side of his nature. He was no more of an intellectual than his brother, but he possessed a quickness of brain that his tutor completely failed to enhance or direct. On the contrary, the dull routine of the York Cottage schoolroom and the emphasis on discipline and obedience at the naval establishments were inimical to any tendency towards originality. Under such pressures, a degree of natural percipience in David degenerated into petulance and the young man's mind was turned into a sort of misguided missile, aimed vaguely in the direction of change but wildly erratic in its course and lacking any precise information as to its actual target. In consequence, he became rebellious and wilful, challenging everything his father appeared to represent but lacking the mental equipment to construct anything new on the site of what he wished to tear down. 'Something must be done,' he said when, as King, he saw for himself the pitiful plight of unemployed miners in South Wales. That was also his attitude towards the monarchical system by then in his care, but in neither instance did he have a clear idea of what could or should be done.

More damaging, however, to both Princes than the method and content of their education was the prevailing atmosphere of the family in which they grew up. It was not simply that their father tended to be a martinet, placing obedience at the head of his personal list of virtues, or that their mother paid too little attention to them. The malaise in the household of George V and Queen Mary went much deeper than that. Theirs was undoubtedly a very successful royal partnership and an outstanding example of mutual loyalty and fidelity, yet as an emotional bond the marriage appears to have left a great deal to be desired. That they genuinely loved each other must be taken on trust, since there is absolutely no evidence to suggest otherwise, no hint of scandal such as attaches to the memory of Edward VII, and plenty of material in the Royal Archives containing expressions of affection. But that very way of showing affection, in writing, leads one to suspect inhibitions between the couple.

Of course, nobody can ever know the intimacies indulged in by two people in private, and royal marriages are particularly difficult to characterise because of the differing demands made on each partner, the separations involved and the veil that is drawn between public appearance and personal life. But in the bizarre circumstances of their engagement and marriage, George and May were certainly shy about expressing their feelings to each other and the testimony of people who were close to them offers no reason to suppose that they ever entirely overcame that early timidity.

'I *love* you more than anybody in the world,' wrote the young Princess May to her fiancé, '& this I cannot tell you myself so I write it to relieve my feelings.' Prince George responded: 'I think it really unnecessary for me to tell you how deep my love for you my darling is.' Eight years later he was writing to his wife, after they had just spent many months together on a colonial tour, 'Somehow I can't tell you, so I take the first opportunity of writing to say how deeply I am indebted to you darling for the splendid way in which you supported and helped me during our long tour . . .' Then in 1930: 'I can never sufficiently express my deep gratitude to you, darling May . . . This is not sentimental rubbish, but what I really feel.' There is more than a hint of embarrassment, both at an inability to express deep feelings and at the thought that in doing so one might be exposed to a loss of dignity. He was a man to whom spontaneity was not natural, other than in the combustion of his temper.

Recollections of May almost all speak of aloofness, coldness, stiffness, an inability to make small-talk and, particularly after she became Queen Mary, an acute consciousness of both her own and her husband's positions. Her innate shyness had been hardened into a protective shield by the barbs of Queen Alexandra and her daughters and by her husband's apparent indifference to the difficulties of her situation, arising from his excessive regard for his mother, which even survived his accession. ('I hope', he wrote when he was forty-six years old, 'that I have gained the approval of my beloved Motherdear.') This barrier of reserve in May was, of course, only strengthened when George became King. It is significant that in 1911, when the new Emperor of India was ready to show himself and his wife to his subjects in the subcontinent and the Empress wished dearly to be able to wear the Star of India at the coronation durbar in Delhi, she did not approach her husband personally to seek admittance to the Order, but did so through an intermediary, Viscount Esher. An ideal couple in some ways, there was nevertheless a sense in which King George V and Queen Mary lived separate lives. Both seem to have been unable to distinguish between their official and their private personae.

As far as their offspring were concerned, this lacuna in the lives of the King and Queen was magnified. Both loved their children dearly, but the Queen admitted that she could not separate sovereignty from fatherhood and the King's way of relating to his sons in particular was much more regal than paternal. 'Remember', he told David when the Prince left for Osborne in 1907, 'that I am your best friend,' yet even during those relatively private years before his accession, contacts with his sons had been for the most part on an excessively formal basis and no spirit of friendship had been established. He was not the unduly harsh and stern father that some writers have pictured and there is no reason to believe that the Princes were generally afraid of him – they simply did not know him, or he them, because there was too great a distance between them.

The most serious effect of these emotional gaps, between father and mother and parents and children, was that personal problems were never discussed, or if they were it was only in a 'pull yourself together' sense. Tears from the thirteen-year-old David, for instance, brought the response that such behaviour was unbecoming for a naval cadet. There was no attempt to understand, and while, in 1920, the King told Bertie that 'you will find me ever ready to help you & give you good advice', such help and advice most often took the form of injunction and exhortation, such as that to the Prince of Wales in 1911: 'In your position it is absolutely necessary that you should ride well . . . and so the sooner you make up your mind to do it the better . . . If you can't ride, you know, I am afraid people will call you a duffer.' The other correspondence between the Princes and their father was certainly copious, but almost always stilted and usually inconsequential. In the House of Windsor created by George V, one did one's duty, obeyed the rules and kept one's feelings to oneself.

So it was that Prince Edward and Prince Albert made the painful transition from boyhood to manhood slowly, incompletely and without help. It was only later and outside the family – or, in the case of the Prince of Wales, beyond the pale – that they would find the support they so desperately needed. Bertie in one way proved to be the luckier of the two. He acquired a wife with the strength and the self-confidence to bring out his qualities as both a man and a king. If David's growth to true manhood was achieved through Wallis Simpson (and even that may be doubted when the pettiness of his later life is considered), it was only at the cost of his kingship. In view of David's abdication and Bertie's early death, both under the strain of what had come to be demanded of constitutional sovereigns, it was a poisoned chalice that George V passed on.

11

The Family Firm

When Prince Albert joined the battleship *Collingwood* as a midshipman in September 1913, he expected, as his father had done before him, to spend the greater part of his life in the Royal Navy and ultimately to achieve command of his own ship. A number of things conspired to make this impossible. To begin with, the Prince was not a natural sailor and, though he enjoyed his naval career, much of his active service was spent battling against endemic seasickness. That in itself, though debilitating, need not have affected his prospects – Lord Nelson, after all, was regularly seasick – but within a year of his posting to *Collingwood*, the gastric troubles from which the Prince suffered intermittently became acute and appendicitis was diagnosed. As a result, Bertie underwent surgery on August 28th, 1914, and spent the early months of the First World War in convalescence and subsequently in command of a desk at the Admiralty. It was not until February 1915 that he was permitted to return to his battleship, and even then many of his duties were carried out ashore, since naval war strategy dictated that the fleet based at Scapa Flow undertook only short patrols in the North Sea.

Three months later, however, the Prince was ill again, attacks of severe abdominal pain striking without warning and sometimes making it difficult for him to attend to his responsibilities. Anxious, depressed and steadily losing weight, he remained with his ship until July but was then forced to take sick leave once more. This time the diagnosis was a mucal disturbance of the stomach caused by muscle weakness, and Bertie agreed to submit to an orderly regimen involving a special diet and daily stomach-pumping, on the understanding that if *Collingwood* should be ordered into action he would be immediately recalled to duty. However, he did not recover as his doctors expected, which caused some worry to his commanding officer and mingled concern and irritation to his father. The captain of *Collingwood* told George V that, in spite of his promise to recall the Prince if action seemed imminent, he regarded it as his duty to accept medical advice, which was that Bertie was unfit for sea-going service. With some impatience the King replied that if his son was so ill, he should be officially declared unfit and sent to a nursing home, though this was not a course that would attract royal favour. 'The King', wrote Lord Stamfordham, 'would prefer to run the risk of Prince Albert's health suffering than that he should endure the bitter and lasting disappointment of not being in his ship in the battle line.' There was a war on and the royal family must be seen to be doing its bit.[1]

If this seems like callousness on the part of the King, it should be remembered that war hysteria was then at its height and Bertie himself was not immune to it. 'We don't want to lose you, but we think you ought to go,' ran a popular song of the time, and the Prince wanted to go as much as anybody else. Stamfordham's letter pointed out in a postscript that the Prince's ill-health was affecting his nerves and that breaking the undertaking to recall him when necessary would only make matters worse. To his son the King wrote soothingly that he should not expect to recover 'in a minute' because 'anything to do with the stomach must take a little time to get right'. Nevertheless, he asked *Collingwood*'s captain to canvass the opinion of another doctor.[2]

Finally, both the King and the Prince were persuaded that active service was out of the question for the time being. At the end of the year Bertie was officially placed on sick-leave and found himself back at the Admiralty engaged in light duties. He did manage to get a taste of the war early in 1916, when he joined the Prince of Wales in France, where David was attached to the Guards' headquarters. The brothers watched an artillery exchange and visited the scenes of earlier battles – spectator sport, if you like, but at least it went some way towards easing Bertie's conscience. He felt even better that spring when, having passed the required examination, he was promoted to sub-lieutenant. In May 1916 he returned to *Collingwood*.

The battleship put to sea with its squadron at the end of May, but Prince Albert was in the sick-bay profoundly depressed by a recurrence of his stomach complaint. This time, though, his incapacity was to be short-lived. In the late afternoon of Wednesday, May 30th, *Collingwood*'s crew was summoned to action stations and the Prince, his ailment forgotten in the excitement, rushed to man the big twelve-inch guns of 'A' turret. The Battle of Jutland, what might be termed the last great face-to-face naval engagement in history, had begun. *Collingwood* missed the main action, but sank one German light cruiser, helped to destroy another and damaged the battle cruiser *Derfflinger*, which had earlier sunk the British cruiser *Queen Mary* and was at that time engaged in the famous 'death ride' close to the British line that helped to save the German fleet from destruction. As night fell the Prince and his comrades manned *Collingwood*'s four-inch guns ready to repel destroyer attacks, but by then the fighting had moved away from them as the German ships smashed through a British cruiser squadron and headed back towards their base. By dawn it was all over.

Twenty-five ships went down during the Battle of Jutland and the casualties on both sides amounted to just under ten thousand men. The action was inconclusive and made virtually no difference to the course of the war, but it certainly had an effect on the morale of Prince Albert, who wrote home complaining that amid all the destruction, 'No one would know to look at the ship that we had been in action.'[3] He knew, though, and his own coolness under fire greatly increased his self-confidence. 'Oh, if only they would come out again,' he wrote to his elder brother, 'and we could meet them, but this time in the early morning, we should have better light and more daylight to deal with them.' His letter also reflected the jingoistic sentiments affecting many at the time:

> In a war on such a scale as this of course we must have casualties and lose ships & men, but there is no need for everyone at home to bemoan their loss when they are proud to die for their country. They don't know what war is, several generations have come and gone since the last great battles.[4]

Twenty-five years later the spirit of defiance would remain but, older, wiser and sadder, he would understand the meaning of such losses as he reigned over a nation that knew only too well what war was.

For a while, the raising of Prince Albert's spirits encouraged him to think that his illness was past, and in July 1916 he was able to report to his father that he had had no further gastric symptoms. By the end of August, however, he was suffering severe pains and was taken first to a naval hospital in Scotland and then to Windsor, where the source of the trouble was finally identified correctly – a duodenal ulcer. So that he could embark on the conventional treatment of dietary care and a way of life as free of stress as possible, he became deskbound again, this time in the office of the commander-in-chief at Portsmouth. A little less than a year later, feeling fitter and promoted to acting lieutenant, he returned to sea in the battleship *Malaya*, but he barely completed two months of duty before finding himself back in hospital in a very low state both physically and mentally. Now the truth had to be faced. 'I feel that I am not fit for service at sea, even when I recover from this little attack,' he told the King.[5] His doctors and the Navy agreed.

The Prince had no wish to remain in the Navy as a desk officer, so he tentatively suggested to his father that he might transfer to the Royal Naval Air Service, which at that time remained distinct from the Royal Flying Corps, though in 1918 the two would be merged into the Royal Air Force. Much to Bertie's surprise, 'my own suggestion for once came off and Papa jumped at the idea,'[6] but before it could be taken up his ulcer laid him low and an operation was performed in November 1917. By the following February he had fully recovered and reported to the flying training establishment at Cranwell in Lincolnshire, which two years later was to become the Royal Air Force Cadet College. It was at Cranwell that he received his first command, though one very different from what he had long imagined. He was placed in charge of Number 4 Squadron, Boy Wing, which 'I am going to run . . . as an entirely separate unit to the remainder of the men'.[7] He did not find command easy and the strict discipline and almost obsessive attention to petty detail for which he soon became known might well provide an indication of the state of his nerves. Apart from that, the creation of the RAF was inevitably a painful business, with dissent and division both within the service and among the politicians who had created it, so that the work at Cranwell was subject to unpredictable changes of policy and practice. 'I am pretty fed up, and don't feel like staying here for good,' the Prince complained after only a few months.[8]

He did not have to stay there. In July 1918 he was transferred to a cadet unit on the south coast and then, after the Armistice in November that year, he joined the staff of the Air Force commander on the Western Front, in Belgium. It was during that spell of duty that he came face to face with one of his royal relatives from the opposing side, the sister of the Kaiser (who had by then abdicated), Princess Viktoria. Bertie was correct with her, but cold. 'She seemed to have very little idea of what our feelings are towards Germany,' he said. 'She asked after . . . the family, and hoped that we should be friends again shortly. I told her politely I did not think it was possible for many years.'[9]

Back in England, Prince Albert became the first member of the royal family to hold a pilot's licence, after a course of instruction at Croydon Aerodrome in 1919. He was not a natural aviator any more than he had been a natural sailor, telling his mother that he preferred the safety of the ground, and he was never allowed to fly solo because of his 'general physical and psychological condition'.[10] On the whole, his naval career was not a great success. In retrospect it appears probable that he was much too highly strung for such a life and that therein lay the root of his health problems. Ultimately, the best that could be found for him was a job at the Air Ministry in London, but by that time there were reasons other than health and temperament for terminating his military service.

Even before the war, George V had realised the fallacy of his idea that the Navy would teach the heir to the throne all he would need to know and as a result the Prince of Wales had spent eight token terms at Magdalen College, Oxford (which had, in fact, added virtually nothing to his knowledge but had satisfied the King). The anti-royal agitation of the war years that forced George V to rename his dynasty, criticism of Prince Albert's long absences from active service, the triumph of Bolshevism in Russia and the social and political upheavals in Britain immediately after the war – strikes, riots and the emergence of the Labour Party as a strong and growing challenge to the established ruling class – convinced the King that the monarchy must work harder both to ensure stability in the nation and to secure its own position. More work for the royals meant greater visibility. The Prince of Wales was already being prepared to set off on a series of tours designed to strengthen the ties of empire. The King and Queen, in their own fashion, were fully occupied in bringing royalty down to the level of petty life at home. Now it was necessary to mobilise other members of the family.

Prince Albert had been introduced to public life during one of his periods of sick-leave from the Navy. In the spring of 1916 he had fulfilled his first, somewhat bizarre, official function by opening a rifle range built for members of the two Houses of Parliament. In spite of his nervousness and his stammer, he had made a creditable speech and had fired the first shot. Shortly afterwards he had been deputed to receive on behalf of his father the visiting Prince Alexander (later King) of Serbia, with whom he had been obliged to converse in French – his success at which may be judged from his own comment that he had had 'a pretty stiff time' because the Prince did not speak English.[11] In 1919 the King decided that Bertie should both undertake a greater public role and complete his 'education' by spending a year at Trinity College, Cambridge, in company with his younger brother, Prince Henry. Quite apart from the unsuitability of the two Princes for academic life, the aims of the King were, of course, incompatible and

Prince Albert had no doubts as to which was the more important. 'My brother is so overwhelmed with work that I am going to help him now,' he wrote. 'It is really the best thing to do, now that there is so much going on in every way.'[12]

He had barely begun the new academic year at Cambridge in October 1919 when he was recalled to London to receive the Freedom of the City and then to welcome, accompany and guide the Shah of Persia on a state visit. A few weeks later he was obliged to interrupt his studies again to escort President Poincaré of France and his wife, who arrived on the first anniversary of the Armistice. Given that during his brief period as an undergraduate, Bertie appeared at more than twenty public engagements and also spent much time with speech therapists in the attempt to overcome his stammer – now a serious embarrassment because of the speeches he was required to make – it is not surprising that he had little to show for his studies. One thing he did do was absorb the precepts of Walter Bagehot. That, in the event, was to ensure the survival of the series of half-truths, misconceptions and outmoded theories which complicates and confuses the position of the royal family today.

But Prince Albert perhaps saw more clearly than his father had done what the application of Bagehot's 'principles' would mean for the future of the monarchy. When, in 1920, he was fined by his college for smoking in academic dress and told that he should set a better example because he was a member of the royal family, he is said to have replied, with some bitterness: 'We are not a family, we are a firm.'[13] Shortly afterwards he was appointed to the board of directors when George V conferred upon him his own former titles, Baron Killarney, Earl of Inverness and Duke of York. Bertie was approaching his twenty-fifth birthday, but his reaction to this honour was more like that of a schoolboy: 'I must . . . thank you again ever so much for having made me Duke of York. I am very proud to bear the name that you did for many years, and I hope I shall live up to it in every way.'[14] He still had a lot of growing-up to do. Fortunately for him, and certainly for the monarchy, he had just met the young woman who would lead him into manhood.

Lady Elizabeth Bowes-Lyon was something of a phenomenon in the determinedly, almost frantically hedonistic London society of the 1920s. The tragedy of the First World War had provoked quite distinct reactions throughout the social strata. Among the entrepreneurial middle classes, many of whom had done quite well out of the war, there was a desire for continued business expansion and quick profits – the sort of attitude that would help to create the conditions for the

Wall Street crash of 1929 and the ensuing Depression. The workers felt a species of anger which showed itself in a sometimes violent determination that their wartime sacrifices should be rewarded by better wages, better conditions, better housing, more leisure and a significant increase in their political power. At the top of the social scale, the older generation adapted as best it could to the fact that life would never again be as comfortable as it had been before 1914, while its children, feeling that the war had robbed them of their youth, resolved to make up for lost time by devoting themselves to pleasure while they still could, recognising that they would soon be obliged to settle down to the grim realities of a world that had become harsher and more serious. The fatalism of war had accelerated the development of a new morality, stripping away some (though by no means all) Victorian hypocrisy, so that the style of sexuality among the young became more overt as its practice became easier through the increasing use of contraceptives. Against this background, Elizabeth Bowes-Lyon, though she had grown up with this new, more liberated generation, was something of an old-fashioned girl.

It was not that she was prim or particularly proper. She liked to enjoy herself as much as anyone else – indeed, she was once described as the best dancer in London – and she had a highly developed sense of fun which made her bridle at the outdated formalities still observed at some social functions. Small, dark and pretty, with large, round, expressive blue eyes, she was well aware of her attraction for men and was not above flirting with them, to the extent that in 1922 alone she received five proposals of marriage. The fact that those proposals were rejected says much about Lady Elizabeth. For one thing, though she appreciated and enjoyed the delights of the London Season, she deplored the main reason for its existence, which was to match the daughters of the aristocracy with young men who would make suitable husbands. Furthermore, from childhood she had possessed an innate sense of her own worth, a degree of self-awareness marked not by any arrogance but by a cautious respect for herself (sometimes manifested in showing-off) that made her determined not to settle for any man simply because his background and fortune made him an acceptable suitor. This self-respect also meant that, unlike many of the bright young things of the 1920s, she was the very opposite of promiscuous. 'Holding hands in a boat, that was her idea of courting,' a close friend recalled.[15] Finally, she was the favourite of a large, closely knit and affectionate family which, together with a small number of intimate friends, provided for all her emotional needs, so that she saw no reason to rush into marriage.

Yet she was the sort of young woman who would appeal strongly to a man with dynastic responsibilities. There was about her, underneath the vivacity and easy charm, an indefinable air of gravitas, a certain strength of character and purpose that marked her out as a prospective wife who would be much more than a decorative addition to one of the best families. In a book published after the Abdication and written 'with the personal approval' of the new Queen Elizabeth, Lady Cynthia Asquith quoted a letter dating from the early 1920s that described Lady Elizabeth Bowes-Lyon's appearance at a British Embassy ball in Paris:

> She seemed to me the incarnation of fresh, happy, English girlhood: so bright, so natural, and with an absolutely enchanting smile and a look of indescribable goodness and sweetness, shot with a delicious gleam of humour and fun. Looking at her, I felt that she was just what should result from her sort of home atmosphere of family affection and fun, laughter, and music, and yet with a sense of the deep eternal realities of life as foundations to it all. That would account for the thoughtful look on the brow, the quiet inner radiance that her little face wears in repose, though superficially it would appear all sparkle and girlish fun. Certainly last night she stood out as an English rose, sweet and fresh as if with the dew still on it.

Small wonder that when her engagement to the Duke of York was announced in January 1923, Chips Channon should write in his diary: 'There's not a man in England today who doesn't envy him. The clubs are in gloom.'

The Duke of York had known his share of gloom, too, during his long campaign to win the hand of Lady Elizabeth. Perhaps one of the main reasons why she had finally capitulated was that, though he seemed in many ways to be far from ideal husband material, he had demonstrated determination equal to her own.

They had met at a London ball during the summer of 1920. There is a story that their very first encounter had been many years before at a children's party, where Elizabeth is said to have presented the Prince with three glacé cherries from the top of her cake at tea; but if such a meeting did take place, Bertie had forgotten it when he was introduced to Cynthia Asquith's 'English rose' in full bloom.[16] A few months later he saw rather more of Elizabeth when he accompanied his sister, Princess Mary, on a visit to the Scottish home of Elizabeth's parents, the Earl and Countess of Strathmore, at Glamis Castle, not far from Dundee. The Princess and Lady Elizabeth had met through their work with the Girl Guides and had quickly become good friends. It was a friendship that provided the shy Bertie with an entrée to Elizabeth's life that might otherwise have been more difficult to arrange. The young woman showed nothing more than polite interest in the Prince who was her friend's brother and the Strathmore family was secure, self-contained and proud enough not to be overwhelmed by such royal contacts.

'It is delightful here,' Bertie wrote to his mother from Glamis that summer, adding that Elizabeth was very kind to him and the more I see of her, the more I like her.' Queen Mary was intrigued. She knew Elizabeth slightly because of her friendship with Princess Mary, but beyond the fact that she seemed charming, the Queen had no impression of how suitable she would be as a prospective royal bride. She wrote to her friend and lady-in-waiting Lady Airlie, whose home at Cortachy Castle was just a few miles from Glamis, and received a glowing report on Bertie's inamorata – Lady Airlie considered her 'a born homemaker'. When, in the spring of 1921, the Duke told his parents that he would propose marriage to Elizabeth, the King and Queen knew enough about her to offer their encouragement. 'You'll be a lucky fellow if she accepts you,' George V told his son. He was not lucky, for Elizabeth turned him down. According to the recollections of Lady Airlie, 'she was frankly doubtful, uncertain of her feelings, and afraid of the public life which would lie ahead of her as the King's daughter-in-law'.

Whether uncertainty or fear was the stronger emotion is hard to say. Bertie was not the most prepossessing of young men, even though, in the manner of suitors, he would undoubtedly have shown his best qualities to Elizabeth. He was small and slight, not particularly good-looking and so lacking in self-confidence as to be, in Lady Airlie's word, humble. Though he was reasonably articulate, the limitations of his mind were only too obvious and he lacked the sophistication of many of the other men Lady Elizabeth would have met on the social whirligig. It is generally agreed that he would not have been sexually assertive and by all accounts his view of morality was very different from that of the Prince of Wales and close to Elizabeth's own, but Elizabeth, with a strong character herself, needed a man who could demonstrate similar strength, and at that point she could not have been sure whether there were hidden resources beneath Bertie's somewhat colourless exterior. Lady Strathmore sympathised with her daughter. She liked the Duke of York, she said, but 'he is a man who will be made or marred by his wife'.[17]

Elizabeth's reluctance to become embroiled in the increasingly public life of the royal family was probably more to do with her age than with anything else. She was not yet twenty-one and her youth had been restricted by the war. She had just begun to enjoy some freedom and independence and would not have been prepared to sacrifice that for a life that, on the one hand, encompassed what was generally acknowledged to be a stuffy and over-formal Court and, on the other hand, promised to be circumscribed by an excess of publicity. Her family, its Scottish title dating back more than three centuries,[18] was accustomed to pleasing itself and jealous of its privacy, so the attention of press and public would have been a serious intrusion. Two years later, however, Elizabeth was quite happy to speak very frankly to reporters – much too freely, in the opinion of the Court – and to delight in the glamour attached to the business of becoming a member of the royal family. She would also throw herself with unprecedented enthusiasm and obvious enjoyment into an array of public engagements that would remain impressive for more than sixty years and, as she passed the age of eighty, cause increasing concern to her household. From her earliest years she had been a performer, always relied on by the family to be a star of home entertainments and house parties. Her talents and her personality found a true vocation in her royal role. Her hesitation in 1921 is more likely to have arisen from doubts about the man who wanted to be her husband than about the position he occupied. Bertie, prince or not, had to prove himself.

Naturally, he was disappointed at his rejection, but his naval career had shown, if nothing else, that once he made up his mind to do something he would overcome any obstacle. He remained in Elizabeth's orbit – visiting Glamis again in the late summer of 1921 for the start of the grouse season, for example – and tried his inhibited best to become part of the open and lively family existence that had made the girl he loved what she was. Nor was he entirely alone in pursuing his dream. The Queen, though wise or perhaps reserved enough not to interfere directly, arranged to spend part of the summer of 1921 with Lady Airlie at Cortachy and during her stay paid a visit to Glamis. She was greatly impressed. Lady Strathmore was seriously ill and Elizabeth was acting in loco parentis as housekeeper and hostess to the stream of summer guests the castle always attracted. Queen Mary reported to Lady Airlie that because Elizabeth had taken her mother's place so charmingly she was more than ever convinced that this was 'the one girl who could make Bertie happy'. The royal visit caused a great stir among the press, but the newspapers knew nothing of the Duke of York's passion for Lady Elizabeth and mistakenly assumed that the Queen was wife-hunting on behalf of her eldest son, who at the age of twenty-seven was considered to be the prime candidate for marriage.

Princess Mary also tried to help her brother's cause. Since Elizabeth was a close friend of the Princess, it was quite natural that she should be one of the eight bridesmaids at Mary's marriage to Viscount Lascelles at Westminster Abbey on February 28th, 1922, but the Princess took care to see that her friend sat next to the Duke of York at the wedding breakfast. Lady Airlie, too, did her part by acting as a sort of go-between. Bertie and Elizabeth visited her frequently but separately in London 'and each talked of the other'. It seems obvious that the royal family had made up its mind to recruit Elizabeth Bowes-Lyon to the firm and exerted whatever influence it could. Equally clear is that as Elizabeth got to know Bertie better, she saw in him qualities that were not immediately apparent and that could, with help, be developed. Not only that, but she fell in love with him, and as her feelings became more intense Lady Strathmore noticed that her daughter seemed 'really worried . . . torn between her longing to make Bertie happy and her reluctance to take on the responsibilities which this marriage must bring'.[19]

The Duke's obvious devotion finally convinced Elizabeth. On January 13th, 1923, in the woods near her family's Hertfordshire country house, St Paul's, Walden Bury, Bertie proposed marriage to her again and she accepted. That evening the Duke, who had fore-warned his parents, despatched a telegram to Sandringham saying simply: 'All right. Bertie.' Three days later the betrothal was officially announced in the Court Circular and preparations for the first great public royal wedding celebration began.

The Duke of York's marriage fulfilled all the aspects of consti-tutional monarchy that Walter Bagehot could have wished for. Not only did it rivet mankind, but it also served to underline the moral superiority that Bagehot claimed for royalty. Here were two young people entirely free from the excesses of what were considered to be the more anarchic and destructive members of their generation. Neither had attracted the merest hint of scandal or even disapproval and the public show of solemnity at the Abbey renewed the ideal of marriage as a sacrament at a time when church-going itself was declining, religious dogma was being seriously questioned and sexual behaviour was perceived as undergoing a change for the worse. The royal family was thus seen as a force for what were considered to be traditional values. The wedding performed another function, too, which might in part have accounted for its very public nature.

The country was in difficulties. An economic boom that had begun as the First World War ended had evaporated in 1921 to produce what *The Economist* called 'one of the worst years of depression since the industrial revolution'. After an upsurge of industrial unrest in 1921, the number of strikes had decreased dramatically but that fall had been accompanied by a steady rise in unemployment, until in 1923 one worker in six lacked a job. The prevailing mood was one of pessimism coupled with nostalgia for what were thought of as the good old days before the war. People had seen what appeared to be the future and did not much like the look of it. The royal wedding diverted attention away from all this, recalling in its splendour and ceremony the glories of the past and, because it acted as a focal point for national loyalty and rejoicing, concentrating minds for a time upon the more positive and hopeful aspects of the present. Profound changes were taking place but, in the best Bagehotian manner, the constitutional monarchy helped to disguise them.

But the wedding also did something to the monarchy itself. It established the Duke of York firmly as the King's favourite son and (though no one outside the family knew it) emphasised the widening gulf between George V and his heir apparent. *The Times* struck a slightly sour note when, in its wedding encomium, it pointed out that Britain awaited another, more important royal marriage, 'which would give a wife to the Heir to the Throne and, in the course of nature, a future Queen to England and the British people'. The newspaper could not, of course, be aware of a letter George V wrote to the Duke of York shortly after his marriage:

> You have always been so sensible & easy to work with & you have always been ready to listen to any advice & agree with my opinions about people & things, that I feel that we have always got on very well together (very different to dear David). I trust that this state of affairs will always remain the same between us & that you will come to me for advice whenever you want it.[20]

The implications are perfectly clear. The King and the Prince of Wales did not get on because 'dear David' did not agree with his father's opinions as to how he should dress, behave, enjoy himself – in short, how he should be a prince. 'You dress like a cad. You act like a cad. You are a cad,' the King was once overheard bawling at his eldest son.[21] It was Bertie in whom George V saw himself reflected and, as time went on, it was Bertie whom he would have wished to see as his heir. After the Abdication, the British people would largely share that view, believing that in George VI they could discern, albeit somewhat diminished, the qualities they had associated with his father.

Bertie certainly shared his father's devotion to obedience and duty combined with, as Asquith had noted in George V, a tendency towards hysteria; but as Duke of York and particularly as King, he was far more aware of the real world, far more adaptable to change and considerably more in touch with the human aspects of monarchy than his father had been. Had he been a more forceful character he might have left a considerable mark on his times. The opportunity was there, with both the monarchy and its subjects in disarray after the shock of the Abdication. But in his anxiety to do no wrong, George VI worked himself to death only to ensure that the monarchy would continue its slide towards irrelevance. One cannot blame him in any way for this. After the trauma of the Abdication he appears genuinely to have believed that the survival of the monarchy was in doubt and that the only way to save it was to pursue with even more vigour the complaisant line his father had taken. In this he was encouraged, if not intimidated, by successive governments which used the monarchy, as Lloyd George had done, to manipulate the loyalty of the people and thus to maintain the power of the mediocracy. 'They all seem to feel George VI is like his father – a safe King,' one of the residents of a Gloucestershire village told the Mass Observation Survey on coronation day, May 12th, 1937. The villagers did not approve of 'any irregularity in their royal family'.

The truth is that it was David who was in many ways more like his father. He inherited the stubbornness, the arrogance and the self-righteousness of George V. That was the main reason why the King and the Prince of Wales could never establish a warm or even a working relationship with each other. Neither recognised that there were ways of doing things other than their own. When George V was seriously ill in 1928, the Prince of Wales mused, 'To think that in a few days I may be King of England.' He was asked what he would do then. 'I shall do exactly what I like!' the Prince said.[22] What he lacked, and what George VI possessed, was the sense of responsibility and the natural caution – the desire to avoid confrontation – that had, at least in public and political terms, tempered the pig-headedness of George V (in his private life there was nothing to restrain him). It has been said that the English monarchy does not excite and therefore it does not inflame. In 1936 it did both, and that in the end was why Edward VIII had to go.

If there had been no Mrs Simpson, the crisis would have arisen in some other way, perhaps infinitely worse, because under Edward the royal firm would not in any case have carried on business as usual. He had little interest in the routine conduct of affairs, the laborious reading and signing of state papers without in any significant way being able to affect their portent, which has fallen to the lot of the sovereign and which, for some arcane reason (or perhaps merely from habit), is still regarded as essential to the business of government. He also held political views, which he was incautious enough to express, that were far to the right of the opinions held by most people in Britain, though shared in certain aristocratic circles. The worshipful company of the English monarchy has, naturally, never been the slightest bit socialistic in outlook – the present Queen is said to have exclaimed 'Oh bother!'[23] when, as Princess Elizabeth, she learned of the election of a Labour government in 1945 – but Edward VIII equated any advance of socialism in Britain with subservience to the Soviet Union and leaned away from 'too much slipshod democracy' and towards aspects of Italian and German fascism.[24] There can be no doubt that he would have been anything but a 'safe' king.

Yet for all his apparent faults, it was Edward VIII, rather than George V or George VI, who left an indelible mark on royal history in the twentieth century and who captured the imagination of people all over the world. He tried to break out of the mould constructed by his father, to introduce a radical style of monarchy that would place itself firmly at the centre of national life, almost an updated version of the Prince Consort's vision but without 'the divinity that doth hedge a king'. It would have been controversial, probably painful, yet it might have worked. Lloyd George understood, writing at the time of the Abdication: 'I cannot help thinking that the Govt. would not have dealt so brusquely with him had it not been for his popular sympathies.'[25] But Edward had neither the strength of purpose nor the intellectual equipment fully to commit himself to what he had started, and in any case his energies were diverted towards establishing his own emotional security, a piece of selfishness and a lack of patience that cost him dearly.

The monarchy paid a price, too. The policy of the family business was to be circumscribed by the Abdication for two generations. Stated quite simply, from 1936 onwards it was safety first.

12

'How Well Did
I Behave?'

When Prince Albert was created Duke of York in 1920, George V told him, 'I feel that this splendid old title will be safe in your hands, & that you will never do anything which could in any way tarnish it.'[1] But the new holder of the title was not to be allowed the years of leisure and privacy his father had enjoyed as Duke of York. It was widely believed that the royal 'firm' was operating in an unfavourable, if not a hostile, market and that it would have to both modernise its products and advertise them more effectively. As the Earl of Cromer pointed out, it seemed 'imperative that in the critical times with which the country is now faced no stone should be left unturned in the endeavour to consolidate the position of the Crown'.[2] Lord Esher expanded on the point in a letter to the King's private secretary, Lord Stamfordham, when he said 'a war-worn and hungry proletariat, endowed with a huge preponderance of voting power,' would require some justification for the monarchy and its cost. Risks would have to be taken, imagination employed and many 'old theories of constitutional kingship' would have to be abandoned.

It was not simply that the Bolshevik Revolution and the fall of the other great European dynasties had made the position of the British monarchy less secure and undermined the theory that while constitutional kingship was not absolutely necessary to the functioning of the state, it was somehow better than anything else. Nor was it merely that the entire class structure over which the monarchy presided was being challenged by the enfranchised workers, that a British Communist Party was founded in 1920 and that the Labour Party was advancing steadily to the point where, in 1924, it would be able to form a government. The entry of the United States into the First

World War had introduced a new player to the game of international power politics, a country rich in resources, manpower and energy which, as a result of its decisive intervention in the European war, was for the first time beginning to see itself as a world leader and guardian of peace and liberty. President Woodrow Wilson, supported by his skilful mobilisation of American public opinion, became the champion of a new kind of international co-operation that made the old imperial powers both suspicious and fearful for their future. Wilson's famous Fourteen Points, a plan for post-war reconstruction, included such revolutionary concepts as an end to secret treaties, free navigation of the oceans in war and peace, the removal of trade barriers, a colonial system placing greater emphasis on the interests of native populations and the creation of a League of Nations to prevent the outbreak of new wars. It was a blueprint for a world in which the nations that had once dominated could not be sure of their place.

Worse still from Britain's point of view was the moral leadership that Wilson established, not only among his own people but also in international terms. His offer to mediate among the European combatants to achieve what he called 'peace without victory' was brusquely rejected because it drew no distinction between the opposing sides, seeming to treat both as wayward children who lacked the maturity to resolve their differences without coming to blows. Here was a man who, simply on the basis of his mundane elective office, claimed the moral high ground Walter Bagehot had reserved for the mystical hereditary sovereign.

Republicanism of that sort suddenly began to look attractive and capable of inspiring the kind of loyalty the British had assumed could only reside in the person of a monarch. As Lord Esher said, 'It is a lesson for us. He has made the "fashion" of a republic.' If it was to survive the increasing surge of discontent both at home and throughout the Empire, the monarchy had to 'go one better'.

Thus all the forces available to the monarchy were deployed. Just nine months after the end of the war, the Prince of Wales was despatched on the first of his Empire tours and even before that his younger brother embarked on the effort to deflect the working classes away from the lure of the Red Flag. However noble the intentions of the royal family in these exercises might have been, their overall effect was to contain the pace of change. It is perfectly obvious that the peregrinations of the Prince of Wales were designed to protect the ties between Britain and its overseas Dominions, Colonies and dependencies, links from which – for both geopolitical and economic reasons – Britain undoubtedly derived the greatest benefit. Equally, Prince

Albert's foray into the industrial world was primarily a public relations exercise devised to counter the republican rhetoric of trade union leaders, Labour Party activists and other groups the mediocracy would classify as undesirable. Though there was a genuine feeling that the condition of the working classes should be improved, Robert Hyde, of the Industrial Welfare Society, gave a clue as to other underlying motives when he noted:

> I feel more than ever certain that if those tendencies which we all deplore are to be checked and guided aright it can only be accomplished if the goodwill which exists in every section of the community is enabled to unite and find expression. The Prince's contribution in this direction is of no small importance.

The spirit of paternalism that had passed from the old landed aristocracy into the hands of the Victorian middle classes was now taken up by the monarchy, its object remaining essentially the same: the maintenance of quiescent masses who generally accepted their lot because their masters knew what was best and were basically kind to them.

In 1928 the *Yorkshire Post* found a tactful way of describing this process when it said:

> It may not have been the case that industry was actually despised, but that members of the Royal House had not found a way to intimacy of touch with it. Even an appearance of neglect could hardly fail to have a bad effect upon the mentality of the worker. At heart he was a little ashamed of manual toil, which to him appeared to be lacking in dignity. Advancement in social status was associated in his mind with black-coated tasks.

All this was true, of course, except that industry actually *was* despised, and not only by the royal house. The trick was to convince the worker that no matter how bad the conditions, his was really a position of dignity. 'The wisest influences in the ranks of industry are nowadays turned to the cultivation of pride in work well done rather than to shame of an overall and grimy hands. And the Duke [of York] is taking part in this task ... He has thrown upon it the glamour and prestige of his position.'

So successful was this sort of tactic that even now, at the dawn of the long-delayed post-industrial age, some trade unions are among the most conservative elements in our society, defending the 'right' of their members to carry out physically demanding, often dirty and sometimes dangerous jobs rather than campaigning for the replacement of men by machines and fundamental improvements in education and training that would offer the real route to dignity.

The purity of the motives of the Duke of York in his industrial welfare work are not to be doubted, and curiously enough he attracted a certain amount of criticism from the more diehard advocates of capitalism, who believed that giving comforts to workers would not only make them soft but might also arouse in them ambitions beyond their station in life. These doughty defenders of privilege need not have worried, however. For one thing, the Duke's activities produced little in the way of real change in working conditions and, for another, he had a fine sense of the traditional distinction between master and man, as he made clear in his final speech to the Industrial Welfare Society as its president in 1935. Without a trace of irony he said:

> I feel there is a change of spirit abroad, recalling many of the best features of working life in the Middle Ages ... In days gone by, the master craftsman lodged his apprentices. Today the employer has to provide houses for his work-people. The master was responsible for feeding his hands. Today he instals a canteen. The ambition of the apprentice was to obtain his independence as a master craftsman. This is not always possible now, but by introducing promotion schemes and pension funds a firm is able to offer security in later life. The master watched over the health of his work-people. Today the employer develops medical services and sickness funds. In those far-off days the master was responsible for the discipline of his young people during their leisure. Today, that responsibility exists no longer, but the wise employer provides, where there is need, facilities for recreation. I may even suggest that the modern works council is in direct following of the close domestic tie which existed between the master and the apprentice which, if the story-books are to be believed, often led to a happy marriage with the employer's daughter ... Much that was best in the relations that existed in the age of the craft and the guild is being re-established today.

There was more than a little of the story-book quality about his assessment of the prevailing conditions – not to mention his rosy view of the Middle Ages – but in any case the mediocracy could look with confidence towards a royal industrial relations expert whose recipe for harmony was based on some of the ingredients of feudal society.

Yet in spite of the limited nature of his actual achievements and his imperfect understanding of the differences between what the leaders of the labour movement sought and what the employers were prepared to concede, the Duke of York did win friends and influence people among the working classes through his obvious and sincere interest in the field of royal endeavour allotted to him and the fact that the interest was maintained over many years. With his presidency of the Industrial Welfare Society and the Duke of York's Camps, he clearly felt that he was doing some good. If visiting factories was not the most glamorous of pursuits, he at least showed no sign of boredom and the absence of formality allowed both him and the people he met to be at ease. He could have been forgiven, however, for casting the occasional envious glance in the direction of his elder brother, who was to be found in Canada, the United States, Australia, New Zealand, India, Ceylon, Malaya, Singapore, Hong Kong, Japan and many other places in between. The Duke of York's ill health during his naval service had limited his professional travels, and now all he got were tours of some of the least prepossessing regions of Britain, combined with the duties of playing host to visiting potentates and various trips to the Balkans to attend weddings and christenings among royal relatives there. It is hardly surprising that shortly after his own wedding, he began to explore the prospects of foreign travel for himself and his bride.

With a perversity that was typical of him, George V resisted his second son's attempts (supported by the then Prime Minister, Stanley Baldwin) to join the royal diplomatic corps by visiting one of the Dominions: it was too soon after the Duke's marriage, the King said with an unarguable lack of logic, and the young couple needed time to settle down. He did allow a visit to East Africa, which was as much holiday as official duty and for which the Duke was profusely grateful, but he chose to wait until the Yorks had a good reason for wishing to stay at home, in the shape of the infant Princess Elizabeth, before sending them on a world tour. Perhaps it was some sort of test, for George V and Queen Mary had themselves, as Duke and Duchess of York, been parted from their fourth child, Prince Henry, shortly after his birth, and for precisely the same purpose – to open the Commonwealth Parliament in Australia. Since that visit in 1901, the Australians had built a new capital, Canberra, and required royal inauguration of the first session of their parliament in its new home in the spring of 1927. This was the task George V selected for the Duke of York, with a new baby, with no experience of such an important occasion, with a dread of public speaking and with a stammer that had so far resisted all attempts to cure it. The Duke and the Australian prime minister, who had requested a royal visit, were equally dismayed at the prospect.

If there was some idea in the King's mind of validating his son's fitness to bear the 'splendid old title' that had once been his own, to establish that here was a chip off the old block in contrast to the increasingly difficult Prince of Wales, then the Duke of York must have made him very proud. As he had done in the past and would continue to do even more in the future, Bertie proved that no matter how awesome the obstacles in his path, he had the capacity to overcome them (though at what cost to himself would only be obvious much later).

The first problem was his speech impediment, and in this the stimulus of the Australian visit was crucial. The complete failure of various forms of therapy had left the Duke disheartened and inclined to believe that he would stammer for the rest of his life. He had, it is true, made a number of public speeches, but they had been an ordeal for both himself and his listeners. In 1925, for instance, he had rehearsed incessantly a speech to mark the opening of the second year of the British Empire Exhibition at Wembley, an occasion that was to be broadcast on the wireless. He said afterwards that it had gone better than he had expected, but there were some nerve-racking pauses and a woman, now in her eighties, who listened to the broadcast, recalls that it was 'an agonising experience to hear him'.[3] The following year, the Duke's attention was drawn to the success of a new specialist practising in London, an Australian (appropriately enough) named Lionel Logue. Of course, therapists had been recommended many times before, and the Duke saw no reason why this one should be any different from the rest, but his wife cajoled him into one last attempt to rid himself of the stammer and in October 1926 he had his first consultation with Logue.

When he arrived, according to Logue, the Duke showed every sign of a man bowed by continual difficulty in speaking, but he left two hours later with a new sense of optimism. Logue had no magic formula, but his strong personality seemed to convince his patients that they could triumph over their impediments and, once this psychological breakthrough had been made, that he could teach physical methods of controlling and eventually banishing the problem. The Duke visited him almost every day for more than two months, frequently accompanied by the Duchess, who became thoroughly familiar with Logue's programme of breathing exercises so that she could help her husband to practise them at home. Within a few weeks, an improvement was apparent and the Duke told his father that, although twenty-four years of speaking in the wrong way could not be set right in a month, he was confident that in time he would be able to talk without stammering. The nervous excitability that underpinned his speech difficulties would never be conquered, but at least its most obvious outward sign virtually disappeared. Even in the presence of the King, when he had habitually stammered even more than usual, the Duke learned how to control himself and for the first time in his life was able to express his thoughts with cogency and fluency. 'I can make him listen & I don't have to repeat everything over again,' he noted with satisfaction.[4] The King for his part, with the irritation of Bertie's stammer removed, began to take more notice of his second son and seemed rather surprised to find him, as he told Queen Mary, 'very sensible' – and, of course, 'very different to D[avid]'.[5]

It was therefore with new hope and confidence that the Duke of York set sail in January 1927 for what had grown into a world tour, taking in as well as Australia such places as Jamaica, Panama, Fiji, New Zealand, Mauritius, Malta and Gibraltar. He was keenly aware of his father's expectations and, in spite of the fact that he was now thirty, an element of the dutiful schoolboy could still be discerned when he wrote to the King: 'This is the first time you have sent me on a mission concerning the Empire, & I can assure you that I will do my very best to make it the success we all hope for.' But if he remained inhibited by a certain immaturity and lack of self-esteem, he now had a wife who suffered from no such handicaps and who in a little more than three years had learned more about the business of popular royalty than her royal-born husband had absorbed in his lifetime. During the early part of the tour, Bertie leaned heavily on Elizabeth, watching her accept gracefully, naturally and unaffectedly the adulation of the people of New Zealand, where the couple were to spend a month. On one occasion, as their train pulled into a station, the Duke jumped on to the platform and, without anyone noticing, joined the wildly excited crowd running alongside the still moving carriage where Elizabeth stood smiling and waving.

Yet while the supportive and educative qualities of such a wife should not be underestimated, neither should they be allowed to detract from the essence of the Duke's own inner resources. Lady Strathmore was probably right when she said that Bertie would be made or marred by his wife, but given that he found what was for him the perfect mate in Elizabeth, there remained through the very nature of his position many things that he simply had to do for himself. The Duchess could soothe his nerves, encourage the growth of his confidence and remind him to do his breathing exercises, but even with her by his side, when he stood up to make a speech he was effectively on his own – and within hours of arriving in New Zealand he had made three public addresses all of which he completed without a hitch. Within two weeks he was literally on his own when Elizabeth (as she had done on her honeymoon and would continue to do throughout her life at times of excessive strain) became ill, being confined to bed with tonsillitis. Once more crisis brought out the best in Bertie and he completed the remaining ten days of the tour in an atmosphere of success that was entirely his. The Governor-General of New Zealand, Sir Charles Fergusson, reported to the King that everybody appreciated the way in which the Duke of York 'threw himself heart and soul into the work of the tour. He never spared himself and went out of his way to give the utmost pleasure to everyone.'

The visit to Australia, which lasted two months, was if anything even more of a triumph. The Duke revelled in his new freedom of speech and, whether it was addressing veterans of the First World War on ANZAC Day (dedicated to the Australian and New Zealand Army Corps) or officiating at the ceremonial opening of the new Parliament building in Canberra, he performed faultlessly. Much public attention was naturally focused on the Duchess, who played up to the crowds in the now familiar way that has helped to make her, as Queen Mother, the most popular royal figure of all time, but the proudly democratic Australians were also captivated by the Duke's lack of formality and 'side'. The Governor-General wrote: 'To say that they instantly made the best possible impression seems almost an impertinence . . .' To which the Governor of South Australia, Sir Tom Bridges, added:

> His Royal Highness has touched people profoundly by his youth, his simplicity and natural bearing, while the Duchess has had a tremendous ovation and leaves us with the responsibility of having a continent in love with her. The visit has done untold good and has certainly put back the clock of disunion and disloyalty 25 years as far as this State is concerned.

That last point was a telling one, underlining the importance of the tour. The First World War and the wide publicity given to President Wilson's vision of a new world order had exacerbated nationalist sentiments in various parts of the Empire, notably India and Burma, while in Britain itself the feeling had grown that changes were necessary both to prevent the decline of British influence and to reduce the cost of maintaining it. At the same time, the Dominions – Australia, New Zealand, Canada and South Africa – already enjoying domestic independence, began to seek the same distance from the British government in international affairs, wishing to pursue foreign policies on their own accounts. For these and other reasons, the imperial conference of 1926 redefined the status of Britain's overseas territories as, in the words of Arthur Balfour, the Lord President of the Council, 'autonomous communities within the British Empire, equal in status, in no way subordinate one to another, though united by a common allegiance to the Crown, and freely associated as members of the British Commonwealth of Nations'. The idea of free association was all very fine, but it left the way open for secession and placed a heavy responsibility on the British monarchy as the sole, symbolic unifying factor.

Little trouble was to be expected from the Dominions, all of which were white-dominated and fundamentally Anglo-Saxon, notwithstanding the Boers of South Africa and the French-Canadians of Quebec. It was necessary, however, for the monarchy regularly to renew the bonds of allegiance, not only to forestall any spread of republican sentiment that might arise in the now even more independent Dominions but also to maintain 'family links' in countries that had racial connections with the motherland. The Duke of York was in no doubt that his visit to Australia was designed, in part at least, to further 'good feeling between the different portions of the Anglo-Saxon race'. The theory appears to have been that the new Commonwealth 'club', constituted formally by the Statute of Westminster in 1931, should be administered by a sort of membership committee consisting of Britain and the Dominions, presumably to ensure that ideas born of European culture continued to dominate and that the non-white members were kept firmly in their place. The titular presidency of this club would in time become one of the last truly essential constitutional functions of the monarchy – simply because of its extra-parliamentary position, which dissociated it from any particular government or party – until even that declined as the Commonwealth ceased to be a potent force and became instead little more than a talking-shop.

It is somewhat ironic that, whereas in the 1920s the Commonwealth was reconstructed as part of a European ideal, it would later be seen as a bar to the 'Europeanisation' of Britain. The Statute of Westminster was part of a strategy devised by the old colonial powers remaining after the First World War – Britain, France and Belgium – to retain traditional spheres of influence and to exclude the new international forces thrown up by the war, the United States and the Soviet Union. It was partly for this reason that the rise of Mussolini in Italy and even, at the beginning, the advent of Hitler in Germany would receive what amounted to a cautious welcome from many so-called statesmen. A strong Europe was a dominant Europe, the continent that claimed to have created the civilised world and would still run it, and Britain, with its empire intact under the guise of the Commonwealth, would remain strongest of all. Thirty years later, the concept of what it meant to be 'a good European' had changed dramatically with a severance of old colonial links and the emergence of the European Community in an attempt to counter the political strength of the new imperialists in Washington and Moscow and the economic power concentrated round the rim of the Pacific Basin. Many in Britain then began to see the Commonwealth and its reminders of the imperial past as something of an embarrassment.

The Duke of York, naturally, evinced no such doubts when he arrived back in England after his 1927 tour. 'I return a thorough optimist,' he said:

> When one has travelled over the vast extent of the Empire; when one has witnessed what our fathers have accomplished; when one has seen how the grit and creative purpose of our kinsmen have triumphed over the most tremendous difficulties, it is impossible to despair of the future of the British race. The same qualities which carried us successfully through the war will, I am convinced, so long as we remain united as members of one family, enable us to surmount all difficulties that may beset us, however formidable or however perplexing. If we hold together we shall win through.

A few years later, he would discover that the Empire would find other uses to which it might put its grit and creative purpose, uses that would conflict with and sometimes directly oppose the interests of the mother country.

His journey had awakened in him a desire to learn more about the affairs and politics of the Empire, especially the Dominions, but he encountered an immovable object of obduracy in the person of his father. George V seemed at times almost to take a pride in ignorance, and he certainly ensured that his sons remained ignorant of matters of state. It may be argued that in the case of the Duke of York, the King saw no reason to involve him in the political business of the monarchy since such things were unlikely ever to fall within the Duke's sphere of responsibility, yet that was hardly a good excuse for denying Bertie the opportunity to pursue something in which he had himself expressed interest. The Duke was required to make speeches which touched on current affairs, but how could he be expected to do so with conviction when he was prevented from learning anything more about them than the average newspaper reader? Furthermore, the bar also applied to the Prince of Wales, whose responsibility it would certainly be to conduct the routine affairs of state that were deemed to be so central to the existence of the sovereign. He was not permitted to be present at audiences with government officials or to see the ministerial communications that arrived so regularly in the despatch boxes over which the King pored each day. The most the King would allow – and then only grudgingly and under pressure – was for his sons to have sight of certain telegrams that passed through the Foreign Office and the special office dealing with the Dominions that had been established in the aftermath of the 1926 imperial conference.

The motives behind this quite irrational behaviour on the part of George V remain obscure. It has been argued that no useful purpose would have been served by allowing the Princes access to state papers that contained confidential information and that indeed such a course might have been harmful, bearing in mind that only the sovereign has the right to attempt to exert any influence over ministers. In support of this argument it has been claimed that while it might have been detrimental to the future of Edward VII to have been refused access to the despatch boxes when he was Prince of Wales, the world had so far changed by the 1920s that, in the words of Frances Donaldson, 'both foreign and internal politics were too complex and too highly charged to be treated as a training ground for kings'.[6] But were such matters more complex and highly charged than they had been between 1901 and 1910, when the First World War was in the making and when Edward VII encouraged his heir to peruse state papers and gave instructions that the then Prince of Wales should see all important diplomatic telegrams? Even if they were, that is surely an argument for allowing greater access to a future king rather than less.

It has also been suggested that state papers are so boring that nobody but a serious student of politics would wish to read them. Yet George V, when *he* was Prince of Wales, studied documents submitted to the King by ministers, and he could hardly be accused of showing any academic interest in political matters.

Such justifications for the behaviour of George V on this point seem spurious. Even if Bagehot's contentious definition of the duties of the constitutional monarch is accepted (as it generally appears to have been), the ideal of the wise and experienced public servant on the throne can hardly be achieved if the person required to perform that role is obliged to begin with a blank page, most often in middle life.

What does seem clear is that the King who was credited as being the first great constitutional monarch had no real idea of what was happening to the monarchy under his stewardship. He knew that he was subject to a great deal more work and a great many more public appearances than, say, his father had been, and he was prevailed upon to involve the rest of the royal family in the huge public relations exercise that the ruling mediocracy believed was an essential part of maintaining national unity and stability, but what all this meant to the future of the dynasty it was obviously beyond his intellectual powers to comprehend. Even if they were not particularly bright, two well-educated and well-informed princes, such as David and Bertie might have been, could have proved to be an enormous asset to the monarchy in uncertain and rapidly changing times. The contribution of George V was to make absolutely sure that this was one asset his royal house did not possess, and the monarchy has been paying the price for it ever since.

Some of the King's doubts about the Prince of Wales were, it must be admitted, well-founded. In spite of his tremendous popularity, there were reservations about his suitability as heir to the throne. These were expressed quite freely in the overseas press, particularly after one of the Prince's visits, and even in Britain there were carefully couched warning noises. As early as 1926, in a book entitled *Certain People of Importance*, the Prince was criticised in the following terms:

> All that has been said about the Prince's charm of manner, friendliness of spirit, and good nature is gladly and universally recognised, but behind this ground for satisfaction is a widespread and growing doubt as to whether other qualities no less necessary to the great place he holds and the still greater place which he will in all probability one day hold, are being cultivated with equal zeal.
>
> There is a feeling that there is a lack of seriousness which, excusable and even natural to healthy youth, is disquieting in the mature man. This implies no disapproval of the Prince's love of sport, of fun and of innocent amusement. Nor does it imply a demand that the heir to the throne should have intellectual tastes that nature has not endowed him with. Least of all does it imply that the qualities of a snob would be a desirable exchange for the Prince's high spirits and companionable temper. But it does mean that the public would be relieved to read a little less . . . about the jazz drum and the banjo side of the Prince's life . . .[7]

The writer, A. G. Gardiner, was right in saying that the Prince of Wales played hard, but at this stage of his life he also demonstrated an enormous capacity for hard work. One of his main difficulties was that his father made no attempt to direct the Prince's energies beyond constantly exhorting him to do what he was told and criticising him with equal constancy when he carried out his duties in ways that did not meet with the King's approval. As for the immaturity to which Gardiner referred, history would show that there were ways in which David never did quite grow up, but equally it would reveal that George V the naval officer had failed to absorb at least one aspect of the theory of command, i.e. that one way of dealing with the irresponsibility of a subordinate is actually to give him responsibility.

Gardiner went on:

> The Prince's future is not a personal affair, but an affair of the nation and of the world. His apprenticeship in life is over. His career is henceforth in his own hands. He commands an affection and goodwill on the part of the nation that cannot be overstated and that a man of his genuine kindliness of heart must wish to repay. He can repay it by emulating the admirable example which is offered by his parents of how a modern democratic throne should be filled.

On the last point he was absolutely wrong. If George V had had any conception of the true meaning of constitutional monarchy in the twentieth century, he would have seen to it that his sons, and especially the heir to the throne, were better prepared. His was entirely a bad example to be offered to the Prince of Wales and he made it worse by deliberately preventing his sons from gaining the experience they would need to take the monarchy beyond the end of his reign. Perhaps he simply did not trust them (he definitely did not trust David, who, to be fair, had given him reason not to); or perhaps it was his own immature, insecure personality that made him so insistent on the rightness of his views and so resistant to any conflicting opinion. As I have already said, the King had told the Duke of York: 'You have always been ready to listen to any advice & to agree with my opinions about people & things' and 'You have done what I asked you to do . . . you have behaved very well . . .' Nothing else was tolerated. Nothing else was offered.

By these standards the Prince of Wales did not behave very well. Sometimes he did not behave well by any standards. Like his father, he was prone to delivering himself of hasty judgments and voicing loud criticism, and he often did so within earshot of people who should not have heard (without the benefit of having Queen Mary to prod him into silence). During a visit to Japan in 1922, he loudly told the British ambassador that he thought the governors of Hong Kong and Singapore were 'fossilised clerks who ought to be kept in a cupboard in Whitehall' and that while Lord Reading was clever he was not the right man to be Viceroy of India (which the Prince had just visited).[8] 'Unfortunately', the ambassador reported to Lord Curzon, the Foreign Secretary, 'this conversation took place when many Japanese were close by and . . . I had to remind him that our neighbours understood English.'

Unlike his father, the Prince was not prepared to submit with dignity and assumed interest to the duller and more routine aspects of royal duties. When something caught his imagination, he could be bold and tireless in pursuing it, but after his world travelling came to an end in the late 1920s it was noticed that he often seemed bored and wearied by the increasing number of petty and mundane ceremonies he was required to attend. At other times he seemed to pay scant regard to the organisers of such functions by failing to adhere to the schedules provided for him and by keeping waiting the people who had turned out to see him. It has been reported that in 1927 one of his own staff became so concerned at the Prince's lack of responsibility that he wrote to the Prime Minister, Baldwin, to ask him to exert whatever pressure he could to improve matters. Some people recall that in the midst of a political crisis, Baldwin so far lost his sense of priorities as to leave Downing Street to accompany the Prince and his brother, Prince George, on a visit to Canada so that he might have time alone with the future king in order to use his influence to good effect.[9]

Whether or not this version of events is correct, Baldwin did go to Canada and for his pains was treated to a blatant example of the Prince's careless attitude in some things. Arriving at the Governor-General's residence for dinner, Baldwin and his wife and their hosts were kept waiting long past the appointed time because the Prince of Wales and his brother had decided to play a game of squash.[10]

On the other hand, as I have already indicated, the Prince endeared himself to many people with his unwearying concern for the unemployed during the years of misery that followed the stock market crash of 1929. According to the National Council of Social Service, of which he was patron,

The Prince knew more than some of his ministers about the problems of the derelict valleys and the silent mills. Nor were the endless ceremonies, openings and presentations accomplished without personal cost in nervous strain and sheer fatigue. On one occasion, worn out with day-long travelling in Wales and the pain of helpless sympathy, the Prince slept exhausted on the shoulder of Sir Percy Watkins, chief NCSS officer for Wales, waking dutifully each time Sir Percy warned him that the car was approaching groups of children waiting to see their Prince.[11]

His initiatives did much to mobilise both funds and volunteers to provide welfare services to the unemployed and their families and in 1932 he made his feelings clear when he addressed a social services rally at the Albert Hall in London: 'I am thinking now of each member of the unemployed population as a single, separate personality, beset by depression, labouring under a sense of frustration and futility.' Many of those who worked with him in this field testify to the fact that one of his greatest contributions was to display a deeply personal concern that both inspired others to help and evoked a warm response from those in need of such help.

What Lloyd George described as the Prince's popular sympathies led some rather less sympathetic souls to link him to left-wing politics, but it was undoubtedly his flirtation with the political right that caused most concern. Not long before his death, George V felt obliged to give his son a telling-off because he had suggested to the war veterans of the British Legion that they should send a delegation to Hitler's Germany. This, the King told him, was directly contrary to the policy of the British government and, in any case, the heir to the throne should not go about expressing political opinions in public. The Prince was unrepentant. A few days later he delivered a public rebuke to the London County Council for banning weapons practice, even with dummy rifles, among the cadet corps of the schools under its control. These, said the Prince, were the misguided views of pacifist cranks.

More privately, he told the German ambassador in London that he definitely intended to be present at the 1936 Olympic Games in Berlin, while Nazi intelligence sources in London reported him as expressing warmth towards Germany and loathing for the policies of the French government. Perhaps even more disturbingly, Hitler's Ministry of Foreign Affairs was informed by its agents that the Prince of Wales had indicated he would feel bound to intervene, as king, if the British government pursued policies conflicting with his own views as to the best way of serving Britain's interests. Those views, the Ministry was led to believe, would be likely to include some sort of alliance with Germany in an effort to preserve the peace of Europe.[12]

Clearly this was a prince of Quixotic proportions, and one the mediocracy would have been hard put to it to control for its own ends. But just out of view was his Dulcinea, the lady-love who would deflect and ultimately provide an excuse for dethroning him. And meanwhile, the Duke and Duchess of York, with their engaging ways and their two pretty daughters, were living useful and respectable lives at Number 145 Piccadilly.

13

Edward the Unacceptable

The blow, when it came, was sudden and unexpected, and to the mass of the British people all the more shocking for that. Yet the very speed with which 'The King's Matter' was concluded allowed no time for a real constitutional crisis to develop, for factions to be formed or for Edward VIII to appeal directly to the people for support and thus to break the convention that the sovereign acts only upon the advice of ministers. The fact that the final, public phase of the Abdication lasted just ten days suggests either that the King colluded in his own downfall or that the mediocracy had decided, for the reasons I have mentioned, that he must be despatched as rapidly as possible. There was probably an element of both those things in the proceedings. Certainly as far as Stanley Baldwin was concerned, the King had only three choices: to abandon any idea of marrying Mrs Simpson; to marry her against the advice of his ministers, who would then be compelled to resign; or to render himself free to marry her by abdicating. So far as is known, this was the extent of the constitutional position placed before the King, who himself only dimly comprehended constitutional law in the very broadest terms and in any case, as his letters of the time show, was in an emotional state more appropriate to a lovesick teenager than to a middle-aged monarch.

But Baldwin's summary of the King's options was heavily weighted towards the conventional Establishment view of how matters stood, and in that there was more than a little self-interest and perhaps a suggestion that abdication might be best for all concerned. As Edward VIII said to his friend and legal adviser, Walter Monckton, in the autumn of 1936, 'I am beginning to wonder whether I really am the kind of king they want. Am I not a bit too independent? As you know, my make-up is very different from that of my father. I believe they would prefer someone more like him.'[1]

The marital activities of the monarchy are regulated by the Royal Marriages Act of 1772. This provides that members of the royal family under the age of twenty-five must obtain the permission of the sovereign before they may contract a lawful marriage. Over the age of twenty-five, they may marry without the sovereign's consent by giving the Privy Council twelve months' notice of their intention to marry, 'except that both Houses of Parliament shall declare their disapprobation thereto'. There is no mention of any regulation governing the marriage of the sovereign. Thus the position of Edward VIII, though extremely delicate, was not quite as clear-cut as it might have seemed. Baldwin must have known that when he outlined those three choices to the King and, as both a shrewd politician and an experienced parliamentarian, he must also have known that, while in general terms the monarch was bound to accept the advice of his ministers, it was highly questionable that the scope of such advice should extend to determining whom he might marry. After all, if the prime minister has the power to decide, allegedly in the national interest, the suitability or otherwise of the sovereign's prospective consort, could he not also dictate, on the same ground, how many children the couple should have, or where and how they should be educated?

There is a popular legend that under what is known as the British constitution, the monarch would have no option but to sign his or her own death warrant if advised to do so by the prime minister on the basis of a parliamentary decision. This is plainly nonsensical and no monarch of sound mind would accept it. Yet it is the logical conclusion of the course that Baldwin and his colleagues followed in deciding that the King should not marry Mrs Simpson and therefore advising him, without any supporting vote in Parliament, not to do so. There was no precedent for their action and it might well be argued that it was entirely unconstitutional. Indeed, the Royal Marriages Act, specifically designed to prevent the sovereign's children from making 'unsuitable' matches, had not addressed the position of an unmarried sovereign. The nearest precedent was that of Queen Victoria, who had simply declared to the Privy Council, in person, her intention to marry Prince Albert and had then left it to Parliament to decide on the details of the Prince's status, finances, household and so on.

In the circumstances, a wiser and more cool-headed king than Edward VIII might have followed Queen Victoria's example, made a declaration to the Privy Council and awaited the outcome of votes in the Commons and the Lords. That such votes would have gone against the King is by no means certain. It must not be forgotten that the people whom the Members of Parliament presumed to represent knew nothing of their King's plight until just ten days before his abdication and therefore had little opportunity to make their views known to MPs. Winston Churchill was certainly prepared to support the King at least in so far as postponing any decision until the level of public support for him could be ascertained, and Churchill was backed by large and influential sections of the popular press. On December 4th Churchill told the King that 'whatever else might happen ... the hereditary principle must not be left to the mercy of politicians trimming their doctrines "to the varying hour",' and the following day he issued a long public statement in which he implied that Baldwin and the Cabinet were railroading the King:

> There is no question of any conflict between the King and Parliament. Parliament has not been consulted in any way, nor allowed to express any opinion ... The question is whether the King is to abdicate upon the advice of the ministers of the day. No such advice has ever before been tendered to a sovereign in parliamentary times ... No ministry has the authority to advise the abdication of a sovereign. Only the most serious parliamentary processes could even raise the issue in a decisive force ... The Cabinet has no right to prejudge such a question without having previously ascertained at the very least the will of Parliament ...

On December 7th the *Daily Mirror*, with the words 'God Save the King' above its masthead, devoted the whole of its front page to an appeal that the people should be allowed to have their say. Its banner headline was: '45,000,000 DEMAND TO KNOW – AND THEN THEY WILL JUDGE!' What those millions demanded to know, according to the paper, were the answers to five questions:

1. What, justly stated and in detail, is the King's request to his Cabinet?
2. What steps were taken to ascertain the views of the people of the Dominions and to explain to them the issues involved in this great crisis?
3. Is the British Cabinet prepared to approach the Governments of the Dominions with a frank request that they should reconsider their verdict against the King and consent to a marriage even if it involved new legislation?
4. Is the British Cabinet sure beyond doubt that the abdication of

Edward VIII would not strike a terrible blow at the greatest institution in the world – our monarchy – and thereby cause irreparable harm?
5. Would the abdication of our King mean that he would be EXILED not only from Great Britain but also from every country in his Empire?

There were spontaneous demonstrations of support for the King outside Buckingham Palace, in Downing Street and near his weekend retreat, Fort Belvedere, at Sunningdale in Berkshire, on the fringe of Windsor Great Park. Some people drove through the streets of London shouting 'God Save the King from Baldwin', while others carried banners threatening revolution if he were forced to abdicate, or daubed pro-Edward slogans on walls. The newspapers indicated that a strong body of opinion, especially among young people, was for the King marrying whomever he wished to, while others said they did not care whom he married. Of course, there was strong opposition, too. Harold Nicolson noted in his diary on December 3rd that 'I do not find people angry with Mrs Simpson, but I do find a deep and enraged fury against the King himself. In eight months he has destroyed the great structure of popularity which he had raised.' The Labour MP Hugh Dalton reported bitterness in South Wales, where the King had recently made his 'Something will be done' promise to unemployed miners. As for the ruling mediocracy, Churchill was howled down in the House of Commons two days after issuing his statement. 'You won't be satisfied until you've broken him, will you?' he yelled at Baldwin before marching out of the Chamber.

Clearly the nation was seriously divided, but division is as much a manifestation of democracy as consensus and demands even more the exercise of democratic rights. This did not happen, partly because the government did not wish it but equally because the King was not aware of the true constitutional position, or else he was not prepared to take the risk that a majority of the people might be against him, or, possibly, he saw marriage to Mrs Simpson and his consequent abdication as a way of escaping from the straitjacket that had been wrapped round the monarchy during his father's reign. It has often been suggested that he never wanted to be king, and his expressed doubts referred to earlier about his royal position indicate that he must have had at least some mixed feelings. But his behaviour after his accession tends to support the belief that he would have been content to remain on the throne – so long as he did so on his own, somewhat idiosyncratic and politically naïve terms. From the middle of October 1936 to the beginning of December, when the matter finally became public, the King negotiated with Baldwin and sought other ways of exerting influence that would persuade the government to agree that he could marry Mrs Simpson *and* remain on the throne. It may well be that his decision to abdicate was reached only after it became obvious to him, first, that the government would never agree and, second, to what degree the sovereign was a prisoner of the politicians. He had suggested a morganatic marriage, by which his wife would not become his queen and any children would be denied succession rights. He had asked to be allowed to broadcast to the people so that he might put his case directly. Both these ideas had been rejected. Considering his character, it is more than likely that he balked at the prospect of being a king who would never be allowed to express his opinions or exercise his will.

There is evidence to suggest that he had made up his mind to marry Mrs Simpson as early as 1934, though he told no one, not even her (she was, of course, still married).[2] Had he wished to avoid the burdens of kingship, he could have begun to make arrangements then: it would have been painful and difficult, given the attitudes of his father, but no more so than the position in which he found himself two years later. He was open, even provocative, in his relationship with Mrs Simpson – his friends, his family and the government were well aware of it. Nobody said anything. He presented Mrs Simpson to his parents in November 1934 at a reception celebrating the marriage of the Duke of Kent, ushering her towards Queen Mary with the words, 'I want to introduce a great friend of mine.' The King was furious afterwards, exclaiming, 'That woman in my own house!' and suggesting that she had been smuggled into Buckingham Palace.[3] But nothing was said to David. In 1936 Mrs Simpson was taken to visit the Duke and Duchess of York, appeared in the Court Circular, played hostess at Balmoral and accompanied Edward VIII on a very public holiday cruise that whipped the American and European press into a frenzy of speculation and anticipation. In Britain, the silence was deafening. The implications seem obvious. David flaunted Mrs Simpson before his family in an attempt to get a reaction, but when none came he lacked the courage to raise himself with his father the question of the relationship and his feelings about how it might develop. He knew that George V would not sanction marriage in the circumstances, and the Queen's views on divorce were well-known. But at the same time, since no paternal reproof was forthcoming (and complaints from the King were common enough on other matters), the Prince took it that this part of his life was considered to be his own business. He began to believe that, freed from parental restraint and as King himself, he would actually 'get away with it' and be able to marry Mrs Simpson. That impression was fostered by the fact that after his accession, there was no mention in the British press of his holiday cruise with Mrs Simpson that had caused such excitement elsewhere.

Since everyone else was keeping quiet, the new King saw no point in announcing his plans. Early in 1936 he asked Ernest Simpson to allow Wallis to divorce him in an undefended action; he even found a solicitor for her who would make sure that the matter would be handled discreetly and, as often happened in those days, away from the London courts. But since the divorce petition would not be heard until later in the year, and because even after a decree nisi was granted it would be a further six months before Mrs Simpson was free to marry again, there was nothing to be gained by disclosing at that stage his desire to be her third husband, though he did introduce her to Baldwin in May 1936, telling Wallis that 'Sooner or later my Prime Minister must meet my future wife.'[4]

Two months earlier Baldwin had received hints of the King's intentions from a third party, but he had refused to take the rumour seriously. As far as he was concerned, there was no possibility of the King marrying Mrs Simpson. The King was the titular head of the Church of England and as such would be crowned in solemn religious ceremony in the spring of 1937 – and while divorce might be legal, it was not recognised by the Church of England. It was not until October 20th, a week before Mrs Simpson's divorce petition was to be heard in Ipswich, that Baldwin took the warning signs seriously enough to attempt an intervention.

The Prime Minister was prompted partly by a great number of letters that had arrived at Downing Street from British expatriates shocked and confused by stories of 'the King's romance' they had read in foreign newspapers and magazines. Baldwin discovered that both Anthony Eden, the Foreign Secretary, and Geoffrey Dawson, the editor of *The Times*, had received similar letters. The other spur to action was a request from the King's own private secretary, Major Alexander Hardinge, that the Prime Minister should approach the King and ask him to use his influence to have Mrs Simpson's divorce proceedings stopped. Hardinge feared (wrongly, as it happened) that the court case would provoke a torrent of publicity in the British press, which he assumed was chafing under the traditional 'gentleman's agreement' that details of the sovereign's private life should not be reported, while its colleagues in the United States (even the staid *New York Times*) and other parts of the world were having a high time publishing all the information they could discover or invent about the King's romance with Mrs Simpson.

An interesting question arises here. It will be remembered that almost ten years earlier, another member of the household had apparently asked Baldwin to intercede with the then Prince of Wales in an effort to modify his behaviour. Now Major Hardinge had taken it upon himself to intervene, to ask – without the prompting or presumably even the knowledge of his master – that ministerial advice should be offered to the King. Where, then, does the courtier's duty lie? Is he bound to act in accordance with the wishes of the sovereign he serves, or is his obligation to the institution of monarchy, regardless of who occupies the throne, so that should he perceive a danger to the institution he must if necessary take steps that are contrary to what the sovereign sees as being in the interests of himself and the monarchy? It may be argued that in this case the interests of the King and the monarchy were not the same, but this is a nice point and begs the question of who makes the decision. Hardinge would no doubt have argued that he felt he was acting in the best interests of the King himself, but Edward VIII would not have accepted that (indeed, he did not accept it) and the private secretary's right or competence to judge is open to serious challenge. Moreover, if the sovereign is the monarchy personified, it is surely difficult to justify a conflict of interest between the two. Edward VIII was to say later: 'I have found it impossible to carry the heavy burden of responsibility and discharge my duties as King as I would wish to do without the help and support of the woman I love.'[5] If we accept that statement at face value (and in the light of his behaviour there is no reason not to), we must assume that he believed it was best for him as King, and consequently for the monarchy, that he should marry the woman of his choice. Hardinge, however, seems to have taken the view that the King could *only* carry his burden of responsibility and discharge his duties *without* the woman he loved. History was never given the opportunity to see who was right, but if Hardinge's actions in attempting to force the King and Mrs Simpson apart are considered to have been justified, then the sovereign becomes even more of a puppet than the conventional restraints of the constitution make him. The fact that the private secretary, having gained Baldwin's support, then explained to the King the motive behind the Prime Minister's request for an audience does not materially alter the case.

The Prime Minister, of course, was in a completely different position. As the head of an elected government accountable to Parliament, he was required to balance the personal needs of the King against the good of the monarchical system and the wider national interest. Though Baldwin has sometimes been portrayed as the villain of the Abdication, there is plenty of evidence that he was sympathetic to the King's position.

[215]

However, he was absolutely convinced that Wallis Simpson would be unacceptable to the British people as a member of the royal family – however that might be arranged, for instance, morganatically – and that marriage to her would render Edward VIII unacceptable. Again, history was denied the chance to judge, but in retrospect it may be significant that the British people, or at least their elected representatives, were not allowed to express their preference.

Suppose that Baldwin had been wrong, that a majority of MPs had supported in a vote the idea of the King's marrying Mrs Simpson. Even if it had been done in such a way as not to imperil the continued existence of the government, it would have been a serious blow, strengthening the position of the sovereign in relation to his ministers and upsetting the constitutional balance so deliberately constructed by the mediocracy. The chances are that in such circumstances we should have had a very different kind of monarchy today. Suppose, on the other hand, that the Prime Minister was right and that Parliament voted overwhelmingly against the King's marriage to Mrs Simpson. Given the firmness of Edward's intentions, he would have had no choice but to abdicate, but in that case it would have been seen that he had been forced to do so by Parliament. Either way, it is likely that there would have been strong opposition, if only for self-serving political reasons – and more so if the parliamentary majority for or against the marriage had been a narrow one. There might have been protests and civil disorder. The mediocracy could not take the risk. The one thing it has always sought to avoid – at least since the Civil War that first established the political potency of the bourgeoisie – is the unleashing of forces that might ultimately demonstrate to the people the power they themselves possess to control the course of events.

Baldwin was alive to the dangers. At his audience with the King at Fort Belvedere on October 20th, 1936, when he discussed Mrs Simpson for the first time with Edward, the Prime Minister voiced concern that 'there might be sides taken and factions grow up in this country in a matter where no factions ought to exist'. The importance of the integrity of the crown, Baldwin said after showing the King some of the letters he had received from abroad, was greater than it had ever been, but the respect that had developed for the monarchy might easily be lost in the face of the sort of criticism to which it was being exposed, and if that happened he doubted whether such respect could be restored. Then, with sophistry that is almost admirable, he said the decline in standards of behaviour since the war meant that people now expected higher standards of their King, that they would tolerate a good deal more in private life than was tolerable in a public personage. There, perfectly summarised, is the basic English hypocrisy that has dogged the monarchy for more than half a century. The royal family is expected to show humanity, but not to be human; to be close to the people, but not to be like them; to be aware of and sympathise with all sorts of problems, but not to share them; to symbolise the spirit of the nation, but not to reflect it.

Edward VIII was many things, but he was not that sort of hypocrite. 'I know there is nothing kingly about me,' he told Baldwin, 'but I have tried to mix with the people and make them think I was one of them.' It was this last that the mediocracy was afraid of. Mixing with the people was one thing: it made them feel important, bringing down the pride of sovereignty to the level of petty life, as Bagehot had expressed it. But if the people began to think of the sovereign as one of them, who could tell where it might lead? It was and is essential to the maintenance of the bourgeois state existing in this country that at all but the most superficial levels the mediocratic establishment acts as both a bridge and a buffer between the monarch and the people. Without that distance, one of two things could happen. First, the people might identify so closely with the sovereign that he or she would become the moving spirit of the state. (It is interesting to note that at various times during the past few years the Duke of Edinburgh and the Queen Mother have emerged from public opinion surveys as most favoured candidates for the presidency were Britain to become a republic.) Second, the people might feel the sovereign so identified with them that they claimed for themselves the traditional moral, social and dignified functions associated with the monarchy. In either case the power of the mediocracy would be eroded as its sense of separateness and superiority disappeared.

It is therefore vital to the mediocracy that the occupant of the throne embodies the accepted qualities and standards of the educated, liberal-leaning, respectable bourgeoisie. Edward VIII did not represent those values. That mattered little while he could be contained and controlled and indulge in his unconventional ways in private, but his infatuation with Mrs Simpson and, even more, his determination to marry the woman threatened to explode the myth once and for all. Hence the action of Hardinge in approaching the Prime Minister. The private secretary believed that Mrs Simpson was the reason for the King's gradual loss of interest in affairs of state, the key to his cavalier way with government papers, the underlying cause of his eccentric and inconsiderate behaviour towards his staff and friends, the spur to his growing arrogance and isolation and even the motivation for his apparently pro-Nazi sympathies. (Wallis was thought to have close contacts in Germany and to be a conduit for Hitler's ambassador in London, Ribbentrop; as a result she, and therefore the King, were under surveillance by the security services for much of the time.)[6] Hence, too, Baldwin's attempt to prevent Mrs Simpson from obtaining a divorce and thereby having the freedom to become even closer to the King.

'Can you not have this coming divorce put off?' the Prime Minister asked at his audience on October 20th.

At this point, the fatal weakness in the character of Edward VIII became apparent. He knew he was going to marry Mrs Simpson when she was free; he had virtually organised her divorce (he and Ernest Simpson were said to have come to blows at one stage);[7] but he lacked the nerve to tell Baldwin the truth. 'That is the lady's private business,' the King said disingenuously. 'I have no right to interfere with the affairs of an individual. It would be wrong were I to attempt to influence Mrs Simpson just because she happens to be a friend of the King.' What he hoped to gain from this deception is not clear. Perhaps he thought that in time people would come to accept Mrs Simpson, as some of his more 'enlightened' friends seemed to be doing, or perhaps, as I have already suggested, he felt it would be unseemly to reveal his true feelings for a woman who was still somebody else's wife. On the other hand, maybe he was simply afraid. 'You and I must settle this matter together,' he told Baldwin as the Prime Minister left. 'I will not have anyone interfering.' As it turned out, that would suit the mediocracy. Whether it suited the King, and indeed the monarchy, is open to doubt. It is clear, however, that the King, for all his reliance on his personal popularity, was at that time as reluctant as the Prime Minister to place the matter squarely before the people.

But there were others who were determined to interfere. One of them was Alexander Hardinge and another was Geoffrey Dawson. On October 26th, the day before the hearing of Mrs Simpson's divorce petition, Dawson visited Hardinge at Buckingham Palace and handed him a copy of what the editor described as 'the best letter I'd had about opinion and comment in USA on HM and Mrs S'. By Dawson's own account he had received 'a spate of correspondence and cuttings from America' which had been growing since the end of September. This particular letter was special, however, so special that Dawson also gave a copy to Baldwin. It ran to nine typewritten pages and it began:

The present letter, touching as it does on what is in England a forbidden theme, is one that in the nature of things I cannot expect to see published in *The Times*, and it may therefore be a rather futile gesture to write it; and yet it involves issues of such great moment that I cannot help unburdening myself by bringing certain facts, for whatever the effort may be worth, to the attention of the organ that is traditionally regarded as the chief moulder of British public opinion ... I might begin by saying that I am a Briton who has been resident in the United States for several years. I have had a deep and continuous interest in everything bearing upon Anglo-American relations, and I have always sought, by depicting British public life in its most favourable aspects, to contribute in my small way to the furtherance of friendly sentiments between the two countries based on mutual respect. It has therefore been with great regret, and even with dismay, that I have watched in the course of the last few months the development of a situation that gravely lowers British prestige in American eyes. I refer to the poisonous publicity attending the King's friendship with Mrs Simpson ...

Dawson must have been delighted as he read this. Here was a correspondent who had apparently learned the craft of writing from the editorial columns of *The Times*. His letter had just the right measured, sonorous tones of a leader Dawson might have written himself. And there was more. The writer discoursed on the advantages of a democratic monarchy over a democratic republic and pointed out that when presided over by a highly respected individual, 'a monarchy ... can be of incalculable behoof in creating the intangible elements that make for international good feeling'. George V, he went on, had been admired by many and respected by all Americans; such, however, was not the case with King Edward VIII. The letter then summarised American press coverage of the King's relationship with Mrs Simpson and drew the conclusion that such publicity was seriously damaging to Anglo-American relations. This was an odd, inverted thought. One of the chief reasons why the American press and public were so excited by what the humorist H. L. Mencken called 'the greatest story since the Crucifixion' was that Mrs Simpson was an American and it was thrilling to consider the possibility that she might become Queen of England. Surely an American consort for the British sovereign would have been a powerful fillip to Anglo-American relations – except, that is, in the mind of a respectable, God-fearing Englishman who apparently thought Americans ignorant and vulgar and signed himself 'Britannicus in Partibus Infidelium'.

Editors generally treat with scant regard such pompous, sanctimonious and contentious letters, and with deep suspicion when they are pseudonymous. Indeed, the signature on this missive adds to its mystery. It has been claimed that the letter bore the name and address of a man in East Orange, New Jersey, but if that is true and the writer, as he said, did not expect *The Times* to publish it, then what was the need for a nom de plume?[8] But Dawson took this letter very seriously. Perhaps it was because of its last paragraph:

It may be presumptuous, and even impertinent, for a person far removed from the centre of events to suggest a remedy; but I cannot refrain from saying that nothing would please me more than to hear that Edward VIII had abdicated his rights in favour of the Heir Presumptive, who I am confident would be prepared to carry on in the sterling tradition established by his father. In my view it would be well to have such a change take place while it is still a matter of individuals, and before the disquiet has progressed to the point of calling in question the institution of monarchy itself.

This was the first suggestion of abdication and Dawson delivered it to Buckingham Palace and to Downing Street just twenty-four hours before Mrs Simpson was to obtain her divorce. Hardinge said he would place the letter before the King; Baldwin said it would be very useful and 'might strengthen his hand in dealing with the King'.

The following day Dawson saw the Prime Minister of Canada, Mackenzie King, who had just returned from an audience at the Palace. Dawson was disturbed to learn that, far from apprising the King of any Canadian anxiety about Mrs Simpson, the Prime Minister had 'made matters rather worse by discoursing on the King's popularity in the Dominions. This impression of personal popularity was in fact becoming a very dangerous factor in the situation . . .' Indeed it was. What if it should prove that the masses actually supported the King? Baldwin and Edward had a row when the Prime Minister suggested that the King's popularity was not sufficient to withstand the strain of his intended marriage. The editor of *The Times* began to write a leading article on the subject for use when the time was right.

Dawson had laid down the first marker for the direction the King might take with the 'Britannicus' letter. The second signpost came from Hardinge. After consulting with Dawson – who, apparently by coincidence, had been at Buckingham Palace – the private secretary sent his own missive to the King on Friday, November 13th:

The Prime Minister and senior members of the Government are meeting today to discuss what action should be taken to deal with the serious situation which is developing. As Your Majesty no doubt knows, the resignation of the Government – an eventuality which can by no means be excluded – would result in Your Majesty having to find someone else capable of forming a government which would receive the support of the present House of Commons. I have reason to know that, in view of the feeling prevalent among members of the House of Commons of all parties, this is hardly within the bounds of possibility. The only alternative remaining is a dissolution and a General Election, in which Your Majesty's personal affairs would be a chief issue – and I cannot help feeling that even those who would sympathise with Your Majesty as an individual would deeply resent the damage which would inevitably be done to the Crown, the corner-stone on which the whole Empire rests.

This time, Hardinge had acted perfectly properly in warning the King of what might be about to happen. Where he failed was in allowing his own prejudices to colour his advice. His summary of the King's position at that time was, like Baldwin's, not entirely complete. Furthermore, Hardinge's personal intervention infuriated the King, who suspected his private secretary of disloyalty and thereafter refused to let him act as an intermediary. It was then that Edward called in Walter Monckton and began to wonder whether he should go. Hardinge's mind was working in the same direction, for after reading the 'Britannicus' letter he had called on the heir presumptive, the Duke of York, to warn him that his sudden elevation to the throne was a distinct possibility.

On November 13th the accession of the Duke became an absolute certainty. The King summoned Baldwin to the Palace that evening and announced his definite intention to marry Mrs Simpson as soon as her divorce decree became absolute. He wished to remain on the throne, but if the government opposed his marriage he was prepared to abdicate. The Prime Minister later told the House of Commons that he had replied: 'Sir, this is most grievous news and it is impossible for me to make any comment on it today.' He made little comment to Dawson when he saw him at the House later that night, but the editor came away with the impression, as he rather smugly noted in his diary, 'that everything was now tending towards abdication'. After the proposal of Britannicus, it could hardly have come as a bolt from the blue to either man. The King, meanwhile, was telling Queen Mary and his sister, the Princess Royal, what he had told Baldwin. He later recalled that with his mother, 'the word "duty" fell between us'.[9] That, of course, was not all: Queen Mary could not possibly imagine her son's feelings or why he was prepared to renounce his throne in such a humiliating fashion for the sake of a woman who was not only a double-divorcee but also an American and, in Queen Mary's own word, a social 'adventuress'. (This last aspect offended many other people, and not only those of noble birth, who sneered at Mrs Simpson's relatively humble background and alleged lack of social poise. Even her hairdresser was heard to comment to another of his clients: 'She may be going to be Queen of England, but she walks like a cow!')[10]

Next day Queen Mary sent her son a note saying that, as his mother, she sympathised with his position and hoped he was making a wise decision for his future. As Queen Dowager, however, she had no sympathy for him at all. She had earlier asked the Cabinet to do something that would turn the King from his folly and now Baldwin – 'Well, Prime Minister,' she said, holding his hand tightly when he visited her at Marlborough House, 'this is a pretty kettle of fish!' – asked her to make one last effort to influence her son. The best that she could do was to plead the unfairness of it all for poor Bertie – who, as his family knew, was weak, in uncertain health, with a tendency to drink too much to steady his nerves, and who was now to be thrust into kingship without any sort of training.[11] None of this had much effect on the King. Bertie had his wife and his family to help see him through, and in any case he would be all right because he was more like his father, more like the sort of king 'they' seemed to want.

Still no final decision was taken and still the newspapers remained silent. Baldwin had discussed 'the value of publicity' with Dawson and had decided that silence was the best course. The King had just made a highly successful visit to South Wales and any criticism of him in the press might inflame public opinion against the government. When, on November 27th, the Cabinet met in emergency session to discuss the King's proposal of a morganatic marriage, the newspapers were told that the meeting was to do with Spain, where the civil war was raging. Dawson knew better and prided himself on an editorial he had written three days earlier in which, though it had nothing to do with the King, he had referred pointedly to the need to keep the crown and its representatives free from public scandal and above public reproach and ridicule. 'The significance', he noted with satisfaction, 'was not lost on the American press or indeed on many people in England.'

But on December 2nd, quite by accident, the first public hint of royal scandal appeared. The previous day, the Bishop of Bradford, Dr A. W. F. Blunt, made a speech to his diocesan conference in which he touched upon the religious significance of the coming coronation. The King, he said, would need God's grace if he was to do his duty faithfully.

> We hope that he is aware of his need. Some of us wish that he gave more positive signs of his awareness . . . His personal views

and opinions are his own, and as an individual he has the right of us all to be the keeper of his own private conscience. But in his public capacity at his Coronation he stands for the English people's idea of kingship. It has for long centuries been, and I hope still is, an essential part of the idea that the King needs the grace of God for his office . . .

That the Bishop chose that moment to make that speech appears to have been purely accidental. He knew Geoffrey Dawson and had actually been with him on October 31st at a church ceremony in Yorkshire, but maintained that 'the King's Matter' was never discussed, that he had never even heard the name of Mrs Simpson, and that his criticisms concerned the sporadic nature of the King's attendance at church. What he said, however, was enough for the *Yorkshire Post* to assume that the Bishop did know what was going on and to become the first British newspaper to break the story by revealing some of what had been said in the American press.

The Duke and Duchess of York were in Scotland that day. Bertie had been told by his brother on November 17th of his intention to marry Mrs Simpson and had subsequently had a number of meetings with Baldwin, Queen Mary and the King. After seeing David on November 24th he had written to the King's assistant private secretary, Sir Godfrey Thomas, saying: 'If the worst happens & I have to take over, you can be assured that I will do my best to clear up the inevitable mess, if the whole fabric does not crumble under the shock and strain of it all.' As always, he was ready to rise to the challenge. Dawson decided to give him a little help. 'The Duke and Duchess of York are coming back from Scotland tomorrow,' he told one of his staff on the day the crisis finally became public. 'Will you write a little piece congratulating them on the success of their visit and welcoming them home? I think this is the opportunity . . . to try and spread the loyalty of our readers a little more widely over the royal family.'[12]

Nine days later the Duke of York was King George VI and the former King Edward VIII was on his way to exile and to Wallis Simpson, who had gone to France to escape the furore. Geoffrey Dawson, the man who had been instrumental in first raising the possibility of abdication as a way out of the crisis, wrote of Stanley Baldwin in his leader of December 11th:

He may have his defects as a party leader or as an administrator; but in handling a great national problem, in which the life and standards of millions of his fellow-countrymen are concerned, he has no comparable rival either among his own colleagues or in any other walk of public life. Every one of us may well be grateful that he remained in office with sufficient vigour to withstand the terrific strain of the last two months, and to have emerged without dividing the nation, which for a day or two was ripe for schism . . . or conceding a jot of his own principles, which he knew at heart to be those of the people behind him.

What that meant, of course, was that the mediocracy had won and in so doing had suffered barely a scratch. A king who was not prepared merely to act as a cipher for middle-class morality and a symbol of mediocratic domination had been despatched quickly, cleanly and, it seemed, of his own volition. The monarchy was back in its box, the Establishment took the credit and the ex-King, together with Mrs Simpson, would for the rest of their lives carry the blame for trying to destroy the illusions that kept Britain going.

Nevertheless, the Abdication broadcast of 'His Royal Highness Prince Edward', as the BBC announced it, moved many people to tears. But Dawson was not one of them. After listening to the words delivered through the wireless in those odd, almost braying tones, the editor of *The Times* was heard to say that the thoughts expressed were worthy of the average bank clerk.[13]

When it was all over, Dawson wrote:

> Of course there were . . . difficult moments in the week when the public crisis lasted . . . when all the forces of evil were bent on getting together in a 'King's Party'. But Providence undoubtedly watches over this country – most notably in this present case by deciding that Lloyd George should have sailed for the West Indies and (with a certain touch of humour) by appointing a guileless provincial bishop to open the floodgates without a notion of what he was doing.

He could afford to be complacent. The new King George VI told his Accession Council on Saturday, December 12th: 'Now that the duties of sovereignty have fallen upon me I declare to you my adherence to the strict principles of constitutional government.' That was what 'they' wanted to hear. After all, hadn't they invented the principles of constitutional government and now retained the right to adapt them as they saw fit?

14

A Clash
of Symbols

'What will endear him to his people', Stanley Baldwin said of King George VI a few days after his accession, 'is that more than any of his brothers he resembles in character and mind his father.' Sadly, that was true – the sadness being in the essentially backward-looking image of monarchy such a statement represented. The abdication of Edward VIII had been a unique event, yet its implications had been barely considered. It had been seen as a national 'problem' that had to be 'solved' and its potential as a political crisis had been wildly exaggerated, so that few people, if any, paused to wonder whether there were any lessons in it for the future of the constitutional monarchy. All that could be seen were the perceived dangers of the situation, the negative aspects, and the overriding impulse seems to have been to restore 'normality' as rapidly as possible. Thus the opportunity for the monarchy to move in new directions as a result of the challenge to normality raised by the Abdication was lost. Instead, external control over the institution as it stood was tightened and the monarchy itself became ever more defensive. Some people thought that made it more democratic.

The fact is that at no time during the Abdication crisis, before and after it became public, was the institution of the monarchy in any danger. Edward VIII understood that, telling Walter Monckton that if he was not the kind of king the Establishment wanted 'Well there is my brother Bertie.'[1] Baldwin knew it, Dawson knew it and even 'Britannicus' knew it. Some political extremists tried to make use of the situation for their own ends – Sir Oswald Mosley's Blackshirts, for example, staged marches in support of Edward – but they received little support. During the Commons debate on the Abdication Bill, the chairman of the Independent Labour Party, Jimmy Maxton, an engaging left-winger of republican conviction, declared: 'We are doing a wrong and foolish thing if, as a House, we do not seize the opportunity with which circumstances have presented us of establishing in our land a completely democratic form of government which does away with old monarchical institutions and the hereditary principle.' When he moved an amendment to that effect he was one of only five MPs who voted to avail themselves of the opportunity.

Commentators and royal biographers have tended to place unwarranted emphasis on Maxton's amendment, claiming that its very existence demonstrated a legacy of bitterness and division left by the Abdication that George VI was called upon to heal. The King himself felt that somehow he had to atone for the action of his brother, telling Baldwin he hoped 'that time will be allowed to me to make amends for what has happened'. Yet there is absolutely no evidence of any serious schism in the nation: for one thing, the manoeuvrings of Baldwin and Dawson (with, it must be said, the collusion of Edward) had left too little time for the formation of factions, and for another, with Christmas just two weeks away people had what seemed to them more important things on their minds. They had lost a king, certainly, but now they had a replacement, so life could go on just as it had before. Nor was there any sense of moral outrage – quite the opposite, in fact. Having banished a monarch allegedly because he wanted to marry a divorced woman, the country promptly accepted a significant liberalisation of the divorce laws which, among other things, reduced the period between the decrees nisi and absolute to six weeks. Hypocrisy was triumphant.

A. J. P. Taylor wrote:

> The abdication left its principal mark in the world of practical politics. By toppling Edward VIII off his throne, Baldwin restored his own moral prestige ... Reluctantly, it seemed, he had voiced the conscience of the nation ... His opponents were routed, Churchill most of all ... Baldwin survived in glory until the coronation. Then he departed with adulation from the public scene.[2]

There was, it is true, some residual affection for Edward VIII. He had, after all, been exceptionally popular as both Prince of Wales and King. But by the day of the coronation, May 12th, 1937, he was generally nothing more than a fond memory. What was important to most people was not the identity of the King but the simple fact that there was one. An observer for the Mass Observation Movement reported from South Devon:

The most noteworthy element in the speeches was that voiced with great sincerity by the local baker – that we had gone through a unique experience that day and it reminded us that there was no country on earth where there was so much happiness, prosperity and freedom as in England, and that we should show 'the foreigner' in no unmistakable terms that we valued our happiness and freedom ... There was no mention of the King and it seemed as if all mention of him was kept in the background as far as possible ...[3]

The very ease of the transition and the consequent speed with which the popularity of Edward VIII evaporated should have given the monarchy and its advisers pause for thought, but George VI was convinced that he had to work ceaselessly to retain the loyalty and regard of the people. In the weeks following the coronation, he and the Queen travelled hither and thither about the country, not forgetting Scotland and Northern Ireland, and after the traditional summer holiday at Balmoral, they plunged once more into the round of visits and public appearances. The mediocracy looked on approvingly and Cosmo Lang, who had first prompted George V to go out and meet his subjects and was by this time Archbishop of Canterbury, felt moved to write to his monarch:

It falls to me as much I suppose as to any public man to meet all sorts and conditions of people, from Cabinet Ministers to 'the man in the street', and to learn what is in their minds. I find everywhere the same testimony to the impression which Your Majesty and the Queen have made upon Your people during the first year of Your reign. At first the feeling was one of sympathy and hope. It has now become a feeling of admiration and confidence ... I *know* this to be true. I have noticed, all who have in any way come into contact with Your Majesty have noticed, how remarkably and steadily, if I may presume to say so, You have *grown* into Your high office. Thus the courage with which a year ago You accepted the burden of a great responsibility suddenly thrust upon You, has been amply vindicated.[4]

A year before there had been doubts among the Establishment as to whether the heir presumptive had either the character or the stamina to carry the great burden of responsibility suddenly thrust upon him, and he himself had exclaimed, 'I'm quite unprepared for it.' Yet within hours of the Abdication he had demonstrated a healthy instinct for survival. Since there were no known precedents in this situation, none of the constitutional experts had any idea what to do about the ex-King, but George VI – as firmly resolved as his father had been to do anything that was necessary to protect the monarchy – quickly found a way to disarm his elder brother as a potential source of opposition. When Sir Claud Schuster, permanent secretary to the Lord Chancellor, called on the King to discuss the problem on December 11th, the day of the Abdication broadcast, he admitted that he did not know precisely what Edward VIII had given up in renouncing his throne. 'I think it would be quite a good thing to find out,' George VI told him tartly. The King was, however, quite clear on one point: his brother could not revert to being simply a private citizen, as Schuster seemed to suggest, and he could not be known henceforth simply as Mr Edward Windsor. 'He was born the son of a duke,' the King said. 'That makes him Lord Edward Windsor anyhow. If he ever comes back to this country, he can stand and be elected to the House of Commons. Would you like that?'

Schuster said he would not like that. Very well, said the King. 'As Duke of Windsor he can sit and vote in the House of Lords. Would you like that?' Again Schuster said no. 'Well, if he becomes a royal duke he cannot speak or vote in the House of Lords . . .'[5] So it was settled. The ex-King would become His Royal Highness the Duke of Windsor, and George VI told him so that evening as he prepared to leave the country. Edward was pleased, believing that in an impossible situation he had behaved with dignity and that in return dignity was being accorded to him. George VI was not that generous, however. On May 28th, 1937, after the coronation and shortly before Edward's marriage to Wallis, the *London Gazette* published the following announcement:

> The King has been pleased by Letters Patent under the Great Seal of the Realm . . . to declare that the Duke of Windsor shall, notwithstanding his Instrument of Abdication executed on the 10th day of December, 1936, and His Majesty's Declaration of Abdication Act, 1936, whereby effect was given to the said instrument, be entitled to hold and enjoy for himself only the title style or attribute of Royal Highness so however that his wife and descendants if any shall not hold the said style or attribute.

The neutralisation of the former monarch was complete. There would be no more royal highnesses on his side of the family, no possible future claimants to the throne in a disputed succession, and – in what appeared to be a peculiarly vindictive stroke – there was to be no recognition of the 'adventuress' who had tempted a king away from the paths of righteousness. 'What a damnable wedding present!' the Duke exclaimed when he received his brother's letter informing him of the decision.[6] It was the royal revenge for humiliation and is generally thought to have been at the instigation of Queen Mary and Queen Elizabeth, both of whom detested Mrs Simpson and would have refused to receive her if she had returned to England with her new husband but would not have been justified in doing so had she acquired the same rank as the Duke of Windsor. But this does less than justice to George VI. He knew what he was doing, and his reasons were not entirely personal.

In his letter to Edward the King said his decision to restrict the use of 'royal highness' was not intended as an insult to the Duke's future wife, and he was probably sincere about that. In a sense, Mrs Simpson no longer mattered. More important was the behaviour of the Duke himself. He had taken to telephoning his brother regularly to offer advice on the conduct of affairs, counsel which, not unexpectedly, often differed from that the King was given by the government. George VI, who had grown up in awe of his elder brother and had always compared himself unfavourably with him, found this extremely difficult to deal with, and may well have suspected that while Edward had relieved himself of actual responsibility he was keen to pursue his own, sometimes dangerous, political ideas from the sidelines. There was also the possibility that once the scandal of the Abdication had dissipated, the Duke of Windsor might wish to take a more active role in matters of state by returning home. Aware of his brother's pride and stubbornness, George VI saw a way of preventing all this, and it worked. 'No HRH for Wallis, no home-coming for me,' the Duke said. That, and his subsequent determination to keep the Duke out of Britain during the Second World War, seems the most likely reason why George VI took a step that many would regard as of doubtful legality, since it denied a wife's traditional right to assume the same status as her husband. At the very least it demonstrated the operation of a double standard: refused a morganatic marriage as King, on the ground that it had no place in English law or practice, the Duke was forced into one after his abdication.

With his brother in safe and impotent exile, the King undertook the for him daunting task of learning about the governance of his country. 'I've never even seen a state paper,' he complained to Lord Mountbatten during the last days before his accession. What for him and the monarchy was a serious disadvantage was viewed with equanimity by the mediocracy, which intended to take no more notice of the opinions of its new King than it had of those of his father. The politicians were not looking for any royal initiatives but merely for a sovereign who would give legitimacy to their rule and would do what was constitutionally required of him, which was in effect nothing. He performed creditably, with the continuing help of Lionel Logue, at his first State Opening of Parliament in October 1937, and thereafter dutifully encouraged the new Prime Minister, Neville Chamberlain, in the policy of appeasement he pursued with Nazi Germany, Fascist Italy and the autocracy of Japan. It was not long before he discovered, as his father had done, that his constitutional punctiliousness resulted in his being taken for granted.

Only when he read the Sunday papers on February 20th, 1938, did the King discover that at a Cabinet meeting the day before the Foreign Secretary, Anthony Eden, had threatened to resign from the government because of his opposition towards Chamberlain's appeasement policy, specifically in relation to Italy. His private secretary, the same Alexander Hardinge who had served Edward VIII, wrote to the Cabinet Secretary:

> His Majesty feels, with, in my humble opinion, much justification, that he should not have been left to learn from an unreliable Press of the difficult situation in which his Government was placed as a result of the Cabinet Meeting on Saturday night. I feel sure that you will agree that some arrangement should be devised to enable The King to receive immediate intimation of any serious developments of this nature . . .

In fact there had been nothing to tell the King, since Eden had not actually resigned and had not even made absolutely clear his intention to do so. That came only on the Sunday evening. Nevertheless, the King insisted that the Cabinet Secretary be responsible for ensuring that he should in future be informed of any impending crisis, and subsequently that he should receive the same draft of Cabinet minutes that the Prime Minister received, before they were officially circulated. His father would no doubt have approved.

While the King was digging himself ever more deeply, and rather fruitlessly, into affairs of state upon which he was to have little influence, the Queen was busy making royalty fashionable. Many people felt, among those who ever thought about such things, that the Abdication had robbed the monarchy of much of its former awesome glamour and certainly of its pre-eminence in social terms. During the reign of George VI this faded glory was to be replaced by an appeal more direct and down-to-earth, and for that new style Queen Elizabeth was most responsible. Before the Abdication it had been their placid domesticity that had established the Duke and Duchess of York in the public imagination and now, as Queen, Elizabeth became a sort of national guardian of the virtues of home and hearth.

She visited community housing projects and took a personal interest in their development, discussing problems directly with the tenants. She became involved with schemes to help the unemployed, talking particularly to the wives of men without jobs and encouraging them to believe that, with the worst of the Depression over, there would soon be an improvement in standards of living. She played a prominent and active role in that most domestically inclined of organisations, the National Federation of Women's Institutes. Most of all, however, she made royalty and its patronage much more accessible to ordinary people than it had ever been before. Those who met her were impressed and charmed by the individual attention she gave them, not only asking pertinent questions but also listening to the replies, and by her ability to relate her own royal life to the everyday concerns of people who had never been within a hundred miles of a palace. At a ceremonial occasion in the city of Norwich, the Queen lightened the proceedings and demonstrated her homeliness by requesting the recipe for home-made mead with which prominent local churchmen and civic luminaries were drinking toasts. It was all a very long way from the ineluctable regality of Queen Mary, but in terms of monarchy for the masses it was a resounding success. This small, rather dumpy woman with the twinkling blue eyes and infectious smile was quickly adopted as the all-embracing mother-figure and national mascot she has remained ever since.

But the Queen also brought hope to people of more refined inclinations. The monarchy had for years been seen as a bastion of Philistinism, lacking both interest in and appreciation of the arts, so when in March 1938 the Queen purchased two paintings by living British artists – Wilson Steer's impressionistic landscape entitled *Chepstow* and Augustus John's portrait of George Bernard Shaw – the reaction among those of cultured sensibilities seemed to indicate that the earth had moved. Geoffrey Dawson's *The Times* surpassed itself in fulsome, fawning rhetoric:

> Even among those with a genuine taste for painting, the number with the courage of their purely artistic preferences, irrespective of fashion subject, is limited. The majority want a lead. It has been given from a quarter above the social uncertainties and complications upon

which a reputation for artistic judgment usually depends. The Queen has decided that contemporary British painting matters – irrespective of subject represented or fashionable tendency in style; and it will be against all experience if, according to their means, the decision is not followed by many of her subjects – to the raising of the general level of taste, and to the practical advantage of good artists, who, less from insensibility to their merits than from uncertainty about the importance of art in life, are apt to be neglected.

Here was social leadership of a kind never envisaged in the days of George V. The pretentious middle classes, agonising over the possibility of committing a social gaffe by hanging the 'wrong' pictures on their drawing-room walls, need fear no longer. What *The Times* was actually saying was the reverse of what it pretended to say, advising that its readers should display their impeccable taste by buying not paintings that they liked, but the sort of pictures that the Queen favoured. The newspaper failed to comment on the fact that the Queen also bought a wood engraving of White Lodge, Richmond Park, for the simple reason that it was a faithful representation of the grace-and-favour residence she and Bertie had occupied immediately after their marriage – a lack of publicity that was no doubt bad news for wood engravers, who might have made their fortunes with studies of the stately homes of suburbia.

The attitude of *The Times*, though perhaps foolish, was nevertheless significant in that it presaged a view of royalty that in later years would send impressionable young girls scurrying to their hairdressers for the 'Princess Di' look or to the nearest department store for a 'Fergie' bow. The acquisition of the so-called common touch has not brought unmixed blessings to the monarchy. Familiarity may not always breed contempt, but it has an unhappy knack of obscuring true value. H. G. Wells drew attention to this as long ago as 1939. Writing in the *News Chronicle*, he declared of the King and Queen: 'These young people are, I believe, a very charming couple, constantly smiling and bowing, but they mean absolutely nothing to the problems of today.' By making such efforts to, as they saw it, 'restore' the popular image of the monarchy allegedly damaged by the Abdication, King George VI and Queen Elizabeth in fact accelerated a process of demystification which has now reached the point where people are asking if the royal family is 'royal' enough. Like George V, they did not see the difference between bringing the pride of sovereignty down to the level of petty life and fostering a sort of pride in the pettiness of royal life.

In the late 1930s, however, when it seemed that at last prosperity was just round the corner and that through the moderate diplomacy of Neville Chamberlain the mistakes of the First World War and its immediate aftermath might be finally rectified and the peace of Europe guaranteed, the people of Britain were for the most part content with a King and Queen who not only reminded them of an earlier stability but also took account of a new spirit of equality. The imagined scars and divisions left by Edward VIII were seen to have been healed, and it now remained only for Their Majesties to present themselves to the Empire, with which, since the Statute of Westminster, they now stood as the most tangible link.

The King had been obliged to forgo the traditional coronation durbar in India in 1937, partly because his doctors doubted whether he could bear the strain of it – coming so soon after the Abdication and the ordeal of his coronation in Britain – but mainly because India was in a ferment whipped up by the nationalist leaders Mahatma Gandhi, Jawaharlal Nehru and Mohammed Ali Jinnah over a new constitution imposed by the British which had unified the country as a single state but failed to recognise that the Indians were capable of governing themselves as a Dominion. Both the Secretary of State for India and the Viceroy believed that a visit by the King-Emperor might go some way towards soothing nationalist sentiments, but George VI, who after all had yet to learn how the government of his own country worked, and his advisers felt it was better to delay. Meanwhile the oldest Dominion, Canada, had used the opportunity of the coronation to present its request for royal attention, and along with that came an even more exciting invitation offering George VI the opportunity to become the first reigning British monarch to set foot in the United States of America. Preliminary approval was granted for both these trips, though at that time nobody could say when they might be made.

The American invitation came from President Roosevelt, who did not share the confidence in the appeasement policy that seemed to sustain the majority of the statesmen in Britain. So far as Roosevelt was concerned, a European war could not be postponed indefinitely, and although the official position of the United States remained one of isolating itself from the political affairs of Europe, the President made a famous speech in October 1937 in which he voiced his personal belief that it was necessary to 'quarantine' those nations adopting an aggressive stance – he meant Italy and Germany specifically – in order to protect the international community. He was preparing the ground for what he saw as the inevitable abandonment of isolationism, but he knew that it could not be done quickly or without a fight and reasoned that a visit to the United States by the

King and Queen of England might create an emotional climate in which a sense of unity between English-speaking peoples might flourish and ultimately grow into a commitment to support the coming struggle against fascism.

Hitler's annexation of Austria in the spring of 1938 and the Czech crisis that summer made Roosevelt more certain than ever that the outbreak of war was merely a matter of time and in August that year he wrote personally to George VI – the first time an American president had ever corresponded directly with the monarch of the former colonial power – and urged him to consider visiting the United States after his tour of Canada scheduled for 1939. The King replied in vague terms, still unsure whether the European situation would be stable enough for him to leave Britain, but in the breathing-space that followed Chamberlain's Munich agreement with Hitler it was resolved that the Canadian tour should go ahead and when Roosevelt pressed the King again in November 1938 the decision had already been taken to include the United States. By now Roosevelt was bombarding Congress with proposals for increased defence appropriations and preparing to amend the American Neutrality Act to permit the sale of arms to Britain and France on the so-called 'cash-and-carry' basis. The increasing territorial claims of Hitler and Mussolini led him to believe that war was only months away and, since France was bitterly divided and rearming in a very desultory fashion, Roosevelt identified Britain as the main line of defence against the dictatorships. But he also knew that Britain would be unable to hold the line without American help, and in order to mobilise public opinion in the United States a successful visit by the King and Queen was necessary.

The circumstances of the tour were of a highly delicate nature. At first Roosevelt proposed only that Their Majesties appear at the 1939 World's Fair in New York and then spend some time at his own home at Hyde Park, in the Hudson Valley. If they wished to go to Washington, that was up to them. The President could not afford to offer his critics – and there were many, as Republican gains in the 1938 mid-term elections showed – the opportunity to suggest that some form of Anglo-American alliance was in the making. Isolationism remained an attractive doctrine and any suspicion of a direct attempt to overturn that policy would have destroyed the President's chances of being able to persuade his people to aid Britain when the need arose. The Americans had to be won over and made to feel ties of kinship that would inspire them to help. The King took the hint from Roosevelt and said that he would visit the American capital, but in order to remove political overtones from the visit it was decided that the Foreign Secretary, Lord Halifax (who had succeeded Eden), should not accompany him. All now depended on the impression the royal couple would make on the people of the United States.

The intention had been that the King and Queen should travel in the battle-cruiser *Repulse*, but with Britain rearming and mobilising in the face of Hitler's latest demands against Poland, whose sovereignty Britain and France had guaranteed, it was actually aboard a chartered ocean liner, *Empress of Australia*, that they left Portsmouth on May 6th, 1939, with a destroyer escort. In one of those fine absurdities that surround royal life, the liner was designated a 'royal yacht' for the occasion and the King, whose naval experience was somewhat limited, regarded as 'supreme commander' of the expedition. Effective command of the 'squadron' was in the hands of Vice-Admiral Sir Dudley North. This needless piece of protocol was to cause difficulties on the voyage.

Frank Knight, who acted as steward to the King and Queen, recalled:

> What a trip it was. Our captain had done it scores of times and knew the Atlantic like the back of his hand. At that time of year you had to watch out for icebergs, and of course the captain was well aware of this. But since we had the King and Queen aboard, some old admiral came down to take charge. [North was three years away from retirement.] Our captain suggested that we follow a certain course, but the old admiral said, 'No, no, we'll go *this* way,' and naturally our captain could do nothing else. We were five days out when we spotted the first iceberg, then a dense fog closed in. For three more days we had to keep our speed down to about five knots, when the engines weren't stopped altogether. Our foghorn was bellowing all the time and there were icebergs everywhere. We were all pretty nervous because we didn't know when the next 'berg would loom up out of the fog.[7]

The King and Queen were told that the icefields had moved much further south than they usually did, a piece of information that appeared to be contradicted by the recollection that in much the same spot and at almost exactly the same time of year the *Titanic* had hit an iceberg and sunk in 1912. 'Incredibly eery, and really very alarming, knowing that we were surrounded by ice, & unable to see a foot either way,' the Queen wrote to her mother-in-law.[8] The King was more matter-of-fact about it, describing the voyage as an interesting experience and taking some comfort from the fact that their arrival in Canada was to be delayed by two days. 'I have been able to have a good rest,' he wrote, 'and the two extra days are all to the good for me.' He admitted that a fogbound icefield was not the ideal place for a holiday, 'but it does seem to be the only place for me to rest in nowadays!'[9]

Frank Knight was impressed by the royal couple's lack of formality and consideration for other people, which would in due course endear them to the Americans. The Queen, he remembered, requested that 'all the staff' should be invited to the ship's cinema one evening, but after the showing of two films she expressed her surprise that the audience had been so small. There was some puzzlement, since her request had been strictly followed, until it was realised that she had failed to distinguish between the 'staff' and the 'crew'.

'She thereupon asked that the following evening the same two films should be shown and that all the staff *and the crew* should be invited,' Mr Knight said. 'They all did so but kept a very respectful distance from the King and Queen. Then one of the Queen's ladies-in-waiting was instructed to ask everybody to close ranks, and we felt very strange when we saw cooks and stokers all clustered round the royal seats.' Democracy, even of a royal variety, had its limits in 1939. But after a while everyone relaxed and Knight's abiding memory of the voyage was seeing the King 'doubled-up with laughter at the antics of Donald Duck'.[10]

The steward also became aware, in a very personal way, of the now famous inquisitiveness of Queen Elizabeth:

She gave me the fright of my life. One day I was sitting in the lavatory, which I should explain was flushed by letting in seawater. Everything was calm and quiet, then suddenly there was a hell of an explosion and freezing seawater shot up and soaked me. I came out of there like a rocket. I thought we'd hit an iceberg or something. I raced up on deck and then found out that the Queen had been responsible. We were escorted by two destroyers and the Queen had seen on their decks things that looked like dustbins. She had asked what they were and been told they were depth-charges. Then she had asked how they worked – and they'd got a destroyer to fire one to show her![11]

With the voyage over, albeit two days late, the King and Queen embarked on a month-long tour during which they visited all of Canada's provinces. The Canadians are among the most royalist of Commonwealth peoples but they are also acutely conscious of the rugged republicanism and independence of their neighbours and during the 1930s there had been some talk of Canada embracing the neutralism then in vogue in the United States with regard to the power struggle in Europe. The royal visit put an end to any thoughts of that kind. 'You can go home and tell the Old Country that any talk they may hear of Canada being isolationist ... is just nonsense,'[12] one member of the party was told, while the Governor-General, Lord Tweedsmuir (better known as the writer John Buchan), overheard First World War veterans shouting 'If Hitler could just see this!' as the Queen unveiled a war memorial. 'She has a perfect genius for the right kind of publicity,' Tweedsmuir remarked.[13]

It was essential that their visit to the United States also attracted the right kind of publicity. 'The British are never polite to us except when they want something,' the *New York Times* warned its readers, adding that there remained in America 'a suspicious nerve where the British are concerned' and that strong in the American consciousness was 'the memory that our independence was won by military resistance to a British king'. The *Chicago Tribune* was even more forthright, directly accusing Roosevelt of using the royal visit to align the United States with what it called British and French imperialism. It was a forlorn hope, the paper implied, because 'the image of a feudal medievalism' did not accord with American national usage, customs and thought. 'Nor can a larger acquaintance with the institutions preserved by the British caste system for its own protection be very stimulating to the American belief that a man's worth is wholly in his own qualities.' The United States welcomed the King and Queen cordially, the *Tribune* concluded, but with reservations.

Nevertheless, some six hundred thousand people turned out to welcome the royal couple to Washington, and by the end of their visit any reservations seemed to have disappeared. The Mayor of New York, Fiorello La Guardia, told the King that simply by being there he had 'negotiated a treaty of friendship that would take many years to revoke' and he had achieved more than 'the sending of twelve ambassadors or the interchange of fifty diplomatic notes'. As always it was the Queen to whom all hearts went out – 'Give her a crowd and she mows them down,' wrote one reporter – but the King made an equally strong, if different, impression, as someone who saw him at the World's Fair observed:

His serious, gravely-smiling countenance, and the faraway look in his eyes as if he were gazing far over the heads of the people in front of him and seeking to penetrate the mysteries of the world of tomorrow in earnest, gave him an appealing aspect that made people feel sympathy for the cares that rest upon a crowned head.

Even the *Chicago Tribune* was to some extent won over, commenting favourably on the 'democratic' approach of the royal couple and admitting, somewhat grudgingly, that 'so far no great harm has been done'.

But the *Tribune* was, of course, quite right in sensing a hidden agenda for the visit and would no doubt have delighted in being party to the discussions that took place between the King and Roosevelt at Hyde Park. Those meetings prepared the way for the later discussions between Churchill and Roosevelt that produced the Anglo-American agreement to exchange destroyers for military bases in the Caribbean and the theory of the eventual Lend-Lease agreement. Lend-Lease allowed the purchase of American goods on credit and thus enabled Britain to place its economy entirely on a war footing (though incidentally to ruin itself for the future as a manufacturing and exporting nation). The President was over-optimistic in his estimation of how quickly the United States government would respond to Britain's needs when war broke out, apparently telling the King that 'if London was bombed USA would come in'.[14] Many bombs were to fall on London before Roosevelt was able to declare war on Germany. But the affection aroused by the royal visit did give him a lever with which to bend the Neutrality Acts and thus to prop up Britain's lone resistance when Europe had been overrun. It also inspired many ordinary Americans to do what they could to help individually during the months when their legislators vacillated.

Back in London in the summer of 1939, the editor of the *Observer*, J. L. Garvin, had no doubts as to the importance of America's exposure to the modern face of the British monarchy:

> Among the victories of peace none is greater than the assuagement of ancient bitterness. In the things that chiefly matter to the world, the American people and ourselves hold the same standard of right and wrong, look with the same eye upon claims of tolerance and mercy and resent with the same intensity whatever violates the precepts of the Christian tradition. When two great peoples have that bequest in common from their searching past, it can be no mere featherweight in the scale of fate.

The King and Queen arrived in London on June 22nd and the reports of their reception suggest scenes of rejoicing reminiscent of the day of their coronation, with great crowds lining the streets between Waterloo station and Buckingham Palace. As the royal procession passed Westminster, the House of Commons suspended its sitting and MPs rushed into Whitehall to add their voices to the cheering. 'We all lost our dignity and yelled and yelled,' Harold Nicolson recorded. 'The King wore a happy schoolboy grin.'[15] If the coronation had been essentially a celebration of Britishness, then so was this. Everyone now recognised that history had entered another momentous phase and, as people most often turn to God in times of trouble, the British people turned to their King in expectation of a great test to come. Events had transformed a reluctant monarch into a national hero, a small, shy and rather unprepossessing man into a symbol of defiance.

Exactly two months later, Adolf Hitler signed a non-aggression pact with the Soviet Union and on September 1st the German armies began their assault on Poland. Appeasement had run its course and failed, and Neville Chamberlain was forced to live up to his promise of the previous March, when he had announced:

> In the event of any action which already threatened Polish independence, and which the Polish government accordingly considered it vital to resist with national forces, His Majesty's Government would feel themselves bound at once to lend the Polish government all the support in their power . . . The French government . . . stand in the same position . . .

By September 3rd Britain and France were at war with Germany. 'I am keeping a war diary now,' the King said, and in that diary he wrote: 'So today when the crisis is over, & the result of the breakdown of negotiations is war, the country is calm, firm & united behind its leaders, resolved to fight until Liberty & Justice are once again safe in the World.'

Like his father before him, George VI was called upon early in his reign to face a cataclysmic armed conflict, but in this case there was to be no cry of 'King and Country', no outpouring of rabid jingoism, no wild enthusiasm for a test of strength among imperial rivals. This time it would prove to be not simply a question of throwing armies at each other and standing back to wait and see which would prevail, but instead a daily battle for survival. In such a situation, the demands made on the monarchy were very different from what they had been a quarter of a century before. George V had fought his war largely alongside the generals and the politicians. George VI would be required to spend much of his time fighting alongside his beleaguered people. In the reign of George V, the First World War was an episode, tragic and bloody, but an episode nevertheless, and if he is remembered at all it is not for his wartime conduct. For George VI, the Second World War was to be not only the apogee of his reign, but also its epitaph.

15

Undertones
of War

Since the British monarchy has remained firmly rooted in the feudal tradition, even now identifying itself with the distant past to the extent of re-inventing 'historical' ceremony and pageantry, it is not surprising that wartime should have presented it with peculiar opportunities. Along with the hereditary principle, the concept of the supreme warrior lies at the very heart of tribal allegiance to a single human symbol of unity and continuity. King George VI was unable to declare war on Germany in 1939 as his father had done in 1914 – at a meeting of the Privy Council, without reference to Parliament, like some warlord of old – and neither was he called upon to lead his armies in the field as his medieval predecessors might have done. But once Parliament had taken the decision to fight, the King slipped naturally into a modern version of the monarch's historic role in the defence of the realm.

Here, perhaps, was some justification for the military nature of his education and early life. Certainly, the connection was not lost on the King himself: 'At the outbreak of war at midnight of Aug. 4th–5th 1914, I was a midshipman, keeping the middle watch on the bridge of HMS *Collingwood* at sea, somewhere in the North Sea. I was 18 years of age . . . Today we are at war again, & I am no longer a midshipman in the Royal Navy . . .'[1] He confessed in his diary to a certain sense of relief that the tortuous and bewildering processes of diplomacy had given way to a straightforward test of strength. 'Hitler had taken the plunge, with the knowledge that the whole might of the British Empire would be against him.'

War may be, as Clausewitz maintained, the continuation of politics by other means; more importantly, it is the pursuit of political aims by simple means. Violence leaves no room for complex philosophical considerations in which the outcome may be blurred by the nuances of argument. As George VI put it in his broadcast to the nation early in the evening of Sunday, September 3rd, 1939:

> Over and over again we have tried to find a peaceful way out of the differences between ourselves and those who are now our enemies. But it has been in vain. We have been forced into a conflict. For we are called . . . to meet the challenge of a principle which, if it were to prevail, would be fatal to any civilised order in the world . . . Such a principle, stripped of all disguise, is surely the mere primitive doctrine that Might is Right . . .

Just so. And it was the very same doctrine that motivated Britain to take up arms against Nazi Germany. Our might was simply perceived as being more right than Hitler's because it was exercised under provocation and in a cause considered to be as noble as Hitler's was evil, but it amounted to the same thing: an attempt to impose a desired solution by force.

No criticism is intended here. I merely point to the manipulation of popular sentiment that is required in order to rouse one nation into armed conflict with another, and to the influence a monarch may bring to bear in that process. Monarchy and making war appeal to tribal instincts that are very similar, a desire for security, a fear of external threat, an urge to display power in an easily recognisable form, and a wish to sublimate any sense of personal responsibility. Germany had its Führer, Italy its Duce, and in purely symbolic terms they fulfilled exactly the same function as the British King, though on a practical level there was, of course, an enormous difference in their powers.

An example of the part George VI was to play in stiffening the warlike resolve of both the British people and the peoples of the Empire is to be found in his wireless broadcast on Empire Day, May 24th, in 1940:

> The decisive struggle is now upon us. I am going to speak plainly to you, for in this hour of trial I know that you would not have me do otherwise. Let no one be mistaken; it is no mere territorial conquest that our enemies are seeking. It is the overthrow, complete and final, of this Empire and of everything for which it stands, and after that the conquest of the world . . .

This, it appears, was simply not true. According to the best German sources, Hitler had, certainly at that time, no designs upon the British

Empire, which he greatly admired. Indeed, even as the King's message was being broadcast, the Führer was explaining to some of his military commanders why the continued existence of the Empire was necessary and extolling the virtues of the civilisation that Britain had brought to the world. One of those who heard him, General Blumentritt, recalled that Hitler said 'all he wanted from Britain was that she should acknowledge Germany's position on the Continent'.[2] Hitler's biographer, Joachim Fest, makes it clear that the Führer had employed stratagem, menace, bluff and trickery to avoid war with Britain and suggests that his statement of July 19th, 1940 – that 'it was never my intention to destroy or even to harm' the British Empire – should be taken at face value. His threat, in the same speech, to annihilate the Empire, Fest argues, was a sign of his recognition that peace with a Britain led by Winston Churchill rather than by Neville Chamberlain was impossible.[3]

Chamberlain's government had entered the war sadly and reluctantly, under irresistible pressure from Parliament. Churchill's first act after he succeeded Chamberlain on May 10th, 1940, was to raise the level of British consciousness so that the war became not an unfortunate necessity but a great moral crusade against evil. In this, essentially a public relations exercise (though a vital one in view of the Germans' rapid conquest of mainland Europe), the Prime Minister received invaluable assistance from George VI, who not only rallied his peoples with a battle-cry on behalf of a supposedly endangered British Empire but also invoked the Almighty: 'Let us with one heart and soul humbly but confidently commit our cause to God, and ask His aid that we may valiantly defend the right as it is given to us to see it . . . with God's help we shall not fail.'[4] Thus, in war, the emotional appeal of the medieval warrior prince was combined with the Victorian principles of constitutional monarchy. On the one hand, the King was presenting himself as the guardian of tribal security and, on the other, he was exercising moral leadership and endowing government with the authority of religion. All this provided a powerful stimulant to morale in the face of the disastrous performance of British and Allied troops against the German thrust to the Channel in the spring of 1940.

Furthermore, if under the conditions of modern warfare George VI could not be a battlefield king, he realised the importance of his leadership on the home front and resolved to join his subjects in whatever hardships and suffering might befall them. Here, though, there arose a curious paradox, which is best exemplified by his attitude towards King Leopold of the Belgians.

As the German armies thundered westwards in May 1940, it was vital that the Belgians held out to protect the northern flank of the British Expeditionary Force, and King Leopold inspired his troops to resist the *Wehrmacht* in spite of the overwhelming odds against them. By the middle of the month, however, it became clear that Belgium would fall: the Germans entered Brussels on May 17th and the government, forced to move to Ostend, pressed the King to leave the country and set up a government in exile, as Queen Wilhelmina of the Netherlands was already doing. The British government supported this advice, but on May 22nd Churchill was informed that Leopold would not desert his army and believed that the best interests of his countrymen would be served if he remained in Belgium, rather than fleeing to form an administration that would be powerless to protect the people it claimed to represent. Three days later George VI sent his fellow monarch a telegram:

> I note that Your Majesty considers it to be your duty to your people and your Allies to remain with your Army in Belgium. In taking this decision Your Majesty will not have overlooked the extreme importance of preserving a united Belgian Government with full authority outside the territory occupied by the enemy, and while paying tribute to Your Majesty's devotion I and my Government must express our grave concern at your decision.
>
> While it would be presumptuous of me to advise you on your duty to your people, I can say that as regards the Allies and the fulfilment of the joint purpose in the war, I do not feel that Your Majesty is called upon to make the sacrifices which you contemplate.

Presumptuous or not, the King went on to suggest to Leopold that it would be best for his people if he remained at liberty to act as 'a rallying-point for the Belgian nation', implying that this would be impossible if he stayed in Belgium:

> Your Majesty must consider the possibility, even the probability, of your being taken prisoner, perhaps carried off to Germany, and almost certainly deprived of all communication with the outside world. Such a position would leave your people bereft of their natural leader without so far as I can see any compensating advantage.

King Leopold, of course, took a different view of his duty and on May 28th, seeing that further resistance was futile, personally negotiated the surrender of the Belgian army, his government by this time having moved to Paris. George VI, while sympathising with Leopold's dilemma, expressed the view that he had confused his roles as commander-in-chief and king, acting impeccably in the former but failing to see that the latter required him to leave Belgium and establish his government in an unoccupied country.[5] The King did not share the widespread suspicion in Britain that Leopold had pro-German leanings and was in effect a collaborationist, and he defended the Belgian king against the opprobrium heaped on him. He understood that Leopold had acted as he did for reasons of conscience, just as King Christian of Denmark had done in remaining in his country when it was overrun by the Germans.[6] Indeed, if faced with the prospect of the same agonising choice himself, the King had no intention of following the advice he had given to Leopold. After the fall of France in June 1940, the landing of German troops on British shores was expected daily, but although a special guard was mounted on the royal family and plans were drawn up for their rapid evacuation from London, the possibility that they might leave the country and set up a government in exile was never seriously considered.

President Roosevelt suggested Ottawa as a base from which the King and British ministers might rally the forces of the Empire even if Britain had been overrun, while his Secretary of State, Cordell Hull, thought Bermuda would be more suitable.[7] But when the Lord Chancellor, Lord Hailsham, wrote to Churchill proposing that Princesses Elizabeth and Margaret be sent to Canada to prevent any possibility of their falling into enemy hands, he specifically ruled out a similar course for the King: 'I think you will agree that it would be disastrous to suggest that he should leave the country – and probably he would not go!' Indeed not. The King installed a shooting-range in the grounds of Buckingham Palace, where he and his family, together with members of their households, engaged in small-arms practice. As Churchill spoke of 'going down fighting amid the ruins of Whitehall', the King travelled in his car with a sten gun beside him and talked of making a last stand at the Palace or of fighting with the resistance movement that would be created if the Germans gained control of Britain. The contradiction between his advice to King Leopold and his own intentions did not seem to occur to him. Perhaps the Queen, who was equally active in pistol practice, gave a clue to the real feelings of the royal family towards their continental colleagues when she said in an unguarded moment, 'I shall not go down like the others.' This was now a British war, and the rules were different.

'Personally,' the King wrote to his mother when France fell, 'I feel happier now that we have no allies to be polite to & to pamper.'[8]

As for the Princesses, they were sent no farther than a heavily guarded Windsor Castle, where their parents joined them every evening they could. 'The Princesses could not go [abroad] without me; I could not leave the King; and of course the King will never leave,' said the Queen.[9]

The German invasion never came, but the Blitz did, in the autumn of 1940, and the King seemed almost to revel in standing squarely with his people against the continual bombardment of the *Luftwaffe*. In the East End of London, in Coventry, Bristol, Southampton, Birmingham and many other places devastated by German air power, the firemen, rescue workers and bombed-out families would suddenly find the King and Queen among them, offering praise, sympathy, encouragement and hope. 'Thank God for a good King,' one victim called out, raising a cheer among his neighbours. 'Thank God for a good people,' the King replied. The royal couple toured the country in a special train, bringing what comfort they could to the regions worst affected and visiting the far-flung sites of anti-aircraft batteries which, after the evacuation of British troops from the European mainland, had become the front line. Royal funds were used to establish a series of relief convoys, known as 'Queen's Messengers', which day by day carried food and medical supplies to the places that had 'copped it' in the heaviest air raids. And in September 1940 there was royal acknowledgment of the importance of the home front in this war when the King created 'a new mark of honour for men and women in all walks of civilian life' – the George Cross, which was to rank next to the military Victoria Cross and to be awarded for 'bravery & outstanding deeds', and the George Medal, intended for wider distribution to people whose work in defence of the homeland was considered to be exemplary. 'Many and glorious are the deeds of gallantry done during these perilous but famous days,' the King said when he announced that he had given his name to these new orders.

Thus, while the destruction and loss of life caused by the Blitz were real enough, it signally failed in its primary aim, which was to destroy the morale of the British population. Crucial to this failure, there can be no doubt, were the unremitting efforts of George VI and Queen Elizabeth, the perception that the highest in the land were sharing in the daily tragedies and sufferings of the most humble, and the knowledge among ordinary folk that their steadfastness and their sacrifices were encouraged, recognised and reflected by those who now, in this desperate crisis, actively symbolised their nationhood. The popularity of the monarchy, having grown steadily for more than half a century as its representatives were seen to be involving themselves to a greater degree in the lives of its subjects and to be working on their behalf, entered a new phase (a particularly important one for the future of the institution) under the pressure of the Second World War. Queen Victoria and King Edward VII had, of course, taken an interest in the people over whom they reigned, but public opinion had not been a significant influence on their lives and, in aristocratic fashion, they had in their different ways exercised almost entirely personal judgments as to the public requirements placed upon them by constitutional monarchy. George V, on the other hand, had placed public duty above nearly everything else, taking with the utmost seriousness the responsibilities of his self-assumed fatherhood in relation to his subjects. He had in a sense, and a very practical one, adopted the people almost in the manner that an ancient tribal chief might have done. George VI approached kingship with much the same attitude, but in his case the enforced closing of national ranks brought about by the disastrous early course of the war, and the King's own determination to take the same risks as everyone else, produced a peculiar element of reciprocity – the people adopted *him*.

Winston Churchill noticed this phenomenon. 'This war has drawn the Throne and the people more closely together than was ever before recorded,' he told the King in January 1941, 'and Your Majesties are more beloved by all classes and conditions than any of the princes of the past.'

Their Majesties were also very much aware of the new bond, particularly after they themselves became victims of the bombing. The first blow was struck against them on September 9th, 1940, when a bomb fell on the north side of Buckingham Palace, just below the King's study. At first it appeared to be a dud and the King continued to use his room, but in the early hours of the following morning a delayed-action fuse triggered an explosion that shattered all the windows on that side of the building, though no damage was done to the structure itself. Three days later, the King and Queen were even more fortunate in their escape when a German bomber dived through heavy rain clouds, flew along The Mall and dropped six bombs in what appeared to be a deliberate attack on the Palace. The couple had spent the night with their daughters in the comparative safety of Windsor and had arrived back in London during an air raid. They were in a small sitting-room overlooking the quadrangle, their quarters on the north side having had the windows blown out, when they heard the noise of the enemy aircraft and saw two bombs fall in the quadrangle, about thirty yards from where they were standing. The explosions left them stunned for an instant, then they and the King's private secretary, Alexander Hardinge, rushed out into a corridor –

'We all wondered why we weren't dead,' the King recalled in his diary. They later discovered that a third bomb had destroyed the chapel, injuring three workmen, two more bombs had fallen in the forecourt and there was a sixth crater in the garden. 'Luckily the Palace is very narrow, & the bombs fell in the open spaces,' the King observed. The chapel had been unlucky because it protruded from the main building into the garden. The King and Queen were uninjured, but they had received a severe shock (the King is said to have taken the bombing personally, speculating that it was the work of some German relative who happened to be serving in the *Luftwaffe*), and their sense of comradeship with those, such as the people of the London docklands, who lived daily under such attacks, was immeasurably heightened.[10]

'Buckingham Palace has been bombed as well as their homes,' the King wrote, '& nobody is immune from it.' The Queen's reaction was to become famous. 'I'm glad we've been bombed,' she remarked. 'It makes me feel I can look the East End in the face.'

The East End felt it too, as did Coventry, flattened by the bombers on the night of November 14th–15th and visited by the King on the 16th, and Plymouth and everywhere else that found its sufferings mitigated and its resolve strengthened by the warmth of royal sympathy and understanding founded on personal experience. There were some who complained that, while the attention of the King and Queen was no doubt appreciated, it was of little practical value to people who had lost their homes, but the news that the Palace had been bombed (though at the time nobody, not even Churchill, was told how close the royal couple had come to extinction) served to strengthen the sense in the minds of the great majority of the population that the monarchy was not only *for* the people – that impression had grown steadily during the reign of George V – but also *of* the people.

Whether this proprietary feeling would have developed without the stresses of the siege of Britain in 1940–41 it is impossible to say. George VI had certainly worked hard enough in the earlier years of his reign to endear himself to, one might almost say to ingratiate himself with, the people, but the war brought out the best in him, as it did in so many others, allowing him to overcome the barriers of both his own diffidence and the conventions of the relationship between the monarchy and its subjects. On the King's part, Churchill found that the chance to share in a very direct way the lives of ordinary people produced a form of exhilaration in him, and a number of men who were regularly in royal company during the war years have testified to the growth of his confidence and maturity, to his calmness and even to a certain lightening of his spirits generally. This may be explained by the fact that, although the work he undertook was exhausting, he had the satisfaction of knowing that what he was doing was right. The questions about the role of the constitutional monarch in such extreme circumstances were all simple and the answers were all obvious. He was permitted to follow his instincts, to be himself, just as he had been in his turret at the Battle of Jutland.

As far as the people were concerned, A. J. P. Taylor has pointed out that the war, and the Blitz in particular, not only cemented national unity but also acted as 'a powerful solvent of class antagonism'. This is perhaps overstating the case somewhat: there is evidence from Mass Observation surveys, for instance, that resentment felt by workers against the managing classes remained strong in spite of appeals to patriotism and the prevailing impression that unity was essential if the nation was to survive. In 1942, Stephen Spender, writing in the *New Statesman*, said that workers, civil defence personnel and even soldiers had no sense that they were sharing the responsibilities of the war – indeed, their consolation was to feel that they were not responsible. 'At a discussion on the loss of Malaya amongst firemen,' Spender wrote, 'the men talked with a certain satisfaction about the hopeless incompetence of the "ruling class" and the "bosses". Convinced that they cannot do anything, they take the satisfaction of the impotent in the guilt, and indeed, today, the punishment, incurred by the potent ruling class.' Nevertheless, if class antagonism was not quite dissolved by the catalyst of total war, it was very considerably diluted and, as those who look back nostalgically to the national spirit of the war years seldom tire of telling us, there was an overwhelming perception, at least, that everyone was 'pulling together'. It was, after all, generally true that social status offered no protection against bombs and that the duke and the dustman were equally likely to be in the wrong place at the wrong time. The refusal of George VI and his family to retreat to a place of safety, and the bombing of Buckingham Palace, at once reinforced the impression of risk spread right across the social strata and, more significantly in terms of public attitudes towards the monarchy, shifted the balance of recognition away from the royals as distant idols who sometimes deigned to touch the earth. It was demonstrated that, in all fundamental respects, they were human beings and had much in common with lesser mortals, to whom they suddenly became considerably more familiar.

The sense of common humanity was reinforced by the royal family's scrupulous observation of the wartime rationing restrictions applied to food, clothing and most other items. The Minister of Food, Lord

Woolton, commented that the meals served at Buckingham Palace during the war, containing such ingredients as powdered eggs and creative concoctions of vegetables, were the same as those to be found in any home in the kingdom (though Eleanor Roosevelt, wife of the American President, was amused to note that, during her stay with the royal family in the autumn of 1942, such simple fare was served on plates of gold and silver). When an American reporter asked the Queen if she had tasted the pie to which Woolton unwisely lent his name – a 'dry and uneatable' mixture of potatoes, carrots, turnips and parsnips covered with white sauce and pastry – she replied that she certainly had, and added with feeling: 'Have *you*?' The King personally supervised the heating arrangements at the Palace in line with the emergency regulations, which meant that vast rooms were heated by nothing more than single-bar electric fires, while at Windsor he took part in the 'Dig for Victory' campaign by ploughing up an extra two hundred acres at the Royal Farm and planting wheat, barley, oats, potatoes and animal feedstuff. All this, of course, was featured prominently in the press for the propaganda value, and had its effect both on national morale and the growing fellow-feeling between royals and people.

Equally important, in view of the traditional links between the sovereign and the armed forces, was the King's symbolic role as military leader, even though he had, in fact, no control over the conduct of the war. He always wore military uniform when he appeared in public, giving the royal penchant for that particular form of dressing-up a significance it cannot possibly have in peacetime, and he paid great attention to the activities of British and Empire troops in the various theatres of war. Throughout 1940 and 1941, and for the first half of 1942, those activities brought no cheer to the King or the nation, though the disastrous attempt by the British Expeditionary Force to defend France and the Low Countries found its way into British legend as a result of the almost miraculous evacuation of 335,000 troops, including more than 110,000 French forces, from Dunkirk. As a mark of his respect for those who had organised and successfully completed an operation that some thought impossible, the King received several of the commanders involved at the Palace on June 5th, 1940. 'I always feel', he confided to his diary some time later, 'that we have to be thankful France collapsed at once after Dunkirk, so that we were able to reorganise the Army at home, & gave us time to prepare the Air Force for the Blitzkrieg.'[11] There is no doubt that he, as much as anyone, was gripped by the sense both of isolation and of mission expressed in Dorothy L. Sayers's poem

The English War, which evoked 'The single island, like a tower, ringed with an angry host'.

The isolation was more keenly felt at first, though in North Africa British forces had some successes against the Nazis' Italian allies and helped to repel the invasion of Greece by Mussolini's forces. German submarines were sinking merchant ships at an alarming rate, which threatened Britain's ability to hold out far more than the Blitz did, and the important Mediterranean naval base of Malta was under siege. Early in 1941 the Nazis moved into Bulgaria and Hitler sent General Erwin Rommel to North Africa to retake territories lost by the Italians – by April 25th Rommel's Afrika Korps had driven the British out of most of Libya and was moving into Egypt. Also in April 1941, the Germans invaded Yugoslavia and Greece: the former surrendered on April 17th and within a little more than a month British, New Zealand and Australian troops had withdrawn from Greece and Crete. In June, Hitler launched a surprise assault on the Soviet Union and quickly overwhelmed large areas. Meanwhile, in South-East Asia, the Japanese took control of French colonies in Indochina and, later in 1941, invaded the Philippines and Malaya, captured Hong Kong and the East Indies, occupied Shanghai and Wake Island and, on December 7th, destroyed most of the United States Pacific Fleet at anchor in its Hawaiian base, Pearl Harbor. In his Christmas broadcast that year, the King said: 'The range of the tremendous conflict is ever widening . . . Truly it is a stern and solemn time.' But with the entry of the Soviet Union and the United States into the war in alliance with Britain against the so-called Axis powers of Germany, Italy and Japan, the British sense of mission overcame the feeling of isolation. 'As the war widens,' the King told his Christmas audience, 'so surely our conviction deepens of the greatness of our cause.'

That conviction was severely shaken, though, in February 1942, when the vast and supposedly impregnable British base of Singapore was overrun by the Japanese, with the surrender of some 70,000 troops. 'I am very depressed,' the King told his mother. 'We are going through a bad phase.'[12] Churchill put it more strongly: the fall of Singapore, he said, was the greatest British military disaster in history. It was now possible, the Prime Minister told the King at one of their weekly meetings, that Burma, Ceylon, some areas of India and even parts of Australia might be taken by the Japanese. 'I cannot help feeling depressed at the future outlook,' George VI wrote. 'Anything can happen, & it will be wonderful if we can be lucky anywhere.'[13] By the end of May, Japan was in control of Burma, as Churchill had predicted, having already landed in New Guinea and bombed the

Australian city of Darwin. In June, Rommel's Afrika Korps captured the British garrison at Tobruk and pushed on rapidly through Egypt.

In London, a Conservative Member of Parliament put down a motion of censure on the government's conduct of the war: Sir John Wardlaw-Milne suggested that the Prime Minister should not also be Minister of Defence, as Churchill had insisted on being, and – with breathtaking eccentricity – proposed that the King's brother, the Duke of Gloucester, should become the commander-in-chief of the army. In the ensuing debate, Churchill routed what he termed the weaker brethren in the House of Commons and the censure motion was heavily defeated.

There was criticism, too, from Australia, where, as the King put it, there was much talk in government circles and among the press about the prospect of a Japanese invasion. The Australian Prime Minister, John Curtin, made it known that he felt Britain was not doing enough to protect his country and that he was inclined to turn towards the United States for aid, which he would do 'free from any pangs about our traditional links of kinship with Britain'. He understood Britain's difficulties, he added – the constant threat of invasion from mainland Europe and the risks inherent in spreading British forces too thinly – but, 'we know that Australia can go and Britain still hold on. We are determined that Australia shall not go.' In the circumstances, an alliance would be formed with the United States to ensure the security of Australia until 'the tide of battle swings against the enemy'.[14]

George VI was seriously alarmed at Curtin's pronouncement and urged Churchill to head off any move towards the Americans by making what concessions he could to Australia. Though grateful for and keen to encourage aid from the United States, he had had serious reservations about the leasing to the Americans of bases in the British West Indies in return for the transfer of fifty aged US destroyers to the Royal Navy in 1940: 'The Americans have got to understand', the King said, 'that in leasing the bases the question of Sovereignty does not come in. These islands are part of the British Colonial Empire & I am not going to see my West Indian subjects handed over to the US authorities.'[15] There had also been difficulties in India, where nationalists led by Nehru and Gandhi had exploited the turmoil of war to press for complete independence, and in South Africa, where the Afrikaners had vainly attempted to institute a policy of neutrality in 1939 and, three years later, had fired another warning shot by trying to persuade the parliament to secede from the British Commonwealth and establish a republic. Now, one of the senior partners in that Commonwealth, Australia, seemed to be turning away from the mother country.

Churchill, however, airily dismissed Australian grievances, pointing out almost with contempt that Curtin's government had a majority of only two and suggesting that it would receive short shrift in Washington anyway. As a concession to the Australians he agreed to the establishment of Pacific War Councils in London and Washington on which Australia was represented. These were no more than a façade, as Churchill later admitted: 'The war continued to be run by the old machinery.' If he thought this would satisfy the Australians, he was wrong; many of them felt that they had been let down by Britain in their hour of greatest need, that they could no longer entirely trust the old country, and that they would in future have to make their own security arrangements. Churchill also failed to foresee the future strategic and economic importance of the Pacific. Both these facts were emphasised by the signing, just six years after the war's end, of a defence treaty involving Australia, New Zealand and the United States, the so-called ANZUS pact. While the King's fears regarding Australia had been overstated, there later proved to have been an element of justification in them. American influence has been marked in Australia since the war, and though the country remains a member of the Commonwealth, it does so with a significant degree of schizophrenia and a strong sense of its own independent identity.

In 1942, however, concern for the future was much more immediate. In Europe, North Africa and the Pacific, the forces of Germany and Japan seemed to be unstoppable. Then, at the beginning of July, came the first breakthrough for the Allies. It happened at El Alamein, an obscure railway halt in the desert sixty miles from Alexandria. There the British Eighth Army stopped Rommel's Afrika Korps in its tracks, and for the first time the Germans lost the initiative. Three months later, after a carefully prepared build-up of forces and under a new commander, General Bernard Montgomery, the Eighth Army launched an offensive at El Alamein and by November 4th the German and Italian forces under Rommel's command were in full retreat. 'A victory at last, how good it is for the nerves,' wrote George VI.[16] It was more than a victory; combined with the Red Army's assault in the summer of 1942 on the German divisions in the Soviet Union, the battle of El Alamein marked the turning-point of the Second World War. As President Roosevelt put it in a letter to George VI that autumn, 'Things for the Axis have reached the peak of their effectiveness.' Just a week after the victory in the desert, British and American forces under the command of General Dwight D.

Eisenhower landed in North Africa to take the first steps in the long and bloody campaigns that would bring about the destruction of Hitler's Third Reich.

Nevertheless, it was in a mood of some despondency that the King concluded his diary for that year: 'Outwardly one has to be optimistic about the future in 1943, but inwardly I am depressed about the present prospect.' There were three main reasons for his depression. The first was simply exhaustion as a result of his and the Queen's ceaseless activity to maintain unity and morale in the face of the battering Britain and the Empire had been receiving during the previous two years. Second, the King had been severely shocked and distressed by the death of his brother George, the Duke of Kent, in a plane crash in August 1942. The Duke, who had waived his honorary rank of air-marshal in the Royal Air Force to become an air-commodore specialising in welfare work on behalf of airmen, had taken off from a Scottish base in a Sunderland flying boat to inspect RAF installations in Iceland, but in appalling weather the aircraft had struck a mountain within thirty minutes of take-off. The Duke, aged thirty-nine, had been with his family only three weeks earlier at the christening of his second son, Prince Michael, which made his death all the more tragic. 'I shall miss him & his help terribly,' the King wrote, comforting himself with the thought that George had been killed on active service. During the funeral service at St George's Chapel, Windsor, on August 29th, he found himself unable to look other mourners in the face for fear that he would lose control of his feelings, and two weeks later he insisted on visiting the site of the crash – 'I felt I had to do this pilgrimage.' The loss brought home in the most intensely personal way the fragility of life in wartime and moved the King to make certain that matters were properly arranged to take account of the possibility of his own sudden death.

The third reason for the King's low spirits at the end of 1942 was less obvious. The invasion of North Africa had stretched British resources to the limit, particularly in view of the fact that German submarines continued to take a heavy toll of merchant shipping in the Atlantic. What that meant in practical terms was greater dependence on the Americans and a certain loss of freedom to conduct the war primarily in accordance with the best interests of Britain and the Empire. 'We shall be in a bad way here in mid-1943,' the King wrote, 'and we shall have to reduce our war effort here, which will prolong the war and put more work on the USA to keep us all going.'[17] Furthermore, the campaign in North Africa progressed less smoothly than it might have done, owing to disagreements and lack of coordination among the Allies, a phenomenon that was to cause difficulties and some disasters during the course of the rest of the war. The involvement of various French factions – including some that had co-operated with the puppet Vichy regime in occupied France – brought further complications as Anglo-American forces campaigned in French North African territories, and the King confessed himself bewildered by it all. It was no longer a British war, or merely a question of fighting for a cause; the scent of distant victory awakened dormant political considerations and aroused rivalries that looked ahead to the possible gains of the post-war world. The questions were not simple any more and consequently the position of George VI, particularly in his own view, was less clear-cut. From now on, he could not be quite so sure of the contribution he was expected to make.

The King had said of his dead brother that the war brought him out in many ways; that was also true of George VI.[18] He gained in confidence, stature and popularity and the demands he made upon himself, while they undoubtedly sapped the strength of a physique that had never been notably strong, also provided a definite and rewarding outlet for his restless nervous energy. In the same way, the dangers and the defeats of the early war years gave positive direction to the inner tensions of his personality – to put it bluntly, he had something tangible and immediate to worry about. In addition, he was exceedingly fortunate in history's selection of his wartime Prime Minister. Unlike George V, who had been frustrated during the First World War because of the disregard shown by Lloyd George and, before him, Asquith, George VI received from Winston Churchill both constant reassurance and the illusion, at least, of being intimately involved in the prosecution of the war. Churchill was an old-fashioned romantic with a mystical view of monarchy (as witness his passionate defence of Edward VIII), a highly developed sense of theatre and an acute awareness of great events unfolding. To him, his weekly luncheon meetings with George VI in the midst of a vast conflict would have taken on something of the character associated with royal councils of war in the age of chivalry, evoking images of Agincourt or Crécy. The very language of his wartime speeches is evidence of the heroic light in which he saw the struggle. As a result, the Prime Minister talked openly and freely with his King, who proudly informed Queen Mary: 'He tells me, more than people imagine, of his future plans & ideas & only airs them when the time is ripe to his colleagues & the Chiefs of Staff.'[19]

The King was equally forthcoming in expressing his views to Churchill, but there is no evidence to support the image conjured up

[255]

by *The Times* in 1943 of King and ministers running the war together. This was based on a rather suspect reading between the lines of letters the King and Churchill exchanged after the defeat of the Axis forces in North Africa. Replying in typically hyperbolic terms to royal congratulations on the successful outcome of the campaign, the Prime Minister said: 'No Minister of the Crown has ever received more kindness and confidence from his Sovereign than I have done during the three fateful years which have passed since I received Your Majesty's commission to form a national administration. This has been a precious aid and comfort to me . . .' *The Times* and, indeed, many subsequent biographers and commentators, took this as a sign that the influence of George VI on wartime policy was rather greater than it actually was. In fact, what Churchill meant was that the King, while offering plenty of advice and encouragement, was much less inclined to warn than his father had been, was more easily reassured that what the government was doing was right, and for the most part did not demur in carrying out precisely what the government required of him.[20] When called upon to strengthen national backbone during the crises of 1940–41, he responded magnificently, as he did also when the time came to demonstrate royal appreciation for the first significant Allied victory of the war.

It is not entirely clear whether Churchill or George VI himself was the moving force behind the King's visit to the troops in North Africa in the summer of 1943. Sir John Wheeler-Bennett says the King put the idea to Churchill in March that year, two months before the Axis surrender, in order to fulfil a long-cherished desire to visit his victorious armies in the field (the fact that they were not 'his' armies, but American and French, too, is ignored). Other accounts indicate that the visit was inspired by Churchill, who had earlier expressed anxiety about the activities of one of the Free French leaders, General de Gaulle, and was trying to stop the General visiting the now liberated French territories in North Africa on the ground that he would foment Anglophobia in the region.[21] What is certain is that final plans for the royal visit were approved by the War Cabinet on June 6th, 1943, but there may be significance in the fact that shortly before his intended departure, the King began to doubt whether it was a good idea for him to be away from Britain at that time.

At all events, the visit was a great success. The King was cheered by the troops wherever he went, was entertained by the Eighth Army's egotistical commander, General Montgomery, and hosted a remarkably good-humoured lunch for General de Gaulle and his rival for the leadership of the Free French, General Henri Giraud. According to Wheeler-Bennett, the King impressed everyone he met with his knowledge and interest, though the memory that remained in the minds of the staff of the commander-in-chief was of Eisenhower and the King travelling for several hours across Tunisia in a jeep together without a word being spoken. The Americans attributed this to shyness on the part of the King and to Eisenhower's awe at such a close encounter with royalty. A year later, when Eisenhower was entertained to lunch at Buckingham Palace shortly before the Allied invasion of Normandy, the Queen revealed that she and the King had been present when the General had been conducted on a tour of Windsor Castle in 1942 but had hidden on hands and knees behind a hedge in the grounds so as not to intimidate the new American arrival. By then more at ease with the royals, Eisenhower told an aide that the lunch had been as comfortable as a visit to friends back home.[22]

Before returning to London, the King visited the island of Malta, which as a vital Mediterranean base had been subjected to months of heavy bombing by the Germans and Italians and to which the King had awarded his own medal, the George Cross. The fact that he was able to be there at all – though the journey remained a risky one – spoke volumes for the change in the Allies' fortunes. Their success in North Africa was followed by the capture of Sicily and the invasion of Italy, which led on September 8th, 1943, to the surrender of Italian forces, though the Germans fought on doggedly. In the King's Christmas broadcast that year there was a strong note of optimism, tempered by caution: 'While we have bright visions of the future we have no easy dreams of the days that lie close at hand. We know that much hard working and hard fighting, and perhaps harder working and harder fighting, are necessary for victory.' Privately he expressed the hope that the war might be over by the next Christmas.

That hope, of course, was not to be fulfilled and events during 1944 seemed to bear out the spirit of his public rather than his private thoughts. At the same time, politics became ever more dominant in the struggle to win not only the war but also the peace that would follow it, and the essential weakness of the position of the British monarchy, notwithstanding its crucial role in wartime leadership, became increasingly exposed. It was Roosevelt, Stalin and Churchill who carved up the world into post-war power blocs, the first two heads of state and the third, technically at least, a head of government. The King, as titular head of state, was permitted to visit the troops in Italy but not to see the Pope or King Victor Emmanuel lest it be thought that he was lending support to the Italian monarchy, which the new government (and the Americans) deemed to be in abeyance pending a plebiscite on the future constitution of the country.[23]

Obstacles were also placed in the way of the King's expressed desire to meet, as head of state, the constitutional leaders of the other great Allied powers, Stalin and Harry Truman, who had become President of the United States on the sudden death of Roosevelt in April 1945. Though Churchill approached Stalin and received his grudging agreement to be a guest with Truman at a luncheon to be given by the King in Berlin during the Potsdam conference of July 1945, the gathering was subsequently cancelled, for reasons which remain obscure. Perhaps the Americans objected and the British government did not wish to upset them. Certainly Truman seemed to do his best to avoid meeting the King, in spite of a personal, handwritten invitation to Buckingham Palace. 'George VI RI sent me a personal letter today,' the President told his wife. 'Not much impressed.' In the end, the two heads of state did meet briefly at Plymouth, where the President's ship called as it took him home from the Potsdam conference.

Nor was the King permitted to announce to his people that the war in Europe had ended. Churchill thought that the final surrender of Germany would involve controversial political issues in which the monarch should not become embroiled and he even suggested that he himself might find it unnecessary 'to make any observations upon this particular event'. But the thought that Churchill might forgo comment at such a moment could not be long sustained, and at three o'clock in the afternoon of May 8th, 1945, his sonorous tones were heard on the wireless with the news that Germany had formally surrendered. The King made his own broadcast that evening, emphasising a spirit of thanksgiving for deliverance and a desire to be worthy of 'those who died for us and to make the world such a world as they would have desired, for their children and for ours'. Three months later, the Americans dropped two atomic bombs on Japan, which ended the war in the Pacific but raised the curtain on an age almost unimaginably more fearful than any that had preceded it.

The King was exhausted by the strain of the war but, as he admitted in his diary, anxiety about the future prevented him from relaxing. Britain was virtually bankrupt, its Empire effectively lost for ever, and a new world order was emerging based on both the opposing ideologies of the new superpowers, the United States and the Soviet Union, and the urgent desire of previously subject or disenfranchised peoples to exercise the right of self-determination. Not only did the simple answers of wartime no longer apply, but it was becoming increasingly difficult to determine what the questions were. To add to the problems of George VI, there was also a new order at home to contend with.

In a general election held immediately after Germany's final defeat, Churchill had been swept from power and the Labour Party, under Clement Attlee, had been elected to govern with a huge parliamentary majority. The King was both shocked and saddened at this outcome, calling the people ungrateful on account of the manner in which they had rejected their wartime leader the minute the war had been won. To make matters worse, Labour had been elected on a programme of industrial and social reform that seemed to the King radical if not extreme. 'My new Government is not too easy & the people are rather difficult to talk to,' he told his brother, the Duke of Gloucester, at the end of 1945.[24]

The real difficulty was not essentially one of substance – though the King, with his natural resistance to change and attachment to tradition, was hardly likely to be enthusiastic towards Labour's reforming zeal – but one of style and circumstance. The illusion fostered by Churchill of the sovereign's influence on affairs was now roughly dismantled: George VI had suddenly to face up to the limitations of constitutional monarchy on the muddled British model. Attlee was far from antagonistic – in fact, he was a strong supporter of the monarchy – and scrupulously observed the conventions, but he did not talk to the King in the confidential way Churchill had adopted. Also, the Prime Minister and his colleagues (with the significant exception of Ernest Bevin, the Foreign Secretary) seemed to pay little attention to the advice offered by the King in accordance with his prerogatives. This caused a certain frustration in George VI. He took seriously Bagehot's view that the very continuity of kingship endowed the sovereign with wisdom and experience often denied to ministers buffeted by the squalls of electoral caprice, and he was irritated when politicians who had never held ministerial office before met royal advice and warning with bland reassurance or polite disregard.[25]

Yet the fact is that George VI was no better equipped than anyone else to navigate the choppy waters of post-war geopolitics. His reign had begun with Britain still a great imperial power and had reached its peak in the heroic stance of the early 1940s, with the United States on the sidelines and the Soviet Union facing extinction. By 1946 the United States had become the most powerful nation on earth, with Stalin's Russia in aggressive competition, as Britain became increasingly marginalised through the break-up of the Empire, economic decline and isolation from the more visionary elements among its neighbours who saw in the concept of a united Europe the prospect of a third force to counteract the influence of the new superpowers. At least the Labour government of 1945 was pragmatic enough to recognise and act within the limits of Britain's reduced circumstances, sublimating what had previously been individual interests in the wider framework of an American-led Western alliance. Whether mistakes were made remains a matter for debate, but surely few would argue with the conclusion that acceptance of America's leadership at least allowed Britain to assume a role at the top of the second rank of international powers.

Of course, there were prices to be paid, political, economic and cultural, and the monarchy was not immune. On August 15th, 1947, George VI ceased to be an emperor when the new independent nations of India and Pakistan came into being, converting themselves into republics not long afterwards. In January 1948 Burma became a republic and severed constitutional links with Britain. The following year Eire rejected the dominion status under which it had chafed since 1922 and became the Republic of Ireland, provoking George VI to ask whether that made him an undesirable alien. Also in 1949 the King, having lost his imperial status, was officially declared head of the Commonwealth: this was a role to which the monarchy would cling tenaciously as its constitutional position in Britain became less and less relevant to government.

Through all this, and the Labour Party's social engineering at home, George VI continued, as his father had done, to slave over state papers, to worry about foreign and domestic affairs and to undertake whatever public duties were required of him. These included an exhausting tour of South Africa in 1947, which failed in its purpose of checking the rise of the Afrikaner Nationalist movement that would soon win power, introduce the abhorrent policy of apartheid and ultimately declare South Africa a republic. The King showed little enthusiasm for the trip and had constantly to be encouraged by the Queen. His thoughts strayed continually back to Britain, where an economic crisis and shortages of fuel coincided with a viciously cold winter, causing real hardship and prompting some criticism of the absence not only of the King and Queen but of their daughters as well. 'He kept saying he should be at home and not lolling about in the summer sun,' wrote the distinguished journalist James Cameron, who was covering the tour. 'He was tense, unbearably nervous, alternating diffidence with sharp bursts of temper. Never was a man so jumpy.' In fact, the strain of the war and the anxieties of the peace had stretched the King's nerves to breaking-point and undermined his always fragile health. His reign had entered its twilight and the world, moving on to what it hoped would be a new dawn, hardly noticed.

Public interest in the monarchy was directed largely towards the heir to the throne, Princess Elizabeth, who in November 1947 provided the kind of royal spectacle not seen since before the war when she married Prince Philip of Greece surrounded by the media circus – including the by then rapidly expanding television service – that was to become one of the main features of royal life in the years that followed. The King continued conscientiously with the tasks of monarchy as he saw them, but his health was now in terminal decline and his spirit more than ever troubled by the courses that domestic and international events were taking. 'Never in the whole history of mankind have things looked gloomier than they do now,' he wrote in the autumn of 1947, 'and one feels so powerless to do anything to help.'[26] On another occasion, in despair at the radical socialist policies Labour was pursuing, he exclaimed: 'Everything is going nowadays. Before long, I shall also have to go.'[27]

In fact, when King George VI died of a coronary thrombosis – after suffering from arteriosclerosis and lung cancer – in the early hours of February 6th, 1952, the monarchy was more secure in public esteem than it had ever been. Any threat to its position came not from socialism but from changing attitudes in society that are not necessarily expressed through politics. Throughout western Europe in the years since the Second World War, the trend has been not towards greater social cohesion and unity but towards division and competition, not towards collectivism but towards factionalism and what is called individual freedom. These are developments George VI, with his strict principles of duty and responsibility, would not have understood, and indeed they are inimical to the British idea of constitutional monarchy, the purpose of which is to symbolise national unity, stability and continuity. As a result, while the monarchy has fulfilled George VI's ideal of being close to its people, it has done so only in respect of what the people see, hear and know of it; in all other respects it has gradually become detached from the mainstream of British life, so that today it is roundly criticised whenever it attempts to become involved in matters deemed to be outside its publicly accepted terms of reference.

It was George VI's triumph that in the early years of the war he achieved, at least in part, the true fusion between sovereign and people which is implicit in the concept of real constitutional monarchy. It was his tragedy that such a fusion lasted only as long as the national emergency and that the sense of familiarity and belonging it engendered would later actually undermine the effectiveness, the authority and even the justification for the existence of the institution which he believed he had been called to the throne to save.

16

Palace in Wonderland

'That which is mystic in its claims; that which is occult in its mode of action; that which is brilliant to the eye; that which is seen vividly for a moment, and then is seen no more; that which is hidden and unhidden; that which is specious, and yet interesting, palpable in its seeming, and yet professing to be more than palpable in its results; this, howsoever its form may change, or however we may define it or describe it, is the sort of thing – the only sort – which yet comes home to the mass of men.' Those were the thoughts of Walter Bagehot in the middle of Queen Victoria's reign, when he characterised the masses as 'scarcely more civilised than the majority of two thousand years ago . . . narrow-minded, unintelligent, incurious . . . unable to comprehend the idea of a constitution'. Much has changed in the intervening century and a quarter, not least the general level of education and sophistication, yet as a description of the way in which most British people view their monarchy, Bagehot's words remain as valid today as they were in the 1860s. Indeed, if anything, they are even more accurate now than they were then.

Royalty has become an obsession in post-war, post-imperial Britain. Hardly a day goes by without a clutch of royal stories and photographs in the popular press or some film of unimportant royal activities at the end of television news bulletins. Royal tours abroad, visits at home and ceremonial occasions are filmed, broadcast and written about *in extenso*, often regurgitated on television several times a day and again in compilation at the end of the week. Women's magazines earnestly discuss the merits and demerits of the Princess of Wales (usually incorrectly referred to as Princess Diana) and the Duchess of York (familiar to all as 'Fergie'), describing in great detail what they wear and why they wear it, speculating on the progress of the supposed competition between the two – though what exactly they are competing *for* is never explained – and on the state of their respective marriages. There are even several publications whose contents are devoted entirely to the lives of the royals; fan magazines, one might call them, not much different in character from those offered to the gullible young in order to promote the careers of pop stars.

People who should know better, or who perhaps have nothing better to do, discourse at length on the character and performance of the various representatives of the monarchy, without really knowing anything about them. As a result, a sort of royal league table or best-seller list has evolved, with individuals moving up and down according to perceptions of their behaviour, public and private, or their entertainment value or the manner and regularity with which they carry out the duties expected of them in return for their Civil List payments. The Queen Mother, for instance, is considered to be the most popular royal figure in history, as well as 'the world's favourite grannie', a real trouper who can teach the ingénues a thing or two and a hard worker who earns every penny she receives from the taxpayer. Princess Anne, once a prime target for the press on account of her alleged grumpiness and lack of co-operation, has now become 'Britain's royal favourite', representing the caring face of monarchy in her work on behalf of the Save The Children Fund, of which she is president.

'She's been called rude, tactless, outspoken. She's been criticised for her dress, her views and her lack of smiles,' five million Sunday newspaper readers were told in 1985. 'But all that is in the past ... Her critics are finally realising that Britain has never before had a Princess like Anne.'[1] Two years later, it was the Duchess of York who had soared up the royal charts, according to another newspaper: 'When she trumped even Princess Anne, until now the Action Woman of the royal family, by learning to fly a Piper Warrior, it won her more kudos with the Queen and Prince Philip than if she had taken a first at Oxford.'[2] So where did all this leave the first young royal superstar? The press pronounced:

> There is little doubt that it was the Di-mania which finally decided Anne to go out and beat Diana at her own game. Both she and Prince Philip became increasingly angry at the attention which the young Princess of Wales was receiving, because they felt Diana hadn't worked for it. The showdown came when Diana put up her hair on the day of the State Opening of Parliament, so stealing the whole show from the Queen. The result was a family row at Windsor Castle ...

From then on it was all downhill:

Once Diana was the darling of the British press, but recently it has been hard for her to do anything right. She has been criticised for her solo excursions to pop concerts and discos, and for her choice of companions such as club-owner Peter Stringfellow, dancer Wayne Sleep, comedian Pamela Stephenson and pop musicians Elton John and Boy George.[3]

One remarkable thing about all this breathless prose – and there is a great deal more in the same vein – is that it resembles nothing so much as a synopsis for one of the popular television soap operas, *Dallas* and *Dynasty*. For example:

In the play of personalities around the Queen it is crucial to grasp the way in which, popular or unpopular, well or badly behaved, the characters continue to reflect well on the monarch herself. Never has she made a single *faux pas*. The royals who don't come up to scratch only serve to highlight the blamelessness of the rest. Few are permanently black sheep, but many have taken their turn, albeit briefly: a restless Prince Philip, a disappointed Princess Margaret; in the next generation, a bolshie Princess Anne and, almost comically, the go-getting Princess Michael. The shadowy mantle has now settled on Prince Edward, currently mooching around at home. Nobody wants the next contender to be the Princess of Wales, but she's significantly closer to it than anyone else. Meanwhile, to everyone's relief, Andrew has been upgraded to another echelon of the family Firm . . .[4]

And the next thrilling episode featured the Prince and Princess of Wales – were they on the brink of divorce? In the autumn of 1987, thousands of column inches were devoted to the subject. It began with the tabloid press speculating about a rift between the couple because they had not been seen together for four weeks and continued with rumours that an obscure titled lady was Prince Charles's mistress. There followed reports of a 'council of war' at the Palace to deal with the crisis, then the popular columnists weighed in with advice to the Prince about how to be a better husband and father and to the Princess about how to save her marriage, followed by expressions of sympathy for the Queen in the midst of her distress. Finally, with no hard facts at its disposal, the press began to write about the press writing about the royals, the more sober newspapers delivering weighty opinions on the constitutional implications (of which there were none) and sneering at the tabloid 'rat pack' while being afraid themselves of missing out

on what might, just might, be the story of the decade. When considering the media coverage of the royal family, it is important to remember
that the British press has never forgiven itself for not reporting the
love affair between Edward VIII and Mrs Simpson and for failing to
discover in advance that Princess Margaret was to marry Antony
Armstrong-Jones.

The Charles-and-Di divorce scenario ran its course like all the
other storylines, as different and perhaps even more appealing ideas
began to ferment in the minds of the scriptwriters. One misunderstanding, one rumour, one unguarded comment, one instinctive action
could be the beginning of a long-running new series. The soap-opera
analogy is inescapable. After all, the British royal family more than
meets the requirements of the genre: unimaginable wealth, ineffable
style, obvious glamour and limitless potential for the clash of wildly
varying personalities in an exotic and claustrophobic setting. The
more serious newspapers have been alive to the similarities. One
commented, ignoring its own role in the process:

> The royal family has become so used to being treated like a soap
> opera by large sections of the media that some of its members are
> beginning to act as if they are in one. This past week alone saw
> Prince Edward play the touchy, misunderstood youth, ready to rage
> against cynical journalists who did not share his passions; Prince
> Charles had a walk-on part as the bad-tempered husband who
> scolds his wife for sitting on the bonnet of his precious sports car,
> only to prang it himself a few hours later (there's soap-opera justice
> for you!); the carefree Princess Diana was meanwhile wandering
> around Ascot playfully jabbing at anybody in sight with her brolly;
> and the Duchess of York was at her jolly-hockey-sticks best (or
> worst) cheering on her team against other royal sports in a television
> charity fundraiser.[5]

But all the commentators, well-intentioned or otherwise, have
overlooked two crucial elements separating the House of Windsor
and the Ewings of *Dallas*, the Carringtons of *Dynasty* or the eponymous
Colbys, differences that reflect significantly on both the modern
monarchy itself and public attitudes towards it. The first is that the
characters in the television series are fictional and therefore behave
exactly as their creators dictate, while the Windsors are real people,
with the ability to exercise at least some control over their own actions.
Unfortunately, they do not appear to be real, and that is partly the
fault of themselves and their advisers. Bagehot believed that there

should always be distance between monarchy and people, mainly in order that the shortcomings of its representatives should not be recognised. Lifting the veil, he believed, would rob the monarchy of its precious mystique. Bagehot was completely wrong. What has happened as the veil has been lifted is that the mystique of the royal family has been intensified, to the point where its members now appear to be no more real than the Colbys, the Carringtons or the Ewings.

As an illustration of this, consider the action of the Sunday newspaper which, in May 1987, published what amounted to the contents of royal wastepaper baskets – cards attached to family gifts, Christmas greetings and so on, provided by a former palace maid who professed to believe that such trivia were of sufficient national importance to warrant not only their collection but also their publication. The newspaper, and therefore presumably its readers, appeared to find deep significance in the fact that the royals called each other by nicknames and pet names. One must assume that they previously imagined the Prince of Wales addressing his mother as 'Your Majesty', like a character in a fairytale, or that the Queen's birthday gifts to her children were endorsed 'The Queen' rather than 'Mummy'.[6] This rubbish (and the word is used literally), suitably illustrated with handwritten examples and occupying two full pages in the newspaper, revealed some of the serious confusion with which we regard our monarchy. On the one hand, we want the royal family to be just like us, and to be reassured that they are, but on the other hand we know that they cannot be just like us, otherwise we would not be interested in them. Thus the air of unreality surrounding the monarchy is reinforced: we do not fully accept the royal family either as mystical beings or as flesh-and-blood ordinary humans.

It is easy to blame the media for this situation, and such criticism is certainly justified in the light of the trivialisation, sensationalism and frequently the sheer invention that accompanies most reporting of matters royal. But newspapers, magazines and television are not in the business of making themselves unpopular, particularly when they are trying to appeal to a mass market, so that the extent and nature of royal coverage must reflect public demand. Surveys have shown that people frequently do not believe what they read in the tabloid newspapers, but they nevertheless continue to read them in large numbers, saying that they do so for entertainment. Hence the attitude that places royal 'news' in the same category as stories about the 'real' lives of the soap-opera stars – and leads to a sort of wonderland somewhere between fantasy and reality.

The psychological, social and political factors influencing this phenomenon are too complex to discuss here, but the historical development of the dichotomy in public perceptions of the monarchy, and the part played by the institution itself in that process, are easy to trace. In the nineteenth century, most people knew next to nothing about Queen Victoria, but she was vividly real to them as their revered sovereign. The next generation knew much more about the personality and proclivities of Edward VII, and so he was even more real in the eyes of the public, because he was recognisable both as a monarch and as a man. It was with George V that the vision started to become blurred. Here was a king, and a man, with no outstanding features, positive or negative: no great qualities of intellect or character, but no easily identifiable vices or deficiencies, either. Queen Victoria and Edward VII had, in their very different ways, been larger than life. George V displayed no particularity of scale; he was, to use his own word, ordinary. The only way to establish him as a popular symbol was to make a virtue of his ordinariness, and the effect of that was to bring the person of the sovereign closer to the experience of everyday life, while the monarchy itself – because of its essentially extraordinary nature – remained remote from it.

This coincided with a period of fundamental social adjustment, when the middle class finally established itself as the ruling class and the by now widely enfranchised working classes sought to improve their conditions and their position in society by combining in political movements that could make the most effective use of their votes. Through a concatenation of political sleight-of-hand on the part of the middle-class rulers and George V's own desire to 'represent' all his people as a father-figure, the notion of the 'people's king' was fostered, so that while the monarchy remained attached to the feudal aristocratic tradition, the sovereign himself began to be viewed as both a public servant and a sort of unelected tribune of the people, a moderating force in relations between the rulers and the ruled. The novelty of the situation, and the growth in the popularity of the monarchy, obscured the fact that the institution was developing in ways that were ultimately irreconcilable.

The eccentric King Edward VIII almost destroyed this cosy arrangement with his colourful and populist style, a curious and, to many people, exciting mixture of old-fashioned aristocratic arrogance, disregard for what had become the accepted images of monarchy and a desire to be the same as other men. A stronger, more astute and less obsessive character might have succeeded, possibly leading the British monarchy into the kind of position now established in Spain under

King Juan Carlos, where the role of the sovereign as head of state is clearly defined and central. But Edward VIII was disapproved of by a political class mostly terrified by the unpredictable nature of populism, and his determination to place his own needs before all others gave the mediocracy the weapon it needed to bring him down. The safe, predictable and obedient George VI restored the desired balance.

George VI was as blameless as and, if anything, even more ordinary than his father. He was also more closely associated with the working classes through his industrial welfare work and the democratic experiment of the Duke of York's Camp. Moreover, his accession took place in the midst of what he perceived as a crisis for the monarchy. In the light of all these factors, the popularity of the monarchy was judged to be more important than its constitutional position, and the early years of George VI's reign were largely devoted to winning popular approval, 'repairing the damage' supposedly (though not actually) caused by the abdication of Edward VIII. For the monarchy, therefore, popularity became an end in itself and provided the principal justification for the survival of the institution.

The rapid spread of television from the 1950s onwards offered new opportunities for the royal family to establish itself ever more firmly in the public consciousness, and new techniques for doing so. By the mid-1960s, documentary programmes about the 'private' lives of Queen Elizabeth II and her family were beginning to appear alongside live coverage of ceremonial events, with a concomitant increase in confusion as to the nature and the functions of the monarchy. More than any other medium, television promotes an impression of participation and familiarity, so that, on the one hand, the viewer can seem to be among the crowd watching the Queen, in full regal splendour, at the ceremony of Trooping the Colour and, on the other hand, can have the sense of accompanying her, in off-duty headscarf and raincoat, walking the dogs at Balmoral. But because television pictures are actually one step removed from reality, there is no distinction between the images they portray. Which is the 'real' Queen: the imposing figure with crown, orb and sceptre at the State Opening of Parliament, or the small and rather undistinguished-looking woman stepping out of the Land-Rover?

This confusion of images was addressed by the cultural critic Judith Williamson in an essay published in 1985 and entitled 'Royalty and Representation'. Williamson wrote:

> In one form of imagery the Royals are just like ourselves, in the other they are delightfully different . . . . Formal 'royal' occasions

such as coronations and weddings give rise to a coinage of heraldic household articles whose charm lies in their combination of the important and the everyday. Conversely, the informal imagery of Royalty takes its interest from the fact that it *is* 'Royals' who are shown in otherwise completely unremarkable situations . . . . The enormous effort the *Sun* photographers took to sneak photographs of Princess Diana bathing when pregnant on holiday is striking for the very banality of the product: the whole point was to get shockingly *ordinary* pictures, far from glamorous, of a woman looking exactly like any other pregnant mum . . . . The urge to find embarrassingly homely pictures of Royals is in part a wish to bring them down, to show that they are not really superior to us at all.[7]

Williamson saw this paradox as part of the essential function of the modern British constitutional monarchy. I would argue that it is in fact nothing more than an example of the complete failure on the part of the people, the politicians and the monarchy itself to answer, or even to ask, the questions, why does Britain *have* a monarchy, what is its purpose and is it needed? The people have been content to be entertained by royal pageant and royal peep-show. The politicians have found it convenient to maintain the monarchy as a bulwark against radical change and as an apolitical rallying-point for national unity during a period of ever widening national division. As for the royals themselves, they are naturally interested most in their own survival and do not wish to take risks by raising awkward questions. They have not forgotten what happened to Edward VIII.

The trouble is that the real lesson of the Abdication lies in its aftermath, the immediate transfer of loyalty to the new King George VI. Public loyalty is both fragile and fickle, public taste changes. Soap operas come and go, but, unlike the stars of the fictional family sagas, the members of the Windsor dynasty cannot simply go out and find other roles to play. Towards the end of 1987, surveys of public opinion began to show that interest in the royal soap opera was declining. Popularity for its own sake carries risks, too.

Which brings us to the second vital difference between the representatives of the monarchy and the television heroes and heroines they have come so closely to resemble in the public mind. An essential part of the fascination of the soap opera on the *Dallas* and *Dynasty* model is that it concerns power and, more particularly, the exercise of that power. The constitutional monarchy, however, has no power; all its trappings are constructed round a vacuum; fundamentally, it is able to do nothing more than exist – its only remaining purpose is to *be*.

Bagehot provided an elegant justification for such an existence, but that was more than a century ago, and much has changed in the meantime (quite apart from the fact that, as I have indicated, it is arguable whether all that Bagehot said was true when he was writing, given his bourgeois prejudices). Let us take Bagehot's four principal reasons in favour of constitutional monarchy and consider whether they remain valid today, if they ever were.

The first advantage of monarchy, according to Bagehot, was that it was the most intelligible part of the political system as far as the vacant masses were concerned – ordinary people, he claimed, really believed that Queen Victoria ruled the country. Even if that were true in the middle of the nineteenth century, and there is plenty of evidence to suggest that it was not, it is certainly far from the reality now, when politics finds its way into almost every aspect of life and the hand of a highly visible government reaches out to touch every inhabitant of these islands. Nobody is in any doubt of the government's responsibilities and nobody believes that the monarchy has anything more than a vague influence on the conduct of national affairs. Indeed, there is a public outcry when any member of the royal family is judged to be acting or speaking 'politically'. Far from being the most intelligible part of the system, the monarchy, as I have already indicated, is probably the least understood, in spite of the fact that it is perceived to be more 'democratic' than in the past.

Bagehot also believed that an important function of monarchy was its endowment of government with the moral authority of religion: not only was the monarch the titular head of the Church of England, the state religion, but it was also widely held that he or she reigned by the grace of God and so was owed allegiance in its most mystical form. This may have been all very well in the 1860s, when religion – no matter how hypocritical those who claimed to practise it – was still a dominant force in society and man, no matter how great his arrogance, still did not place his own laws above the laws of God. Today, when the state religion has lost almost all its moral authority and secular institutions, such as the courts, tend to exercise greater influence on most forms of belief and social behaviour, the phrase 'by the grace of God' has become merely a quaint form of words evoking nothing more than the lost glorious past so dear to British hearts daunted by the complexities of the post-industrial revolution. The mysticism of that old-time religion, even in significant sections of the Church of England itself, has given way to a pseudo-rationalist, pseudo-political sloganising in a desperate attempt to make the Church 'relevant' to a secular society. Where does that leave the moral authority of the monarchy?

Thirdly, according to Bagehot, the sovereign was the head of the society and the state and, as such, was essential to the pageantry of nationhood. Certainly, the pageantry still exists, but who now believes that the rituals of monarchy have any meaning or any purpose other than to provide entertainment? Who, indeed, remembers or cares very much about the original significance of such ceremonies? Again the images have become confused. No distinction is made between the State Opening of Parliament and the royal wedding: both are mere spectacle. Furthermore, it can be argued that the maintenance of such rituals serves narrow political ends both by helping to obscure change and by disguising the need for change. Come the microchip and the space shuttle and the growth of Islamic fundamentalism and the economic power of the Pacific Basin, good old England will always remain an island of civilisation protected by its traditions from the antics of those damned foreigners.

The visit of King Hassan of Morocco to London in 1987 prompted one tabloid journalist to refer to him as a so-called monarch, implying that our own dear Queen was endowed with much more legitimacy than some jumped-up little Arab who called himself a king. The fact is that Hassan is his country's head of government and as such might claim a somewhat greater degree of importance than Elizabeth II, who is little more than an adornment. Pageantry and ceremonial have always been used to appeal to the basest instincts of nationalism, whether in Nazi Germany, the Soviet Union, the People's Republic of China, the United States or Britain itself. The political nature of such practices was dramatically demonstrated by the 'victory parade' following the grubby little war in the Falklands, when the chief ceremonial figure was not the Queen but the Prime Minister, Margaret Thatcher. The fact that public spectacle is dressed in the accoutrements of a medieval power structure merely serves to emphasise that the people to whose emotions it is intended to appeal have allowed themselves to be manipulated for that much longer.

As for the position of the sovereign at the head of society, Judith Williamson has dealt with that in properly sceptical fashion:

> Post-Victorian royalty seems to have combined both the structure of a feudal aristocracy and the culture of the capitalist bourgeois and petit-bourgeois, incorporating the most conservative elements of both systems. Moreover, the fact that the structure itself belongs to an earlier system, historically, keeps those at the bottom of the

present social structure in a state of emotional feudalism, looking backwards instead of round about. It is, however, the petit-bourgeois – the class with the least clear place under capitalism – that this opportunity for looking backwards really appeals to, and for whom the royal family is an especially important focus.[8]

But what of Bagehot's fourth basic reason for the retention of the constitutional monarchy, the sovereign's role as head of the nation's morality? The moral hypocrisy of the Victorians has become legendary, but in the case of public perceptions of the royal family it has also continued unabated. To put it shortly, the royal family has been and still is expected to live up to a standard of morality that the majority of the rest of the population has long since abandoned; it must remain trapped in its Bagehotian time-warp.

The abdication of Edward VIII, allegedly because of his desire to marry a divorcee, was followed by a significant relaxation in the laws governing divorce. Princess Margaret was widely condemned in 1955 because she wanted to marry a divorced man, Group-Captain Peter Townsend, and her popularity as a royal figure has declined markedly since 1978 when she herself was divorced from Lord Snowdon, even though the divorce rate in general has risen steadily since the Second World War until now one marriage in every three is legally dissolved. *The Times* enshrined this hypocritical attitude in an editorial on the Townsend affair, claiming that the Queen was a mirror 'in whom her people see their better selves reflected, and since part of their ideal is of family life, the Queen's family has its own part in the reflection'. That the illusion remains intact is evidenced by the furore that surrounded suggestions that the Prince and Princess of Wales might divorce. At the time, William Deedes, a former MP and ex-editor of the *Daily Telegraph*, commented:

> Looking back over English history, I doubt if there has ever been a period in which, taking it all in all, the Royal Family, under the Queen, has led such blameless lives. Nor has there been any period when it has suffered more from downright offensiveness by sections of the press ... The Royals would have fared better on an island inhabited by republican-minded cannibals and surrounded by piranhas.[9]

It appears, then, that we have shredded Bagehot's criteria and there is no longer any justification for the retention of the constitutional monarchy as Britain steps somewhat fearfully towards the twenty-first century. But while it is true that the Bagehot version does not now apply – if it ever really did – there is a future role for the monarchy if both it and the people over whom it reigns can cast aside the web of fantasy, myth, assumption and confusion that surrounds the institution.

A good beginning might be the recognition of the real importance of a politically impartial monarchy, which is not generally understood. Since Britain has no written constitution, no Bill of Rights, no single body of law that, irrespective of party politics or ideology, defines what the nation is, there is in effect no state. Rather, the notion of the state as a political entity changes according to the principles of the party in government. Thus, since 1945, when the first Labour government with real power came into office, Britain has veered wildly between collectivism and individualism, between self-interest as an engine of progress and its opposite, the subordination of self-interest to the good of the country as a whole. One result of this has been the now widespread acceptance of the idea of rights without responsibilities, the assumption that the state provides irrespective of the contributions individuals make to it, the belief that somehow the government is independent of the people who both vote for it and provide it with finance in the form of taxes. Such confusion is inevitable when the only absolute manifestation of statehood is the monarchy.

The same is not true of a democratic republic. In order to function a republic must have a constitution defined as a single entity, whether it invests actual power in the hands of the president or, as in the case of the United States, allows for a separation of powers between an executive branch headed by the president and a legislative branch represented by the Houses of the Congress. In either case, presidents may come and go, may pursue differing ideological aims, may act benevolently or malignantly, but the state remains a historical fact basically unchanged, except superficially, by the activities of particular presidents. In Britain, the state would in effect cease to exist if the monarchy ceased to exist. Ironically, the same situation applies in a dictatorship, where the state and all its works are embodied in one person: when that one person is removed, the entire state has to be recreated. Under the British system, however, the single person upon whom the whole concept of statehood depends, the monarch, has no political power and is even deemed to have no political existence. Since that condition actually renders the state unworkable, we have seen the growth of the presidential premiership: the prime minister has become, in effect, the ruler and the monarchy has become irrelevant to the political process, except in the most peripheral sense.

[273]

Such a situation can continue indefinitely where there is a broad consensus within the country, where political parties and their supporters differ only in matters of detail and there is general agreement as to what is best for the country and all its citizens. In Britain that consensus no longer exists. The electorate is deeply, perhaps irrevocably split on matters of defence and national security, of social policy, of industrial and economic policy and in its visions of the future. Such ideological differences are inflamed by the British electoral system, which militates against coalition because of its insistence on simple numerical majority and therefore effectively disenfranchises those who do not vote for a particular government for the entire period during which that government is in power. What all this means in practice is that governments are becoming less and less representative of the population as a whole and the sense of national cohesion that the extension of participatory democracy was designed to promote is being eroded. As a result, a growing minority of people is losing faith in parliamentary representation and resorting to extra-parliamentary 'direct' action in an attempt to influence the policies of a government with which it disagrees. Confrontation has replaced consensus, ideology has begun to obscure notions of the national interest. Since the state, other than in the institution of the monarchy, does not exist independently of the party in power, it is not difficult to foresee the possibility, at some point, of a descent either into anarchy or into an authoritarian regime.

If one of these should come to pass, the British will have only themselves to blame, because they have continued to subscribe to the fantasy of statehood embodied in a powerless, apolitical monarchy. They have been encouraged to do so in part by every sovereign since George V, all of whom have interpreted their duty as a matter of taking the line of least resistance, though with the best of intentions in all cases except that of Edward VIII. The history of the monarchy in the twentieth century has been one of effectiveness sacrificed on the altar of popularity, of continuing retreat into a never-never land of empty glamour and fairytale simplicity, of steady decline towards irrelevance and, unless there is a change, ultimate extinction.

I hope that in this book I have provided some clues as to how and why this happened: a queen of exceptional longevity and capricious nature; a king too old, too self-indulgent and too set in his ways to be more than an historical apostrophe; the headstrong and wayward Edward VIII; and the two Georges, both promoted beyond their expectations and their capabilities. It should have been different with Elizabeth II, who came to the throne young, with an alert mind and a strong consort – but the legacy of her father and grandfather was overwhelming, for both the Queen and her subjects, and the dreams of a new 'golden age' that accompanied her accession have not been fulfilled. No doubt I shall be accused of being anti-monarchy, but those who have read this book with some care and an open mind will see that what emerges from it is not a case for the establishment of a republic, but an argument for a stronger, healthier and more useful monarchy.

The opportunity is there. The Prince of Wales, unlike his mother, his grandfather and his great-grandfather, was born to succeed to the throne. He has grown up and learned the business of monarchy in relatively stable and peaceful times. He is better educated than any heir to the throne this century and has shown himself to be more thoughtful and more cultured than most (even if the intellectual elite dismisses him as 'middlebrow'). Like the last Prince of Wales, later Edward VIII, he has shown an exceptional degree of interest in the least favoured members of British society – those to whom participatory democracy is virtually meaningless – and he has not been afraid to make statements and speeches that have been interpreted as 'political'. Already warnings have been sounded by politicians, mainly those of the so-called 'new Right', who do not like the old-fashioned liberal tone of what he says, while even those who broadly agree with his sentiments and defend his right to express them caution that he must do no such thing when he becomes king. These are signs that the monarchy can still be a force to be reckoned with. What it needs is a framework within which it can use its influence to restore the cohesion that is being destroyed by recent trends in politics.

One solution would be finally to discard the constitutional model to which Britain has clung so tenaciously and so illogically, and to recognise Bagehot's exposition for what it is, the interesting and illuminating view of one man at a particular period in history. Once freed from the mythical concept of state-as-monarchy, the British could then set about providing themselves with a real constitution, making themselves citizens rather than subjects, defining their rights and responsibilities and those of the people who presume to lead the nation. There is no need to sweep away the institutions of the past, so long as the people, the citizens, are clear about what it is they require those institutions to do. What is needed is a state that exists in itself, independently of the changing fortunes of political parties, so that there is a level of politics that transcends partisan sympathies.

If the monarchy were to be allowed to represent such a state, it would automatically become a useful political force, as the Prince

Consort, and others, believed it could and should be. The sovereign would be a citizen like everyone else (though without a vote), able to express his or her opinions whether or not they reflected the policies of the party in power. There would be constitutional guarantees of the impartiality of the monarchy and a solemn duty upon it to act in the national interest. The relationship between the sovereign and the government would be closely defined and, with a written constitution, any dispute concerning that relationship could be referred to the judiciary. The French have experienced the successful 'cohabitation' of a socialist president and a conservative prime minister; American presidents have for years worked successfully with Congresses controlled by an opposing political party. There is no reason why, with the main elements of a system already in place, Britain cannot have, instead of an increasingly presidential premiership, a presidential style of monarchy. Then, perhaps, the concept of the sovereign as representative of all the people could become a reality, rather than the fiction with which George V and George VI deluded themselves and which has led to even greater delusions.

Notes

Except where otherwise stated, the royal letters, diary entries and memoranda quoted in the text are preserved in the Royal Archives at Windsor Castle. The author is grateful for permission to reproduce such material, the copyright of which is held by Her Majesty the Queen. Thanks are also due to the publishers of the various books mentioned in the following list, and in the text, for permission to quote from them, and to the National Library of Wales, which holds the copyright of quoted letters written by Lloyd George.

Introduction   Monarchy and Mediocracy

1. In *George V*, published in February 1936, shortly after the death of the King.
2. In an essay entitled 'The Eighteenth Century', published in *The Oxford Illustrated History of Britain*.
3. This comment was made in the autobiography of the Duke of Windsor, *A King's Story*.
4. In *A Thousand Years of British Monarchy*.
5. *The British Constitution*.

Chapter 1   Albert's Memorial

1. Quoted in *Victoria R.I.* by Elizabeth Longford.
2. Quoted in *Melbourne* by David Cecil.
3. Quoted in *The Prince Consort* by Roger Fulford.
4. In a little-known book, written late in his career, and entitled *In the Fourth Year*. Looking back to the beginning of the twentieth century, and lamenting the decline of republicanism, Wells wrote of the royal family: 'The marriages, the funerals, the coronations of this amazing breed of idols were matters of almost universal worship.'
5. In a letter to Lord Granville, the Foreign Secretary, on December 3rd, 1870.

Chapter 2   'Peculiar to Himself'

1. Quoted in *King Edward the Seventh* by Philip Magnus.

Chapter 3   The Education of Princes

1. Rumours about the involvement of the Duke of Clarence in the 'Ripper' murders arose from descriptions of a suspect who had actually been seen leaving the scene of one horrific killing. Eyewitnesses said he was of medium height, with a small, fair moustache and that he wore a deerstalker hat and 'collars and cuffs'. Eddy wore a blond moustache and had been photographed wearing a deerstalker; his father's nickname for him was 'Collars-and-Cuffs', from the Prince's habit of wearing high collars and wide cuffs to disguise his unusually long neck and arms. It has been established that police officers in Whitechapel, where the murders took place, were among those harbouring suspicions against the Prince. No real evidence was ever found and, notwithstanding the many theories that have appeared during the past century, the identity of the killer remains a matter for speculation.
2. The phrase was used by the Queen in a letter to King Leopold of the Belgians dated June 8th, 1865, at which time the Queen had not yet seen the new baby.
3. The Queen expressed her views in a letter to the Prince of Wales on June 13th, 1865.

4. The misgivings of the Teck children, in particular, are recorded in *King George V, A Personal Memoir* by John Gore.
5. *George V.*
6. This was part of the Queen's reply, on February 15th, 1877, to a memorandum from Dalton arguing in favour of naval training.
7. Commander G. W. Hillyard, in a BBC schools broadcast after the death of George V.
8. From Nicolson's official biography, *King George V: His Life and Reign.*

Chapter 4   Bred to the Sea

1. Dalton told the Prince of Wales, in a letter dated May 16th, 1882, that the book would appear in the names of the Princes and would 'redound to their credit and to that of Your Royal Highness, I hope'. The tutor even went to the length of dedicating the book to Queen Victoria from her 'affectionate and dutiful grandsons'.
2. Commander G. W. Hillyard, *op. cit.*
3. *Ibid.*
4. Letter to the commander of HMS *Canada*, Captain Francis Durrant, signed by both the Prince of Wales and the Queen. Quoted by Nicolson, *op. cit.*
5. In a letter dated October 21st, 1886.
6. The quotation comes from a letter written to Prince George by Princess Alexandra on April 11th, 1890. The antagonism of the Princess towards Germans stemmed from the fact that in Bismarck's establishment of his 'Greater Germany', Alexandra's father had lost the duchies of Schleswig-Holstein and her sister's husband, the Duke of Cumberland, had been 'robbed' of his private fortune.
7. These revelations were found by Harold Nicolson in the diary of Prince George for the year 1888. They are reported in *Harold Nicolson: A Biography* by James Lees-Milne.
8. Letter quoted in *Queen Alexandra* by Georgina Battiscombe.

Chapter 5   Grand New Duke of York

1. Newspaper reports of the case reveal that the Prince was ill at ease in court and answered the questions put to him in a voice so low that his replies were frequently inaudible. This helped to reinforce the impression carefully presented by Gordon Cumming's counsel, Sir Edward Clarke, that his client was a victim rather than a villain, so that when the verdict went against him, there was an outburst of hissing in the court.

2. The Queen's view was expressed in a letter to her eldest daughter, Princess Victoria, the German empress.

3. Prince George was writing to Captain Stephenson, his former commanding officer and a family friend, in April 1891. The letter is quoted by Gore, *op. cit.*

4. John Gore refers to a letter, written by an unnamed member of the household to the Queen's secretary, which suggested that the severe shock suffered by Prince George on the death of his brother would not be alleviated by a period of inactivity. According to Gore, the Prince himself came to share that view.

5. Dawson's biographer, Francis Watson, revealed in an article in the December 1986 issue of *History Today* that while researching his book he had discovered from Dawson's diary that the doctor had, for humanitarian reasons, administered to the dying King a fatal dose of morphia and cocaine. Watson was quoted in *The Times* as saying that he had not included this information in his book, published in 1951, because Dawson's widow had thought it too controversial.

6. The fact that the possibility of altering the succession was seriously considered is reported on two separate occasions by Dermot Morrah, in books written with the co-operation of the royal family (see Bibliography). Morrah says that 'some men of authority in the state' as well as members of the royal family and the Household discussed the idea that the Duke of Kent should become king after the abdication of Edward VIII. One reason given was that the Duke had a son who could have become Prince of Wales. According to Morrah, the Duke of York 'would never on his own account have repudiated the new load of responsibility; but he shrank from imposing the burden eventually on his daughter'. Morrah summed up the constitutional position of 1936 thus: 'Since Parliament must be asked to alter the laws of succession so as to transfer the Crown from the heir designated by the Act of Settlement to some other person, it was not a legal necessity that the person selected should be the next in hereditary order.' It was, of course, the Abdication that required an alteration in the laws of succession – the fact that the designated successor had renounced his claim. It seems logical to assume that the situation

would have been the same had the Duke of Clarence renounced *his* claim to the throne, even before his succession.

7. Magazine articles of the time concentrate on the smallness of York Cottage and, with obvious disappointment, its lack of grandeur and style. In 1901, Edward VII tried to persuade his son to move his family to Osborne House, commenting in a letter that 'I can hardly look on the Cottage as a country house'.

Chapter 6 Royal 'Regiment' of Wales

1. Queen Victoria expressed her wishes to the Duke of York just three days after the birth of the new heir to the throne, saying that 'The country would expect that dear Grandpapa's name should follow mine in future to mark the Victorian era.' The Duke responded on July 1st, drawing the following comment from the Queen the next day: 'My chief object and anxiety about *Albert* is that it should *mark* the Dynasty which becomes on dear Papa's succeeding me, like the Norman, Plantagenet, Tudor (fr. the grandfather of Henvy VII), Stewart [*sic*] and finally Brunswick & all will be united in the Coburg dynasty.'

2. The source for this is Lord Esher, recalling an incident that occurred shortly before the coronation of Edward VII in August 1902. At dinner, the Prince of Wales told Esher of the prophecy, made some forty years earlier, and begged him not to tell the King, who was of a superstitious nature. 'One of Prince Edward's names is David,' said Esher in great excitement, and he commented: 'I don't think the Prince of Wales is altogether free from superstition himself, but he is reconciled to a short reign.' Esher's *Journals and Letters*, edited by Maurice V. Brett, were published in four volumes between 1934 and 1938.

3. This is an undated letter among Queen Mary's papers in the Royal Archives, quoted by John Wheeler-Bennett in his official biography of King George VI.

4. Reported by Bryant in *George V*.

5. In *Edward VIII*, Chapter 1.

6. Chapter 1 of *King George VI* by Denis Judd.

7. In a letter to his wife dated September 10th, 1910.

8. *Lord Derby: King of Lancashire*.

9. *Diaries and Letters*.

10. This was in April 1900 and the new arrival was Prince Henry. The story comes from George V himself; he wrote: 'David, of course, asked some very funny questions. I told him that baby had flown in at the window

during the night, and he at once asked where his wings were and I said they had been cut off.' From a manuscript collection at the Imperial War Museum.

11. The remark of the Empress is recorded in *Queen Mary* by James Pope-Hennessy.
12. *Thatched with Gold.*
13. In a letter to her husband, reproduced by Pope-Hennessy, *op. cit.*
14. *George V.*

Chapter 7   An Honest Man's Conviction

1. Christopher Hibbert, *Edward VII: A Portrait.* The King's state of mind is also referred to in the memoirs of Princess Daisy of Pless.
2. *George V.*
3. The government issued an Order in Council prohibiting banks from paying money to anyone considered to be acting against the national interest. The King pointed out that this was an inflammatory step, given that the strikers were displaying extremely moderate behaviour. 'Anything done to touch the pockets of those who are now only existing on strike pay might cause exasperation and serious reprisals on the part of the sufferers,' he told the Cabinet, adding that it would be 'a grave mistake to do anything which might be interpreted as confiscation . . .' See Nicolson's *King George V,* Julian Symons's *The General Strike,* and others.
4. *Diaries and Letters.*
5. Introduction to the Fontana edition of *The English Constitution.*
6. Quoted in *The Peoples of Ireland* by Liam de Paor.
7. In *The Great Hunger.*
8. Interviewed in the Channel 4 television documentary series *Crown and Shamrock.*
9. This comment was reported in the *New York Times.* Although it was denied at the time, it was subsequently revealed that the conversation on which it was based – between the American reporter and the editor of *The Times,* Wickham Steed – did in fact take place, though Steed had apparently believed it to be off the record. According to Nicolson and others, the comment accurately reflected the King's views.
10. In *Conservatism,* published in 1919, quoted by Grainger.
11. In *Patriotisms, Britain 1900–1939.*

Chapter 8 The People's King

1. In a letter to his wife dated May 8th, 1910.
2. There may have been an element of deception here on the part of Lord Knollys, one of the King's private secretaries. Knollys did not tell the King of Balfour's expressed willingness, in April 1910, to form an alternative government: George V did not know of it until 1913, after Knollys had retired. Such knowledge, the King noted on the relevant documents in the Royal Archives, would have had 'an important bearing and influence with regard to Mr Asquith's request for guarantees'. However, Balfour had in fact told Knollys in October 1910 that the situation had changed and he would no longer feel justified in taking office if Asquith were to resign. As Kenneth Rose has indicated in his biography, *King George V*, this was something of a snap judgment, and Balfour's response might have been different had he actually been asked to form a government, but Knollys chose not to suggest this to the King, or even to bring to his attention Balfour's two statements. Though George V was annoyed by the omission, with hindsight we may see that Knollys was probably wise: history demanded that the Lords' veto should go and, on a more practical level, any minority government formed by Balfour could not have lasted long. Given the Liberal ascendancy, another general election would have left the King in exactly the same position.
3. In conversation with Lord Esher.
4. Quoted by Gore, *op. cit.*
5. In *Parliamentary Government in England.*
6. In a telegram preserved in the Royal Archives and quoted in *King George V* by Nicolson.
7. D. C. Somervell, quoted by Gore, *op. cit.*
8. Somervell in *ibid.*
9. Letter from Wigram to the Archbishop of Canterbury, January 1919, preserved in the Wigram papers and quoted by Rose, *op. cit.*
10. Dalton had written: 'Self-approbation enormously strong, becoming almost the only motive power in Prince George ... The slightest difficulty discourages him and when he frets he finds it hard to subdue himself.' Wigram was also irritated by the King's reaction to criticism.
11. Diary entry, January 22nd, 1924: 'I held a Council at which Mr Ramsay MacDonald was sworn in a member. I then asked him to form a government ... Today 23 years ago dear Grandmama died. I wonder what she would have thought of a Labour Government!'

12. Reported in Lord Birkenhead's autobiography, *F.E. The Life of F. E. Smith, First Earl of Birkenhead*.
13. Quoted in *Victor Cazalet* by Robert Rhodes James.
14. In his memoirs, *Twenty-five Years, 1892–1916*.

Chapter 9 'Royalty of Virtue'

1. The revolution actually began in Petrograd on March 8th, 1917, according to the Gregorian Calendar introduced in 1582 and adopted by most European countries during the following two centuries. The Russians, however, retained the Old Style or Julian Calendar until 1918, so in their terms the month of the revolution was February. Similarly, the October Revolution that brought Lenin and the Bolsheviks to power in 1917 took place in the New Style Calendar month of November.
2. Lloyd George wrote to his wife on September 2nd, 1920, partly in Welsh: 'Hen gachgi ydi'r benhin [The King is an old coward]. He is frightened to death & is anxious to make it clear that he has nothing to do with it . . .' (see Bibliography).
3. In *English History 1914–45*.
4. After a prolonged correspondence and audiences with the King on the Home Rule question, Asquith wrote to Venetia Stanley in January 1914: 'I found the main preoccupation of the Other Party to my interview at the Palace was with his own position, and the "terrible cross-fire" to which he conceives himself to be exposed.' Quoted in *H. H. Asquith: Letters to Venetia Stanley*.
5. According to his biographer, Francis Watson, Dawson's diary entry read: 'Hours of waiting just for the mechanical end when all that is really life has departed only exhausts the onlookers and keeps them so strained that they cannot avail themselves of the solace of thought, communion or prayer. I therefore decided to determine the end and injected (myself) morphia gr. 3/4 and shortly afterwards cocaine gr. 1 into the distended jugular vein . . . Then the Queen and family returned and stood round the bedside. Intervals between respirations lengthened, and life passed so quietly and gently that it was difficult to determine the actual moment.' Reported in *History Today*, December 1986.
6. Newspaper reports quoted in *Abdication* by Christopher Warwick.

Chapter 10 Damnosa Hereditas

1. *A King's Story.*
2. Lord Mountbatten's comments have been quoted by John Terraine in *The Life and Times of Lord Mountbatten* and by Philip Ziegler in *Mountbatten.*
3. Winifred's husband, William Dudley Ward, was Liberal MP for Southampton and Vice-Chamberlain of the Royal Household. The Prince of Wales, before his affair with Mrs Simpson, once made the mistake of telling his father that Freda Dudley Ward was the only woman he had ever really loved. The response of George V was a contemptuous reference to 'the lacemaker's daughter': her father, Colonel Charles Birkin, was a highly successful manufacturer of lace.
4. Quoted in *The Windsor Story* by J. Bryan III and Charles J. V. Murphy.
5. Quoted by Warwick, *op. cit.*, and others.
6. These comments are recorded respectively by Kenneth Rose and Lady Airlie.
7. Quoted in *Baldwin* by Keith Middlemass and John Barnes.
8. Recorded in *A Diary with Letters, 1931–1950* by Thomas Jones.
9. The evidence for this determination is given by Frances Donaldson, *Edward VIII*, Warwick, *op. cit*, and others.
10. The letter is quoted in the Duchess of Windsor's autobiography, *The Heart Has Its Reasons.*
11. Viscountess Coke, daughter-in-law of the Earl of Leicester.
12. These rumours are reported by Frances Donaldson and others.
13. In an interview, towards the end of her life, with Dennis Eisenberg.
14. Quoted in *King George V: His Life and Reign* by John Wheeler-Bennett.
15. According to Wheeler-Bennett, the doubts were expressed to the Princes' tutor.
16. Wheeler-Bennett, *op. cit.*

Chapter 11 The Family Firm

1. Wheeler-Bennett, *op. cit.*
2. Lord Stamfordham told Captain Ley that the King 'would prefer to run the risk of Prince Albert's health suffering than that he should endure the bitter and lasting disappointment of not being in his ship in the battle line'. As a result of further medical consultation, however, the Prince left the hospital ship to which he had been transferred and spent a month recuperating at Abergeldie. Admiral Sir Stanley Colville told the King

in a letter that it would simply be bad luck if 'The Day' – i.e. a naval battle – should come while the Prince was absent from his ship.

3. Wheeler-Bennett, *op. cit.*
4. George VI Collection in the Royal Archives, quoted in *ibid.*
5. Papers of George V, quoted in *ibid.*
6. In a letter to his tutor, Mr Hansell.
7. Letter to the King.
8. Letter to the King in June 1918.
9. Letter to his parents.
10. Wheeler-Bennett, *op. cit.*
11. *Ibid.*
12. Letter to one of his officers at Dartmouth, July 1919.
13. This famous remark is quoted in *Destiny Called to Them* by A. B. Baxter (Oxford University Press, 1939).
14. Wheeler-Bennett, *op. cit.*
15. Quoted by Lady Cynthia Asquith in *Queen Elizabeth: Her Intimate & Authentic Life*.
16. Though of Scottish descent on her father's side, Lady Elizabeth was born in London and her mother was a Cavendish-Bentinck. The family's main homes were in London and at St Pauls, Walden Bury, Hertfordshire, though they usually spent the summer at their Scottish seat, Glamis Castle. Thus while Cynthia Asquith claimed Lady Elizabeth for England, she would later be celebrated as a Scottish queen.
17. According to Lady Airlie.
18. The full Scottish title is Earl of Strathmore and Kinghorne and it dates from 1606. The English title Earl of Strathmore was created in 1937, the year of the coronation of King George VI and Queen Elizabeth.
19. Quoted in *The Queen Mother* by Elizabeth Longford.
20. Wheeler-Bennett, *op. cit.*
21. Quoted by Warwick, *op. cit.*
22. *Ibid.*
23. Quoted in *The Little Princesses* by Marion Crawford.
24. It was Chips Channon who, knowing Edward VIII as he did, said that the King was 'against too much slipshod democracy'. An American journalist, Marietta FitzGerald, reported that in 1945 the then Duke of Windsor told her one thing she could be certain of was that if Labour won the general election the Soviet Union would take over Britain within a few days. The King's sympathy with certain perceived advantages of fascist rule is well documented by Italian, German and British sources, and such views were not uncommon among members of the ruling classes in the 1930s.

25. Letter from Jamaica dated December 9th, 1936. On Christmas Eve that year, Lloyd George sent a cable to the ex-King deploring 'the mean and unchivalrous attacks' on 'a monarch who sympathised with the lowliest of his subjects' (see Bibliography).

Chapter 12   'How Well Did I Behave?'

1. In a letter to his son dated June 7th, 1920.
2. This was written in 1918 and quoted in an article in the *Bedfordshire Times and Independent* in August 1921. Wheeler-Bennett, *op. cit.*
3. Interview with the author.
4. In a letter to Lionel Logue.
5. Letter dated August 29th, 1927.
6. In *Edward VIII.*
7. The book, by A. G. Gardiner, was published by Jonathan Cape in 1926.
8. Quoted by Warwick, *op. cit.*
9. Donaldson, *op. cit.*
10. Middlemass and Barnes, *op. cit.*
11. Official history of the National Council of Social Service.
12. Revealed in German documents captured after the Second World War.

Chapter 13   Edward the Unacceptable

1. Quoted by Warwick, *op. cit.*
2. *Ibid.*
3. Donaldson, *op. cit.*
4. Duchess of Windsor, *op. cit.*
5. In his abdication broadcast.
6. Mrs Simpson's alleged German connections were principally the subject of dark hints and social gossip, but, as Frances Donaldson points out, they were taken sufficiently seriously by the authorities – along with the King's open expression of a certain sympathy towards Germany – for the security services to be instructed to maintain surveillance. At the time, the fear was mostly of 'indiscretion' on the part of the King, though Sir John Wheeler-Bennett and others made it clear they believed that Mrs Simpson was being used by Ribbentrop to gain information from her unique contact with the British Establishment. Details of the action

taken and the suspicions harboured may be found in *Baldwin: The Unexpected Prime Minister* by H. Montgomery Hyde, and Hugh Dalton's *The Fateful Years, 1931–45*.

7. Warwick, *op. cit.*
8. Reported in *The Abdication – Twenty-five Years After* by Lewis Broad.
9. *A King's Story.*
10. First-hand account given to the author.
11. Sir Henry Channon in *Chips: The Diaries of Sir Henry Channon*.
12. Quoted in *Geoffrey Dawson and Our Times* by John Evelyn Wrench.
13. Eyewitness account given to the author.

Chapter 14   A Clash of Symbols

1. Monckton, quoted by Donaldson, *op. cit.*
2. In *English History 1914–45*.
3. Reported in the Mass Observation survey of coronation day, May 12th, 1937.
4. In a letter dated December 10th, 1937.
5. Memorandum written by the King and quoted by Wheeler-Bennett, *op. cit.*
6. Quoted by Judd, *op. cit.* According to the recollection of Walter Monckton, the King said to him, 'This is a nice wedding present.'
7. In an interview with the author.
8. May 15th, 1939.
9. In a letter to Queen Mary, May 17th, 1939.
10. Interview with the author.
11. *Ibid.*
12. Remark made to Alan Lascelles, quoted by Wheeler-Bennett, *op. cit.*
13. Reported by Lord Tweedsmuir in a letter, quoted in *ibid.*
14. Memorandum written by the King.
15. *Diaries and Letters.*

Chapter 15   Undertones of War

1. Diary entry, Sunday, September 3rd, 1939.
2. Quoted in *The Last Emperor* by Peter Townsend.
3. In *Hitler*.
4. Broadcast on Empire Day, May 24th, 1940.
5. Reported by President Roosevelt's envoy, Harry Hopkins, in a letter to the President, quoted by Robert E. Sherwood in *Roosevelt and Hopkins*, published in New York by Harper & Brothers in 1948.
6. In fact, King Christian had had little choice in the matter, since Copenhagen had fallen within twelve hours.
7. Hull thought Roosevelt's political opponents would make capital out of the presence of the British king in Canada, seeing it as an attempt to re-establish monarchy on the North American continent.
8. June 27th, 1940.
9. Quoted by Christopher Hibbert in *The Court at Windsor, A Domestic History*.
10. Expressed in a description of the incident written by the King at the request of Winston Churchill for inclusion in his monumental history, *The Second World War*.
11. February 7th, 1941.
12. In a letter dated February 16th, 1942.
13. Diary entry dated February 28th, 1942.
14. In a statement reported by the Australian press on December 27th, 1941.
15. The King himself, during his visit to the United States in 1939, had helped to lay the groundwork for the eventual Lend-Lease agreement by mobilising American public opinion behind Roosevelt's policy of supporting Britain, but when the details of the deal were produced, the Americans appeared to be seeking far greater control in the Caribbean than the King had foreseen. His comment here appeared on December 30th, 1940, in a written instruction of Sir Alexander Hardinge, his private secretary, for transmission to Lord Lloyd, Secretary of State for the Colonies, who was negotiating with Washington. Hardinge told Lloyd that while the King understood Roosevelt's difficulties with the isolationists, Britain must not be seen to be jeopardising the sovereignty of the West Indies in agreeing to US bases there. But he added: 'We may well feel obliged to make concessions and submit to off-hand treatment, such as we would not tolerate in ordinary times.' Lend-Lease was satisfactorily concluded in March 1941.
16. Diary entry, November 4th, 1942.
17. Diary entry, December 29th, 1942.

18. Diary entry, August 9th, 1942.
19. Letter to Queen Mary, February 2nd, 1943.
20. Sir John Colville, Churchill's private secretary, makes it clear in his diaries (published under the title *The Fringes of Power*) that Churchill almost always got his own way in any disagreement with the King. Exceptions were the Prime Minister's plan to accompany the invasion troops on D-Day in 1944 and the suggestion in January 1944 that Princess Elizabeth should become Princess of Wales.
21. There is an interesting account of the political situation in North Africa by David Eisenhower in his biography of his grandfather, *Eisenhower at War 1943–1945.*
22. *Ibid.*
23. When the plebiscite was held in 1947 the Italians, to their own surprise as much as anyone else's, voted for a republic.
24. In a letter dated January 21st.
25. 'Bevin is very good and tells me everything that is going on,' the King noted in 1946. 'The others are still learning to run their departments, & their efforts have not made life any easier so far.' By the following year he had begun to suspect that he was being ignored and fobbed off, writing in his diary on January 30th, 1947: 'I have asked Mr Attlee 3 times now if he is not worried over the domestic situation in this country. But he won't tell me he is when I feel he is. I know I am worried.' He had, he said, told a friend that 'I was doing my best to warn them that they were going too fast in their legislation and were offending every class of people who were ready to help them if they were asked to, but were swept aside by regulations, etc.'
26. In a letter to Queen Mary, September 14th, 1947.
27. Remark to Vita Sackville-West when she told the King that the National Trust was to take over her family's home.

Chapter 16   Palace in Wonderland

1. *News of the World* colour magazine, July 7th, 1985.
2. *Sunday Times* colour magazine, July 19th, 1987.
3. *News of the World* and the *Sunday Times*, both as above.
4. *Sunday Times, ibid.*
5. Editorial in the *Sunday Times*, June 21st, 1987.
6. *Sunday Express*, May 10th, 1987.

7. Collected in *Consuming Passions: The Dynamics of Popular Culture*.
8. *Ibid*.
9. *Daily Telegraph*, November 2nd, 1987.

Bibliography

Airlie, Mabell, Countess of, *Thatched with Gold*, ed. Jennifer Ellis (Hutchinson, 1962)

Alice, Princess, Countess of Athlone, *For My Grandchildren* (Evans Bros, 1966)

Arthur, Sir George, *King George V* (Cape, 1929)

Asquith, Lady Cynthia, *Queen Elizabeth: Her Intimate & Authentic Life* (Hutchinson, 1937); *Diaries 1915–18* (Hutchinson, 1968)

Asquith, H. H., *Memories and Reflections 1852–1927* (Cassell, 1928); *H. H. Asquith: Letters to Venetia Stanley*, ed. Michael and Eleanor Brock (Oxford University Press, 1982)

Avon, Earl of, *The Eden Memoirs* (Cassell, 1962)

Bagehot, Walter, *The English Constitution* (Fontana edition, 1963, with an introduction by R. H. S. Crossman)

Baldwin, A. W., *My Father, the True Story* (W. H. Allen, 1955)

Battiscombe, Georgina, *Queen Alexandra* (Constable, 1969)

Beaverbrook, Lord, *Men and Power, 1917–1918* (Hutchinson, 1956); *The Abdication of King Edward VIII* (Hamish Hamilton, 1966)

Birkenhead, 2nd Earl of, *F.E.: The Life of F. E. Smith, First Earl of Birkenhead* (Eyre & Spottiswoode, 1959).

Briggs, Asa, *Victorian People* (University of Chicago Press, 1955)

Broad, Lewis, *The Abdication – Twenty-five Years After* (Frederick Muller, 1961)

Bryan, J. III, and Murphy, Charles J. V., *The Windsor Story* (William Morrow, 1979)

Bryant, Arthur, *George V* (Peter Davies, 1936); *A Thousand Years of British Monarchy* (Collins, 1975)

Buchan, John, *The King's Grace, 1910–1935* (Hodder & Stoughton, 1935 – also published as *The People's King*, Houghton Mifflin, 1935)

Buxton, Aubrey, *The King in his Country* (Longman, 1955)

Cameron, James, *Yesterday's Witness* (BBC, 1979)

Cecil, David, *Melbourne* (Constable, 1965)

Channon, Sir Henry, *Chips: The Diaries of Sir Henry Channon*, ed. Robert Rhodes James (Weidenfeld & Nicolson, 1967)

Churchill, Randolph S., *Lord Derby: King of Lancashire* (Heinemann, 1959)

Churchill, Winston S., *The Second World War*, 5 vols (Cassell, 1948–54)

Colville, John, *The Fringes of Power: Downing Street Diaries 1939–1955* (Hodder & Stoughton, 1985)

Cooper, A. Duff, *Old Men Forget* (Rupert Hart-Davis, 1953)

Cowles, Virginia, *Edward VII and his Circle* (Hamish Hamilton, 1956)

Crawford, Marion, *The Little Princesses* (Cassell, 1950)

Cust, Sir Lionel, *King Edward VII and his Court* (John Murray, 1930)

Dalton, Hugh, *The Fateful Years 1931–45* (Frederick Muller, 1957).

Darbyshire, Taylor, *King George VI* (Hutchinson, 1937)

de Paor, Liam, *The Peoples of Ireland* (Hutchinson, 1986)

Donaldson, Frances, *Edward VIII* (Weidenfeld & Nicolson, 1974)

Dugdale, Blanche E. C., *Arthur James Balfour* (Hutchinson, 1936)

Edwards, Anne, *Matriarch, Queen Mary and the House of Windsor* (Hodder & Stoughton, 1984)

Eisenhower, David, *Eisenhower at War 1943–1945* (Collins, 1986)

Esher, Reginald, Viscount, *Journals and Letters*, ed. Maurice V. Brett, 4 vols (Nicholson and Watson, 1934–38)

Fest, Joachim C., *Hitler* (Weidenfeld & Nicolson, 1974)

Fulford, Roger, *The Prince Consort* (Macmillan, 1949)

Gore, John, *King George V, A Personal Memoir* (John Murray, 1941)

Grainger, J. H., *Patriotisms, Britain: 1900–1939* (Routledge & Kegan Paul, 1986)

Grey of Fallodon, Viscount, *Twenty-five Years, 1892–1916* (Frederick A. Stokes, 1925)

Hardinge, Lady Helen, *Loyal to Three Kings* (William Kimber, 1967)

Harrison, Michael, *Clarence: The Life of HRH The Duke of Clarence and Avondale, 1864–92* (W. H. Allen, 1972)

Hibbert, Christopher, *The Court at Windsor, A Domestic History* (Longman, 1964); *Edward VII: A Portrait* (Allen Lane, 1976)

Howarth, Patrick, *George VI* (Hutchinson, 1987)

Hyde, H. Montgomery, *Baldwin: The Unexpected Prime Minister* (Hart-Davis, MacGibbon, 1973)

Jenkins, Roy, *Mr Balfour's Poodle* (Heinemann, 1954); *Asquith* (Collins, 1964)

Jennings, Ivor, *The British Constitution* (Cambridge University Press, 1943)

Jones, Thomas, *A Diary with Letters, 1931–1950* (Oxford University Press, 1954)

Judd, Denis, *King George VI* (Michael Joseph, 1982)

Lacey, Robert, *Majesty: Elizabeth II and the House of Windsor* (Hutchinson, 1977)

Lascelles, Hon. Mrs Frances, *Our Duke and Duchess* (Hutchinson, 1932)

Laski, Harold, *Parliamentary Government in England* (Allen & Unwin, 1938)

Lees-Milne, James, *Harold Nicolson: A Biography* (Chatto & Windus, 1981)

Lloyd George, David, *War Memoirs* (Nicholson and Watson, 1936); *Family Letters 1885–1936*, ed. Kenneth O. Morgan (University of Wales Press and Oxford University Press, 1973)

Longford, Elizabeth, *Victoria R.I.* (Weidenfeld & Nicolson, 1964); *The Royal House of Windsor* (Weidenfeld & Nicolson, 1974); *The Queen Mother* (Weidenfeld & Nicolson, 1981)

Magnus, Philip, *King Edward the Seventh* (John Murray, 1964)

Mayne, Richard, *Postwar, The Dawn of Today's Europe* (Thames and Hudson, 1983)

Medlicott, W. N., *Contemporary England 1914–1964* (Longman, 1967)

Middlemass, Keith, and Barnes, John, *Baldwin* (Weidenfeld & Nicolson, 1969)

Morgan, Kenneth O. (ed.), *The Oxford Illustrated History of Britain* (Oxford University Press, 1984)

Morrah, Dermot, *Princess Elizabeth, Duchess of Edinburgh* (Odhams, 1950); *The Work of the Queen* (William Kimber, 1958)

Nicolson, Harold, *King George V: His Life and Reign* (Constable, 1952); *Diaries and Letters*, ed. Nigel Nicolson, 3 vols (Collins, 1966–68)

Philpott, H. R. S., *The Right Hon J. H. Thomas* (Sampson, Low, Marston, 1932)

Pless, Princess of, *Daisy Princess of Pless by Herself* (Dutton, 1929)

Ponsonby, Sir Frederick, *Recollections of Three Reigns* (Eyre & Spottiswoode, 1951)

Pope-Hennessy, James, *Queen Mary* (Allen & Unwin, 1959)

Rhodes James, Robert, *Churchill: A Study in Failure 1900–1939* (Weidenfeld & Nicolson, 1970); *Victor Cazalet* (Hamish Hamilton, 1976)

Rose, Kenneth, *King George V* (Weidenfeld & Nicolson, 1983)

Sinclair, David, *Queen and Country, A Life of Elizabeth the Queen Mother* (Dent, 1979)

Symons, Julian, *The General Strike* (Hutchinson, 1957)

Taylor, A. J. P., *English History 1914–1945* (Oxford University Press, 1965)

Terraine, John, *The Life and Times of Lord Mountbatten* (Hutchinson, 1968)

Townsend, Peter, *The Last Emperor* (Weidenfeld & Nicolson, 1975)

Warwick, Christopher, *Abdication* (Sidgwick & Jackson, 1986)

Watson, Francis, *Dawson of Penn* (Chatto & Windus, 1951)

BIBLIOGRAPHY

Wheeler-Bennett, John W., *King George VI, His Life and Reign* (Macmillan, 1958)

Williamson, Judith, *Consuming Passions: The Dynamics of Popular Culture* (Marion Boyars, 1986)

Windsor, Duchess of, *The Heart Has Its Reasons* (Michael Joseph, 1956)

Windsor, H.R.H. The Duke of, *A King's Story* (Cassell, 1951)

Woodham-Smith, Cecil, *The Great Hunger* (Hamish Hamilton, 1962)

Wrench, John Evelyn, *Geoffrey Dawson and Our Times* (Hutchinson, 1955)

Young, G. M., *Stanley Baldwin* (Rupert Hart-Davis, 1952)

Ziegler, Philip, *Mountbatten* (Collins, 1985)

Index

mediocracy – *cont.*
　suspicious of extremism, 139
　George V's acceptance of, 141
　successful challenge to nobility of
　　descent, 151
　challenged by working class
　　aspirations, 151
　and marketing benefits of royal
　　visits, 153
　power maintained by using
　　monarchy, 192
　and Abdication, 209, 212, 216,
　　217, 218
　approves of George VI, 227
　intends to ignore George VI's
　　opinions, 229–30
Mediterranean Fleet, 61, 63
Melampus, HMS, 70, 80
Melbourne, William Lamb, 2nd
　Viscount, 14, 15–18, 21
Mencken, H. L., 219
Menzies, Sir Robert, 152
Metcalfe, Lady Alexandra, 169
middle classes, 3, 4, 22, 23, 26, 32,
　33, 34, 49, 104, 112, 113, 119,
　139, 141, 146, 153, 185, 196,
　232, 267
Minimum Wages Act, 133
monarchy
　survial of, 2, 10, 53, 78, 86, 118,
　　120, 135, 145, 146, 192, 195
　and middle class, 3, 4, 25, 26, 49,
　　112, 113
　surrender of authority, 3
　influence of Prince Albert, 3, 5,
　　13, 14, 19, 20, 21, 23, 24
　mystique, 4, 14, 23–4, 25, 34–5,
　　104, 116, 117, 119, 123–4,
　　142, 166, 195, 255, 266
　evolution in modern times, 5
　'new' popular, 6
　passivity of, 8
　'romance' surrounding, 9
　views of, 27
　expectations of, 35–6, 39
　and links with military, 58–9

　as 'family firm', 60, 185, 193, 194,
　　264
　loss of identity, 104
　overthrow of, 145–6
　reaction to xenophobia, 147–8
　concerned with safety after
　　Abdication, 193
　new challenges to, 194–5
　takes up spirit of paternalism, 196
　and Abdication crisis, 210–12,
　　215–20, 230, 232
　becomes more defensive, 225
　new appreciation of the arts,
　　231–2
　demystification of, 232
　new demands made on in Second
　　World War, 239–40
　appeal to tribal instincts, 242
　new phase of popularity, 246–7,
　　267, 268
　clings to Commonwealth role, 260
　and modern media, 262–9
　lack of power, 269, 273, 274
　future role, 273–6
　see also Bagehot, Walter
Monckton, Walter, 209, 221, 225
Montgomery, General Bernard,
　253, 256
Mordaunt, Sir Charles, 31
Morley, John, 106
Morning Post, The, 16, 157
Mosley, Sir Oswald, 225
Mountbatten, Lord Louis, 150, 165,
　229
Munich agreement, 234
Mussolini, Benito, 141, 202, 234,
　251

National Council of Social Service,
　207
National Federation of Women's
　Institutes, 231
National Insurance Act, 133
nationalism, 34, 201, 271
Nehru, Jawaharlal, 233, 252
Neutrality Acts, 238

New Romney, 158
New Statesman, 249
New York Times, 214, 237
New Zealand, 200–201, 251, 253
Newfoundland, 161
News Chronicle, 232
Nicholas II, Tsar, 37, 72, 147, 148, 149, 150
Nicolson, Harold, 51, 52, 81, 93, 95, 107, 108, 109, 212, 239
North, Vice-Admiral Sir Dudley, 235
North Africa, 251, 253–7
North American Squadron, 60, 65
Northumberland, HMS, 64
Norwich, 231

Observer, 238
Olga, Queen of Greece, 61, 63
Olympic Games (1936), 208
Ophir, SS, 117
Osborne, John, 10
Osborne House, Isle of Wight, 46, 79, 100
Oxford, Bishop of, 28
Oxford University, 175, 184

Pacific War Councils, 253
Pakistan, 260
Palmerston, Henry Temple, 3rd Viscount, 14
Paris, Louis Philippe, Comte de, 65–6
Parliament Bill/Act, 126–9, 131, 150, 175
Passchendaele, 138
Pearl Harbor, 251
Pearse, Padraic, 113–14
Peel, Sir Robert, 14, 17–19, 22
Persia, Shah of, 185
Pless, Princess of (formerly Daisy Cornwallis-West), 37–8, 39
Plymouth, 248, 258
Poincaré, President, 185
Poland, 235, 239
Ponsonby, Sir Frederick, 38, 165–6

pornography, 32
Potsdam Conference (1945), 258
Potter, Henry C., 151, 152
press secretary, 135, 136
Princess Elizabeth Land, 161
prostitution, 32, 62
Protestants, 19, 66
Prussia, 65

Queen Mary (cruiser), 182
'Queen's Messenger', 246

radicalism, 15, 22, 27, 31, 33, 85, 112, 121, 124, 125
Raj, the, 118
rationing, 249–50
Reading, Lord, 206
Reform Act (1832), 14
Reform Act (1867), 111
Reith, John (later Sir John), 153
republicanism, 24, 27, 30, 32, 146, 149, 195, 202, 236
Repulse (battle-cruiser), 235
revolutionary movements, 3
Ring, Anne, 161
Robertson, Sir William, 138
Romanovs, 34, 146
Rommel, General Erwin, 251, 252, 253
Roosevelt, Eleanor, 250
Roosevelt, Franklin D., 233, 234, 237, 238, 245, 253, 257, 258
Rothschild, Constance de (later Lady Battersea), 44
Royal Air Force, 183, 250, 254
Royal Air Force Cadet College, Cranwell, 183
Royal Archives, 108, 177
Royal Family
  increased popularity, 113, 162
  as public relations organisation, 135, 205
  Princesses as 'juvenile leads', 162
  as a 'firm', 60, 185, 193, 194, 264
  seen as force for traditional values, 190